Ripley's Believe It or Not! 2007

Ripley's Believe It or Not!® 2007

Expect... The Unexpected

CENTURY

Developed and produced by Miles Kelly Publishing Ltd
in association with Ripley Publishing

Executive Vice President Norm Deska
Vice President, Archives and Exhibits Edward Meyer
Archives Assistant Viviana Ray
Researcher Lucas Stram

Publishing Director Anne Marshall

Managing Editor Rebecca Miles
Text Geoff Tibballs
Interviews Jo Wiltshire
Editors Judy Barratt, Sally McFall
Editorial Assistant Philippa Geering
Indexer Hilary Bird

Art Director Jo Brewer
Project Designer James Marks
Cover Designer Warris Kidwai
Reprographics Stephan Davis, Ian Paulyn, Mike Coupe
Picture Researchers Philippa Geering, Laura Faulder
Production Manager Sally Knowles

Sales and Marketing Morty Mint

First published in the UK by Century, The Random House Group Ltd,
20 Vauxhall Bridge Road, London, SW1V 2SA

Random House Australia (Pty) Limited
20 Alfred Street, Milsons Point, Sydney, New South Wales 2061,
Australia

Random House New Zealand (Pty) Limited
18 Poland Road, Glenfield, Auckland 10, New Zealand

Random House South Africa (Pty) Limited
Isle of Houghton, Corner of Boundary Road & Carse O' Gowrie,
Houghton 2198, South Africa

The Random House Group Limited Reg. No. 954009

www.randomhouse.co.uk

ISBN 10: 1-8460-5149-5
ISBN 13: 978-1-8460-5149-4
10 9 8 7 6 5 4 3 2 1

British Library Cataloguing-in-Publication Data
A catalogue record for this book is available from the British Library

Printed in China

PUBLISHER'S NOTE
While every effort has been made to verify the accuracy of the entries
in this book, the Publishers cannot be held responsible for any errors
contained in the work. They would be glad to receive any information
from readers.

WARNING
Some of the stunts and activities in this book are undertaken by
experts and should not be attempted by anyone without adequate
training and supervision.

Contents

ROBERT RIPLEY, creator of the world famous daily cartoon strip "Ripley's Believe it or Not!" combed the globe in a relentless quest for odd people, places, and things.

In December 1918, while working as a sports columnist for the *New York Globe*, Ripley created his first collection of odd facts and feats. The cartoons, based on unusual athletic achievements, were almost called "Champs and Chumps," but his editor wanted a title that would describe the incredible nature of the content, so it was changed to "Believe It or Not!" The cartoon was an instant success and the phrase "believe it or not" soon entered everyday speech.

Ripley's passion was travel and by 1940 he had visited no fewer than 201 countries. Wherever he went, he searched out the bizarre for inclusion in his newspaper cartoons—these achieved worldwide distribution, were translated into 17 different languages, and boasted a readership of 80 million. Although he died in 1949 (after collapsing on the set of

Ripley with female shrunken head with long hair

his weekly television show), Ripley's "Believe It or Not!" cartoons are still produced on a daily basis—just as they have been every day since 1918—making it the longest running syndicated cartoon in the world. Intrepid researchers follow in Robert Ripley's footsteps, continually scouring the world and enabling Ripley's to remain the undisputed king of the strange and unbelievable. With a huge database of incredible facts, people, and events, a massive photographic archive, and a warehouse stuffed with unique and fascinating exhibits, Ripley's is able to present a celebration of the amazing diversity of our world, without ever passing judgment.

Ripley poses with a large surfboard on a Hawaiian beach

On a CBS phone in Alaska, Ripley gives a radio interview

In 2005 Ripley's took possession of a preserved elephant's head with two trunks
page 13

A company sells solar-powered glow-in-the-dark gravestones that appear normal during daylight, but glow after dark
page 14

A woman was arrested by customs officials for hiding 51 live tropical fish in her skirt
page 17

In Manchester, England, a boa constrictor 10 ft (3 m) in length appeared in an apartment toilet bowl
page 23

WORKERS DYED THE CHICAGO RIVER green as part of the city's annual St. Patrick's Day celebrations on March 11, 2006. This was first done in 1962 when pollution-control workers used dyes to trace illegal discharges and then hit upon the idea of dying the river to celebrate St. Patrick's Day. They used 100 lb (45 kg) of dye that lasted a week! Now only 40 lb (18 kg) is used, and the color lasts several hours.

STRANGE

A Burmese python tried to swallow a 6-ft (1.8-m) American alligator in Florida
page 31

Japan has an indoor beach with 13,500 tons of salt-free "sea" and surf up to 11 ft (3.4 m) high
page 34

A cyclist riding backwards traveled an amazing 16.7 mi (26.9 km) in one hour
page 37

WORLD

CRAZY HORSE

The detailed face of Crazy Horse stands 87 ft 6 in (26.7 m) high and took 50 years to complete—the lips alone took two years and the nose is 27 ft (8.2 m) long!

More than 8 million tons of rock has been blasted from a South Dakota mountain to create a sculpture depicting Native American chief Crazy Horse, who led the Oglala Sioux at the battle of the Little Bighorn in 1876. At the invitation of local

With arm outstretched toward his ancestral homeland, astride a stallion over two football fields long, Crazy Horse will be 641 ft (195 m) long and 563 ft (172 m) high. By comparison, the heads of Mount Rushmore are a mere 60 ft (18 m) high.

Indian leaders, Boston-born sculptor Korczak Ziolkowski began work on Thunderhead Mountain back in 1948.

The crew uses precision explosive engineering to remove and shape mountain rock, the explosives being loaded into holes drilled to a depth of 35 ft (11 m). The final surface is smoothed by a jet torch, which operates at 3,300°F (1,815°C).

With the face complete, work is now progressing on the horse's head, which will stand 219 ft (66.7 m) high—the equivalent of a staggering 22 stories—and for which another 4 million tons of granite must be removed.

The final memorial will also feature a poem written by Ziolkowski, which will be carved into the hard mountain rock in letters 3 ft (1 m) tall.

June 1988

April 1990

June 1991

August 1993

August 1996

Sharpshooters

Since 1971, the World Peashooting Championship has been held in the village of Witcham, England. Some competitors take the event so seriously that they fit their shooters with laser or telescopic sights for a better aim.

In SADIEVILLE, Kentucky, property owners are **banned** by law from **mowing** their lawns, but **fishing** in the **nude** is legal.

Mud Slinging

In South Korea each summer, families, friends, and complete strangers indulge in hours of mud slinging—and enjoy every minute of it. They are taking part in the annual Poryong Mud Festival, a mad, muddy mess that features mud baths, mud sculpture, mud body-painting, and even a mud beauty contest. Hundreds of willing competitors seize the opportunity to get grubby, encouraged by the beneficial minerals in the local mud, which are believed to reduce wrinkles and wash away excess oils from the skin.

Quick Service

At Lambert's Café, Sikeston, Missouri, they don't bring bread rolls in a basket—they throw them at you! One day in 1976, the restaurant was so busy that proprietor Norman Lambert was unable to get through the crowd to serve the rolls. A customer shouted, "Throw it!" and Lambert did—and the tradition began.

▶ **How Many Hooves?**
This six-legged calf was born on a farm in Poland in February 2005. It belongs to farmer Jaroslaw Garbal, who has named the animal "Star."

Message in a Bottle

William T. Mullen's wife warned him that if he didn't stop drinking she would humiliate him after his death. He paid no attention and died in 1863, whereupon she carried out her threat by giving him a gravestone—at Clayton, Alabama—in the shape of a whiskey bottle.

Barking Beach

Believe it or not, Barking Sands Beach, on the Hawaiian island of Kauai, has sand that barks like a dog! The dry sand grains emit this strange sound when you walk on them in bare feet.

Chocolate Moose

Lenny the Moose is made from 1,700 lb (771 kg) of the finest milk chocolate! A life-sized chocolate moose, Lenny resides at Len Libby Handmade Candies in Scarborough, Maine. He was born in 1997 at the request of the store's co-owner Maureen Hemond, and created on-site in four weeks by local sculptor Zdeno Mayercak. The moose is 8 ft (2.4 m) tall and over 9 ft (2.7 m) from nose to tail. He began as a metal armature onto which 10-lb (4.5-kg) chocolate blocks were placed. Melted chocolate was then used as the mortar to hold the blocks together.

Two-trunked!

Ripley's took possession of this preserved head in August 2005—the elephant itself had been shot in Zimbabwe on November 9, 2004. It is estimated that the animal was about five years old. The head was preserved, and DNA analysis has determined that the two trunks contain identical DNA patterns and that they were indeed from the same animal.

Dearly Departed

★ Scotsman Alexander, Duke of Hamilton, spent more than £11,500 ($20,000) on a genuine ancient Egyptian coffin. But, when he died in 1852, he was found to be too long for it and so his legs had to be cut off before he could fit inside.

★ In 1876, an American gang of grave robbers tried unsuccessfully to steal Abraham Lincoln's body and hold it for ransom in return for the release of a convicted forger, Ben Boyd.

★ When the body of King George IV of England became badly swollen in his coffin, court attendants feared that it would explode through the lining. So, they hurriedly drilled a hole in the casket to let out some of the rotten air.

Dead Weird!

Wacky gravestones are all the rage in Japan. In a land where household altars and ornate headstones are the norm, specialist shops sell extraordinary-looking sculptures for remembering the dead. A gravestone shop in Fuji stocks such offbeat stone sculptures as Godzilla, a hippopotamus, and a baby dinosaur breaking through an egg. At a gravestone design competition in Japan in 2005, every taste was catered for, as shown above, left, and below.

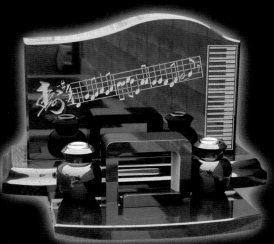

⬆ Glow in the Dark

An Austrian company is selling solar-powered glow-in-the-dark gravestones. The grave appears normal during daylight hours, but once it gets dark the grave begins to glow. A family grave, large enough to hold 12 bodies, has already been constructed. The standard single version comes with a glowing gravestone, a solar roof, and a digital text display that allows relatives to program in names, the date of death, and personal blessings.

Miracle Putt

There should be no cursing on a miniature golf course at Lexington, Kentucky—because the 54-hole course has a biblical theme throughout. The first 18 holes are based on events in the Old Testament, the second 18 are related to the New Testament, and the final 18 are the toughest—the miracles. Where else can you play through Jesus's tomb and Jonah's whale, or conquer Mount Sinai with a putter?

Luxury Hearse

An Australian funeral director is offering a highly unusual hearse with its own minibar, DVD player, and fresh coffee-maker. The luxurious mint-green vehicle, which can be hired from Tobin Brothers of Melbourne, is fitted with chrome handrails, tinted windows, pop-out cup holders, and atmospheric lighting. It can hold up to 12 mourners and a coffin.

Novelty Coffins

Coffin-maker Vic Fearn, from Nottingham, England, likes to offer a funeral with a difference. Mr. Fearn makes novelty coffins to cater for every taste and interest, in such diverse shapes as a sports bag, a kite, a canal boat, and a guitar.

Every year, the **Israeli post office** in JERUSALEM sorts up to **3,000** letters addressed to **"God"** and forwards them to the **Western Wall**, where they are inserted into the **cracks** at the **holy site**.

Dolphin Mystery

In August 2003, locals reported a strange sighting on Florida's Gasparilla Lake—a dolphin. Yet the lake is totally landlocked, with no access to the Gulf of Mexico!

Duck March

Guests at the Peabody Hotel, Memphis, Tennessee, witness a truly strange ritual. Twice a day—at 11 a.m. and 5 p.m.—ducks march in a line from their rooftop penthouse to the hotel elevator and then travel down to the marble fountain situated in the hotel lobby. The Peabody Ducks have been a tradition for more than 70 years, dating back to when the hotel manager, Frank Shutt, returned from a drunken hunting trip and thought it would be fun to place some of his living decoy ducks in the hotel's fountain.

◥ Dining on Toilets

A family settle down to a meal in a toilet-themed restaurant named Martun ("toilet" in Chinese), in Kaohsiung, China. Diners sit on toilet seats and the food arrives in bowls shaped like Western-style toilets or Asian-style "squat pots."

Long Payment

At one time, Filipinos could wear their hair long only if they paid a fee of 78 cents a year.

Biggest Cap

Visitors to Rocanville, Saskatchewan, may be amazed to find it is home to an enormous baseball cap. More than 13 times the regular size, it was built from fiberglass in 1988 and sits perched on top of a pole.

▶ Planting the World

For the last five years Ernst and Nelly Hofer have planted a giant maze on their farm. In 2005, they planted a world map. Laid out with GPS, the landmasses are made from feed corn and the oceans are soybeans. One step or stride on the ground in the maze is equal to traveling 43 mi (69 km) on the Earth's surface—that means it would take just 54 strides to cover the breadth of America!

Bathtub Race

The summer of 2005 witnessed the 39th staging of one of Canada's strangest events—the Great International World Championship Bathtub Race, at Nanaimo on Vancouver Island. Motor-powered fiberglass bathtubs—some costing up to $3,000—take to the waters on a 36-mi (58-km) round course. When the race was held back in 1967, the sea was so choppy that only 47 of the 200 starters finished.

Expensive Wind

During the 18th century, in the village of Zaanse in the Netherlands, the government forced windmill owners to pay a tax on the wind.

Free Electricity

John Lorenzen of Woodward, Iowa, who has never paid for electricity, has run his 100-acre (40.5-ha) farm using windmills for over 60 years.

Wheel of Fire

In 1928, a windmill on a farm in Kaltendorf, Germany, began spinning so fast in high winds that it eventually caught fire and burned to the ground.

Reindeer Parking

A hotel in the Siberian city of Nadym announced in March 2005 that it was offering free parking for reindeer! The hotel aimed to cash in on the area's major industry—reindeer breeding.

Park and Pray

Daytona Beach, Florida, boasts its own drive-through church. The congregation park their cars and then listen to sermons delivered from a balcony. During choral songs, some motorists toot their horns instead of clapping.

Inn-credible!

The town of Stafford, in England, lost an entire pub! Workmen dismantled the historic White Lion Inn in 1978 to make way for a new road, but forgot the storage location.

Country for Rent

Located in the Swiss Alps, the entire country of Liechtenstein (with an area of 62 sq mi/160 sq km) can be rented for corporate conferences.

In-flight Catering

In Canada, a grounded airplane has been turned into a restaurant—Super Connie's Airplane Bar, in Mississauga, Ontario.

Invisible Bar

For years, the town of Nothing lived up to its name. With a population of just four, it was nothing more than a gas station on Hwy 93 between Phoenix and Las Vegas. Then Ben Kenworthy decided to build an invisible bar. Drivers can't see the bar in daylight because the building is camouflaged by thousands of light bulbs, reducing it to a glitter in the Arizona Desert. Passersby can see the light, but assume it is just the sun's reflection.

◀ Hidden Fish

Having flown in from Singapore, a woman was arrested at Melbourne Airport in 2005 after customs officers heard "flipping and flapping noises from the vicinity of her waist." She had 51 live tropical fish in 15 water-filled bags attached to a purpose-built apron hidden under her skirt.

RED APPLE HOUSE
This apple-shaped store and restaurant lay on a dirt road in Missouri. It had windows all around, a chimney for a stem, and measured 30 ft (9 m) in height and 100 ft (30 m) in circumference.

HERCULEAN HOME
Jim Ryan lived in a giant redwood tree called "Hercules," near Dyerville, California. His house had one large circular room that measured 15 ft (4.6 m) in diameter.

HUGE RED PIANO
The home of the California Piano Supply Co. in Los Angeles was red, shaped like a giant piano, and played piano music on a loudspeaker.

HOME ON WHEELS
John Martie, a sightseer who lost his sight in an accident, built himself a house on his car and covered 50,000 mi (80,465 km) in the U.S.A.

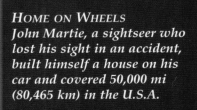

RADIO STORE
Built to resemble an Atwater-Kent radio (c.1935), this storefront in Niles, Michigan, measured 14 ft (4.3 m) high, 9 ft (2.7 m) wide, and 5 ft (1.5 m) deep.

BOTTLE FACTORY
In the 1930s, the Asseline Dairy in Norway, Michigan, was built in the shape of a giant milk bottle. There were three floors of office space for 30 people, connected by a spiral staircase.

CLIMBING HIGH
For 40 years, this magnolia tree in Kent, Ohio, was used to train students of the Davey Tree Expert Co. No man graduated until he could climb the tree without spurs.

CAR MAIL
An automobile owned by E.G. Hadley from Casper, Wyoming, was covered with 37,770 foreign stamps, from 60 different countries.

PAPER HOUSE
This two-room paper house in Rockport, Massachusetts, has walls and furnishings made entirely from over 100,000 newspapers.

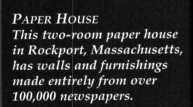

Looking Back

October 25, 1799 English captain **Lord Edward Russell** hosted a party where his fountain was used as a punch bowl, into which were added 25 hogsheads (560 gal/2,120 l) of brandy, 25,000 lemons, and 1,300 lb (590 kg) of sugar. **December 28, 1929** When a **boiler** exploded in Canton, Ohio, a man was blown completely through a house 400 yd (366 m) away.

Big Boot

A cowboy boot, 39 ft (12 m) tall and weighing 40 tons, looms over Edmonton, Alberta. It was built to promote the Western Boot Factory in 1989, at a cost of $200,000.

Rooftop Goats

A store at Coombs, on Vancouver Island, British Columbia, has goats on the roof! They stay up there during the summer but come down for the winter.

Swimming in Beer

In 2005, an Austrian holiday resort offered guests the chance to swim in a pool of beer. The resort, at Starkenberger in the Tyrol, filled seven pools with around 42,000 pt (20,000 l) of beer, claiming that beer helps to heal a variety of skin diseases.

Green Monument

In 1971, when war broke out with Pakistan, archeologists in India draped the famous Taj Mahal monument with green cloth to try to camouflage it.

Eye Surgery

Dr. Agarwal's eye hospital in Chennai, Bangalore, India, is shaped like a human eye.

Old Stairs

Archeologists in Hallstatt, Austria, have discovered an ancient wooden staircase, which was preserved in a salt mine, and is more than 3,000 years old.

Scented Food

An Argentinean restaurant has started adding designer perfumes to its dishes. Sifones and Dragones, in Buenos Aires, call their cuisine Pop Food. The menu includes oysters flavored with Anaïs Anaïs, and Chanel No.5 ice cream.

Batman Hotel

At the Hilton, Buenos Aires, Argentina, you can stay in a replica of the Batcave! The room is dedicated to Batman and there is even a secret passage leading from the "cave" to the next room.

LA TROBE

▶ **Inverted**
Situated in central Melbourne, Australia, this upside-down statue, entitled La Trobe, *was made by Charles Robb in 2005. Robb said that the inversion of his* La Trobe *questioned the purpose of public monuments and their meaning in contemporary society.*

To promote its art exhibition **The Naked Truth**, the **LEOPOLD MUSEUM** in Vienna, Austria, announced in 2005 that it was offering *free admission* to anyone who turned up in the nude!

On The Line

Norwegian slackliner Eiliv Ruud, 30, walks across crevasses and canyons thousands of feet above the ground—balancing on a moving rope that is 1 in (2.5 cm) wide.

How did you discover slacklining?

❝I'm a professional mountain guide, and climb all over the world. In 1999 in Australia I saw some climbers who had strung a climbing rope between two trees and were balancing on it—a rest day activity. The line, or webbing, is about an inch wide, or less—it's called a slackline because it's not taut. It bounces and sways when you step onto it. ❞

What is a highline?

❝It's a slackline that is fixed much higher off the ground. Slacklining was started by American climbers in the late 1980s, although similar acts have been going on in circuses for years. The only difference between walking a low slackline and a highline is a mental one—it's all in your head. ❞

Where did you do your first highline?

❝My first one was across a crevasse on a glacier in Chamonix, France. On a high one like that, I have to empty my head of all thoughts—if you're not totally in the moment you will fall off. Highlining is almost like meditation. The lowline is more gymnastic—you can do more because you're not afraid to fall off. ❞

What is the highest line you have ever walked?

❝I did the Lost Arrow Spire in California's Yosemite National Park. It was 20 m long and 1,000 m high, and the rigging took us two days to put up. I don't think highlining has been done anywhere higher. I had been training on the same length line lower down and was completely comfortable, but when I first stepped onto it up there my feet just wobbled. I could barely stand, but I kept trying and eventually did it. That was a big one. ❞

How do you train and prepare?

❝You can learn the basics of slacklining in a couple of days—after that, it's just practice. The only training for the high ones is mental. You have to be confident in your skills. Before a highline walk I check the rigging, and check it again. ❞

Have you ever lost your concentration or your balance?

❝I've started to relax too soon and thought 'Oh I'm almost across now' and then lost it. People do tricks like going backwards, turns, sitting or lying down on their backs, even back flips and handstands, but you still have to really concentrate—if you don't you'll just get halfway across and get thrown off. ❞

What is the worst thing that could happen on a highline?

❝If you don't do the rigging properly, the equipment could fail! On a highline, the results could be fatal. If I fall, I usually catch myself with the crook of my knee on the line and hang upside down. You actually get more injuries from the low lines because they bounce and can turn you upside down onto your head. ❞

Is there anywhere you still want to do a highline?

❝I would love to do a highline between the spires on the 3500-ft Troll Wall in Norway. But it doesn't matter really where you do it, as long as you are having fun. I've done it over lakes, rivers, glaciers, canyons, and across waterfalls. Being out in the nature surrounded by magnificent scenery is an important part of the experience. But once you're high up on a difficult line you often don't pay much attention to the scenery, because you have to stay so focused on the task at hand. ❞

Eiffel Replica

If you go to Paris, you expect to see the Eiffel Tower, but not one that is only 60 ft (18 m) tall. But that's what you'll find at Paris, Tennessee—a replica of the French original created by Dr. Tom Morrison using 6,000 steel rods and 500 pieces of Douglas fir. The American tower was originally on display at Christian Brothers University in Memphis, but in 1992 it was moved to Paris.

▼ Dish of the Day

Most people cook beneath the hood of an oven, but Bob Blumer prefers cooking beneath the hood of a car. Hollywood's Surreal Gourmet, Blumer has championed cooking meat and fish in aluminum foil on car engines. His recipes often begin: "Preheat the engine for 20 miles...." He has also toured the States promoting his unusual recipes in his "Toastermobile," a trailer equipped with a professional kitchen, and topped with two slices of toast, 8 ft (2.4 m) high!

Cosy Rabbits

William Schultz of Grants Pass, Oregon, heats his greenhouse with the body heat of 350 caged rabbits!

Army Decoy

During World War II, the British magician Jasper Maskelyne was recruited to create an entire fake seaport to hide the Suez Canal and to disguise the activities of the army by building decoy troops. He acheived this amazing deception by using mirrors, flashing lights, and an array of wooden props.

Dead Ends

Alliance, Ohio, is the only town in the whole of the U.S.A. that has a main street that is a dead end at both of its ends.

Paperweight Museum

A museum at Cambridge, Ohio, boasts over 4,000 paperweights. The Degenhart Paperweight Museum houses the collection of former glass-factory owner Elizabeth Degenhart, who picked up her paperweights between 1947 and her death in 1978.

Going Nowhere

Eccentric British tycoon Joseph Williamson dug a network of tunnels under the city of Liverpool, England, 200 years ago. Most of the tunnels lead nowhere.

Banana Stamp

There was once an official stamp issued by the country of Tonga (in the South Pacific) shaped like a banana.

Mountain Job

In August 2005, executives of ImageNet Co. gave job applicants an initiative test by holding interviews at 12,388 ft (3,776 m) at the summit of Mount Fuji! They wanted to make sure that new employees would have what it takes to scale the heights of business.

Interviewing a prospective candidate on Mount Fuji.

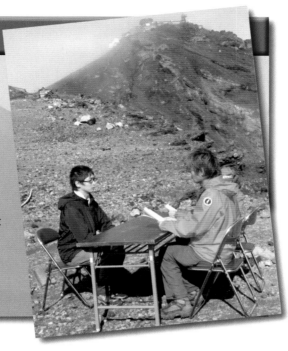

Revolving Jail

At Council Bluffs, Iowa, is a curious three-storey jail known as the Squirrel Cage. Built in 1885, the cells used to revolve constantly so the jailer could watch his prisoners at all times.

Snail Mail

A letter sent to the German town of Ostheim-vor-der-Rhoen in 1718 arrived in 2004, surviving 286 years in the postal system.

The King's Stamp

The king of rock 'n' roll, Elvis Presley, is the only person whose image appears on a U.S. postage stamp approved by a public vote.

Sewer Constrictor

In October 2005, in Manchester, England, a 10-ft (3-m) boa constrictor appeared in an apartment toilet bowl. A concrete block was placed on the toilet lid to prevent the snake escaping before firefighters and plumbers arrived. Using hi-tech fiber-optic equipment, they checked the sewage pipes, but could find no evidence of the snake. Another resident in the apartment building then captured the snake, having found it on his bathroom floor. The snake appeared to have been living happily in the apartments' sewage system!

Tree Hotel

The Hotel Woodpecker, Vasteras, Sweden, sits 43 ft (13 m) above ground in an oak tree in the middle of a park. To reach their rooms, guests must climb a ladder (which is then removed) and meals are served via a basket attached to a pulley.

Luxury Cave

Kokopelli's Cave Bed and Breakfast is surely the world's most luxurious cave. Carved into the side of a mountain in Farmington, New Mexico, the cave covers 1,650 sq ft (153 sq m) and has every modern convenience for guests, including hot and cold running water, carpets, and a kitchen.

Cross Garden

William C. Rice, who died in 2004, erected hundreds of crosses on his land at Prattville, Alabama. It took him more than 20 years to create his garden of faith. Beside the crosses he painted messages of redemption on recycled window air-conditioner covers, refrigerator doors, and auto parts.

State View

On a clear day you can see five states from the top of the Empire State Building in New York City—New York State, New Jersey, Connecticut, Massachusetts, and Pennsylvania.

Dem Bones Dem Bones

A chapel in the Czech Republic contains beautiful decorations and furnishings—and they're all made from human skeletons.

Below is one of the chapel's bone chalices. The use of bones to create this and all the other decorations was intended to give the visitor an impression of the shortness of life and the inevitability of death.

Centuries ago, the abbey at Sedlec was a major burial site. Around 1400, a church was built in the middle of the cemetery and a small chapel was used as an ossuary for the mass graves unearthed during construction.

The task of exhuming skeletons and stacking their bones was given to a half-blind monk.

In 1870, wood-carver Frantisek Rint was employed by the Schwarzenberg family, who owned the church, to put the bone heaps in order. He turned 40,000 skeletons into amazing artistic creations, producing crosses, columns, and chalices of bone. From the center of the nave hangs an enormous chandelier featuring every bone in the human body several times over. Garlands of skulls drape the vaults, four bell-shaped bone mounds occupy the corners of the chapel, monstrances of bones flank the altar, and there is even a bone replica of the Schwarzenberg coat-of-arms.

Above is a detail from a pinnacle: a decorative pyramid of bones. Each pinnacle in the chapel is crowned with a cherub.

The image on the left shows a cross-shaped decoration above the entrance to the chapel. Below is one of the two solar crosses that are placed in the recesses on either side of the altar.

The bones come mainly from victims of the Black Death plague that swept across Europe in the 14th century, when 30,000 people were buried in Sedlec Cemetery. Some, however, are also casualties from the Hussite Wars of the 15th century—on some of the skulls the marks of battle wounds are clearly visible.

Climate Change
Mount Waialeale on the island of Kauai, Hawaii, often has 350 days of rain a year. Yet a few miles away at sea level, the annual rainfall is as low as 20 in (50 cm).

Highs and Lows
Mount Whitney, California, which is the highest peak in the U.S.A. outside Alaska, and Zabriskie Point in Death Valley, which is the lowest point in the U.S.A., are fewer than 80 mi (130 km) apart.

Barrel Boat
Japanese sailor Kenichi Horie, aged 60, spent three months sailing alone across the Pacific Ocean on a yacht made out of beer kegs.

Pepper Shakers
Some people collect stamps, others collect coins, but Andrea Ludden collects salt and pepper shakers. Her 20-year obsession is displayed at the Salt and Pepper Museum in Gatlinburg, Tennessee. And with more than 17,000 shakers from all over the world, her collection is definitely not to be sneezed at!

An **advertisement** in the 1860s for the PONY EXPRESS COMPANY read "must be expert riders, **willing to risk death daily**. ORPHANS preferred."

Tree Huggers
If you thought climbing trees was only for small boys, think again. In August 2005, 52 tree-climbers from across the world scrambled up trunks at a staggering pace for the International Tree Climbing Competition in Nashville, Tennessee. Judging is strict, with penalties for unsafe maneuvers and bonuses for creativity, confidence, and use of equipment. The top prize of $1,000 went to the newly crowned world champions, Dan Krause of Seattle, Washington, and Chrissy Spence from New Zealand.

Windmill King
Frank Medina was acknowledged as king of the windmills. He built up a collection of more than 2,000 windmills at Stockton, in California. At the age of 96, he also had all his own teeth and had never had a cavity!

▶ Ice Sculpture
Randy Finch, from Grand Rapids, Michigan, has built a double Ferris wheel out of ice— that actually works! The sculpture is made from over 30 separate pieces of ice, most less than 1 in (2.5 cm) thick. Each of the individual carts turns on an ice axle. Finch has also made a full-sized ice pool table (above), complete with ice balls and cues.

Cave Music

The Great Stalacpipe Organ, in the Luray Caverns of Virginia, is a gigantic musical instrument that covers 3.5 acres (1.4 ha). Invented in 1954, the organ uses natural stalactites instead of metal pipes to make beautiful music. Its inventor, mathematician and scientist Leland Sprinkle, walked the length of the caverns, deliberately choosing stalactites that would perfectly match the musical scale.

Colorado Keys

The Baldpate Inn in Estes Park, Colorado, has more than 20,000 keys on display. The collection boasts keys from Mozart's wine cellar, the Pentagon, and Westminster Abbey.

Underground Church

The amazing 750-year-old Church of St. George in the Ethiopian village of Lalibela is built vertically downward! It has been cut out of the rock in the shape of a cross and is surrounded by a trench. The top of the church is flush with ground level. There are 10 other underground churches in the area, many connected by tunnels.

Kicking the Bottle

Bottle Kicking (and Hare Pie Scrambling) competitions have taken place on Easter Monday in Leicestershire, England, since 1771. Yet this curious sport involves neither bottles nor kicking. The contest—often bloody and brutal—takes place between the neighboring villages of Hallaton and Medbourne. The rival villagers fight over three small beer barrels and attempt to manhandle two of them over their opponents' line. The respective goal-lines are two streams a mile apart. The free-for-all has no other rules and the game can last for several hours.

Unexpected Guests

Visitors to a luxury manor house in Kenya are likely to be joined at the dinner table by some unusual guests—a herd of giraffes! Set in 120 acres (49 ha) of forest on the outskirts of Nairobi, Giraffe Manor has welcomed the likes of Mick Jagger, Johnny Carson, Brooke Shields, and Lee Remick. But it is the rare Rothschilds' giraffes that have been the star attractions since moving in to the manor in 1974.

Long Overdue

Padma Maya Gurung, of Nepal, spent an extra six years in jail because a letter of release from the supreme court, issued in 1997, was lost in the mail.

RIPLEY'S FIRST, OLDEST, AND LARGEST permanent museum, St. Augustine was opened on December 9, 1950. It is situated in a historic 1887 building that was once a hotel where Ripley himself stayed several times in the 1940s. The museum features a full-size Ferris wheel made from Meccano.

SNAKE MASK
This colorful Ceylonese mask, is used to help exorcise evil spirits.

IRON MAIDEN
A medieval German torture device, this was used on heretics to ensure a painful death.

MUMMIFIED CAT
This cat lived over 2,000 years ago in the ancient Egyptian city of Bubastis.

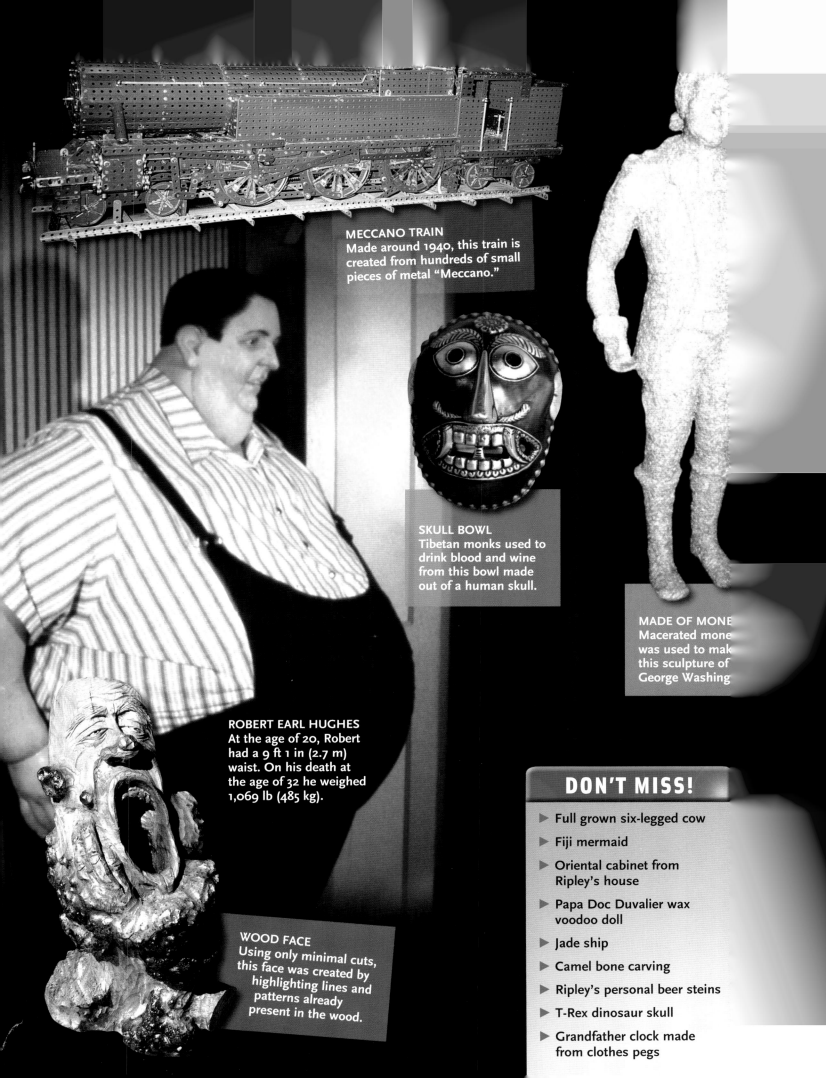

MECCANO TRAIN
Made around 1940, this train is created from hundreds of small pieces of metal "Meccano."

SKULL BOWL
Tibetan monks used to drink blood and wine from this bowl made out of a human skull.

MADE OF MONE
Macerated mone was used to mak this sculpture of George Washing

ROBERT EARL HUGHES
At the age of 20, Robert had a 9 ft 1 in (2.7 m) waist. On his death at the age of 32 he weighed 1,069 lb (485 kg).

WOOD FACE
Using only minimal cuts, this face was created by highlighting lines and patterns already present in the wood.

DON'T MISS!

- ▶ Full grown six-legged cow
- ▶ Fiji mermaid
- ▶ Oriental cabinet from Ripley's house
- ▶ Papa Doc Duvalier wax voodoo doll
- ▶ Jade ship
- ▶ Camel bone carving
- ▶ Ripley's personal beer steins
- ▶ T-Rex dinosaur skull
- ▶ Grandfather clock made from clothes pegs

⛰ Pet Cemetery
Jean Pyke has buried 22 pets in her garden on Hayling Island in England. Alongside the pets are also buried the ashes of her dead husband.

House of Clocks
In 1960, Ray Thougen rescued a grandfather clock from a garbage truck and bought three other junk clocks for $5. That was the start of a clock collection that now stands at almost a thousand pieces—all in full working order. For 17 years, Thougen lovingly restored damaged clocks, often without diagrams, before the collection was bought by Ray Sweeney in 1977. Unable to deny the passing of time, both Rays are now dead, but their legacy ticks on at the House of Clocks, in Waukon, Iowa.

Nuts and Bolts

★ The Grand Mosque Djenne in Mali is 328 ft (100 m) long and 131 ft (40 m) wide—and is made from mud!

★ There are over 130 million items on about 530 mi (853 km) of bookshelves in the Library of Congress, Washington D.C.

★ An old-style red telephone kiosk in Huddersfield, England, was converted into a tiny public bar.

Dog Paddle
Among the 500 swimmers that competed in the South End Rowing Club's annual Alcatraz Invitational in 2005, one stood out—Jake the golden retriever. The only four-legged competitor in the field, Jake jumped from a boat near Alcatraz and swam 1.2 mi (1.9 km) to the San Francisco shoreline, finishing a creditable 72nd.

Kahului, *Hawaii*, is home to a museum devoted solely to **paper airplanes**. There are more than **2,000** models ranging from postage-stamp size to paper planes with wingspans of more than 6 ft (1.8 m).

Bone Cabin
Near Medicine Bay, Wyoming, is a cabin built entirely from dinosaur bones. Thomas Boylan began collecting discarded bone fragments from a nearby paleontological dig in 1916. Seventeen years later, he had managed to amass an amazing 5,796 bones, weighing a total of 102,116 lb (46,319 kg), which he then decided to use to construct a lodge measuring 29 ft (8.8 m) long and 19 ft (5.8 m) wide.

Duck Walk
Carp collect in such numbers and at such a high density at the base of the spillway of the Pymatuning Reservoir near the town of Linesville, Pennsylvania, that ducks are able to walk across the backs of the fish and hardly get their feet wet!

Symbolic Pot
Towering over the town of Davidson, Saskatchewan, is a coffee pot 24 ft (7.3 m) tall that could hold 150,000 8-oz (227-g) cups of coffee. The giant pot is intended as a symbol of Davidson's friendliness and hospitality.

⛰ A Meal Too Far
A Burmese python 13 ft (4 m) long bit off more than it could chew when it tried to swallow whole a 6 ft (1.8 m) American alligator. Both animals were found dead, floating in the water. Experts think the alligator was still alive when the snake swallowed it snout first, and that repeated kicks from its hind legs ruptured the snake's stomach wall.

Gone to Pot

The site of the Sky Kingdom religious sect in Kampung Batu, Malaysia, was dominated, until its demolition in 2005, by a two-storey building in the shape of a giant pink teapot. The teapot was apparently inspired by the dreams of one of the sect's followers.

Horn Tree

Believe it or not, at Junction, Texas, there is a Christmas tree made entirely from deer horns!

Doll Habit

At Indian River, Michigan, is a museum with around 525 dolls, all dressed as nuns. The Cross in the Woods Nun Doll Museum is the brainchild of Sally Rogalski, who, as a young girl in 1945, used to dress her dolls in nuns' habits to preserve Catholic history. The Rogalskis received a special blessing from Pope John Paul II for their work "in helping to promote vocations to the priesthood and religious life through their doll collection."

Beer-can Castle

Faced with a growing pile of empty beer cans, Vietnam veteran Donald Espinoza from Anonito, Colorado, decided to put them to good use. He spent the following 25 years building a fortress—named Cano's Castle— from the cans, as well as from hubcaps and strips of aluminum.

Ship Shape

A car wash at Eau Claire, Wisconsin, is shaped like a cruise liner, complete with two smoke stacks.

Large wads of alligator skin were found in what remained of the snake's stomach, and the alligator had also sustained wounds behind the eyes and on the shoulder. Until an alligator's spinal cord is severed, it can still move its legs, so its sharp claws could have torn through the snake's skin, causing the gaping hole.

After the snake died, its head was probably eaten by another alligator.

The alligator's tail and hind legs are protruding from a large hole where the python's body literally burst under the pressure of its meal! The stomach of the python still surrounds the head, shoulders, and forelimbs of the alligator.

Moving Land

The fastest-moving place on the Earth is the South Pacific island of Niuatoputapu. It is moving at a rate of 10 in (25 cm) a year.

Fish Parade

The town of Aitkin, Minnesota, hosts an annual Fish House Parade. Fish houses (the sort used for ice fishing) are dressed in weird and wonderful themes and paraded through town for eight blocks before up to 6,000 enthusiastic spectators.

▼ Grape Time

Revellers frolic among grape pulp during the annual grape battle in Binissalem on the Spanish island of Mallorca. The town celebrates its wine tradition with the fiesta every year at the end of the grape festival.

Silent Mourning

Women of the Warramunga tribe of Australia do not speak for a year after the death of their husbands—communicating instead only with hand and arm gestures.

Tiny Congregation

A wooden church in Drumheller, Alberta, is just 11 ft (3.4 m) long and 7 ft (2 m) wide. Originally built in 1968, Little Church has six one-person pews and a pulpit.

Bank Pets

Customers at the Union Federal Savings and Loan Bank in Kewanee, Illinois, can watch two otters, Andy and Oscar, romping in a climate-controlled play pool in the middle of the bank. They were introduced in 1991 by the bank's president.

Firm Bite

Australian Rugby player Shane Millard was treated for an unusual head wound after a match. Doctors found a tooth from one of his opponents embedded in his skull.

Pyramid House

Jim and Linda Onan wanted a house with a difference, so they created a six-storey building shaped like a pyramid and made out of 24-carat gold plate. The Gold Pyramid, which is in Wadsworth, Illinois, has an interior that measures an enormous 17,000 sq ft (1,580 sq m). Furnished in the style of the ancient Egyptian pharaohs, it contains a replica of King Tutankhamen's tomb, while the grounds feature a triple-pyramid garage and a 64-ft (19.5-m) statue of the Egyptian king Ramses.

Wreck Replica
The world's most bizarre Stonehenge replica can be found near Alliance, Nebraska, made entirely from wrecked cars. Built by Jim Reinders in 1987, "Carhenge" has 38 cars, positioned in a circle 96 ft (29 m) in diameter, echoing its famous English counterpart.

Roadside Oddity

In 1930, to catch the eye of passing motorists, brothers Elmer and Henry Nickle built a roadside gas station at Powell, Tennessee—in the shape of an airplane. More recently the airplane building, complete with wings and a propeller, has been used as a car lot.

Junk House

When eccentric sculptor Art Beal bought a hillside plot at Cambria, California, in 1928 he set about building a junk house. He spent 50 years realizing his dream and, as the town's garbage collector in the 1940s and 1950s, he used the junk he collected in the construction. He called the result Nitt Witt Ridge, Beal's alias being Captain Nitt Witt.

Elephant Hotel

In 1881, James T. Lafferty built a hotel in the shape of an elephant. Nicknamed Lucy, this historical landmark is now located in Margate, New Jersey. Lucy is 65 ft (19.8 m) tall and weighs 90 tons. For $4 you can wander through its pink rooms and get an elephant's-eye view of the city.

Easier than ABC

Rotokas, a language of the South Pacific, has an alphabet with only 11 letters, comprising six consonants and five vowels.

Trans-Australian Swim

A group of 60 swimmers swam their way across Australia in a pool attached to the back of a truck traveling at 56 mph (90 km/h).

Petrified Dog

Loggers at Waycross, Georgia, looked inside a hollow tree—and found a mummified dog. It was thought the dog had died after getting stuck in the tree, probably 20 years earlier. The petrified dog is now a local tourist attraction and is displayed inside a cross-section of log.

Deep Sleep

Near Västerås, Sweden, is a hotel where guests sleep in an underwater room. The brainchild of artist Mikael Genberg, the bedroom at the Utter Inn is situated 10 ft (3 m) below the surface of Lake Mälaren, with a window offering a panoramic view of passing marine life.

Fish Hotel

Chicago's newest downtown hotel caters solely for fish. This "fish hotel" is a series of small gardens densely planted with pondweed to satisfy the scaly inhabitants of the Chicago River. Some gardens are floating, others submerged, and all of the "rooms" are fitted with underwater cameras so that humans can catch a glimpse of the action.

In **Cleveland**, *Ohio*, stands a gigantic office **rubber stamp**. Made by artist **Claes Oldenburg** in 1985, the steel structure is 28 ft (8.5 m) **tall** and 48 ft (14.6 m) *long*.

Remote Island

The uninhabited Bouvet Island in the South Atlantic is probably the world's most remote island. The nearest land—Queen Maud Land in Antarctica— is 1,050 mi (1,690 km) away, and is also uninhabited.

Turtle Power

At Dunseith, North Dakota, a giant turtle has been welded together from over 2,000 steel wheel rims. The head alone weighs more than a ton.

Big Smoke

This giant cigar, made in Miami, Florida, in 1994, is 6 ft (1.8 m) long, 11 in (28 cm) in diameter, and weighs 55 lb (25 kg)—holding enough tobacco to make 3,000 regular no.1-sized cigars! It took two men two weeks to hand roll.

Look Who's Talking

You never know who's talking to you at Vent Haven, as this museum at Fort Mitchell, Kentucky, is home to over 600 ventriloquists' dummies. It is the legacy of W.S. Berger, who collected ventriloquism memorabilia from the early 20th century up until his death in 1972.

Foam Home

At Centralia, Washington State, is a house covered in Styrofoam®™. The owner, former art teacher Richard Tracy, has been working on the house for more than 20 years.

Giant Chair

A steel chair, 33 ft (10 m) high, stands next to a furniture store in Anniston, Alabama. Built in 1981, the structure can withstand winds of up to 85 mph (137 km/h).

Indoor Beach

With 3,350 sq yd (2,800 sq m) of white sand, the Ocean Dome beach, at Miyazaki, Japan, is one of the world's finest. But what makes it unusual is that it is indoors. The beach features plastic palm trees that sway in an artificial breeze, and 13,500 tons of salt-free "sea." A machine creates surf up to 11 ft (3.4 m) high, and even when the giant roof is open the temperature is a warm 86°F (30°C). There's no danger of sunburn or shark attacks and even the surrounding volcanoes are fake. But perhaps the oddest thing about the dome is that the real beach and sea are only 300 yd (275 m) away!

Movie Theater

The 2,908-ton Shubert Theater in Minneapolis, Minnesota, was moved in one piece to a new site three blocks away in 1999. The theater was transported on rubber wheels for a short journey that took 12 days.

Prophetic Name

When Nancy Araya opened a new restaurant in Santiago, Chile, in 2005, she decided to call it Car Crash because the area was an accident blackspot. But within a few weeks the restaurant had to close after a passing car crashed through the entrance of the building.

Lobster Derby

In a spoof of the Kentucky Derby, lobster racing takes place every May in Aiken, South Carolina, on a track called Lobster Downs. The track is a series of water-filled tanks where progress can be painfully slow. Indeed some lobsters have been known to die mid-race.

Icy Weather

Gale-force north-easterly winds brought freezing temperatures and freakish weather to Lake Geneva, Switzerland, in January 2005. With 70 mph (120 km/h) winds and temperatures of 10°F (−12°C), waves swept over the lake's banks and droplets of water froze instantly on everything they touched.

Canadian Moulette

A popular pastime in rural areas of North America is cow patty bingo. To play, a field is divided into squares, which are wagered on by contestants. The prize goes to whoever has picked the square on which the cow deposits a pat. In 2003, a Canadian firm introduced a variation on this theme, moulette, using a 50-ft (15-m) long roulette board instead of a field. However, protestors said it was cruel to deprive a cow of dirt and grass on which to answer a call of nature.

Pub Grub

A restaurant in Germany enjoyed a rush of bookings in 2005 after adding maggots to the menu. The Espitas restaurant in Dresden served up such delicacies as maggot ice-cream, fried maggots with cactus and corn, maggot salads, and maggot cocktails. Owner Alexander Wolf said, "We were fully booked for weeks. Most people were disgusted but tried them out of curiosity or for a dare, and were amazed at how good the maggots tasted."

Fence Forte

Musician Simon Dagg from Kent, England, is so obsessed with his first love that he spent a whopping £60,000 ($105,000) fine-tuning the fence around his house so that it would play like a giant glockenspiel. He worked 12 hours a day for five years tuning the metal bars to play like the real thing.

Simon Dagg's musical garden fence measures 120 ft (36.5 m) long.

Tree Village

Believe it or not, the grounds of Alnwick Castle, England, are home to a remarkable tree house—or, rather, a 60-ft (18.3-m) high tree "village"—set among the branches of 16 lime trees. The brainchild of Jane, Duchess of Northumberland, it opened in January 2005, having cost over £3.3 million ($5.7 million). There are five rooms, which include a restaurant, and 6,000 sq ft (557 sq m) of suspended walkways.

Seasonal Snowman

A smiling snowman, 35 ft (10.6 m) tall, stands near Beardmore, Ontario. Made of wood over a steel frame, the snowman was built in 1960 to promote the community and the local ski hill. He even dresses for the time of year—in summer he has sunglasses and a fishing pole; in winter he wears a scarf and carries a curling broom.

On the Border

The Hotel Arbez at Les Rousses straddles the French–Swiss border and offers guests a choice of rooms in either France or Switzerland.

◀ Upside-down Bed

Fancy sleeping in an Upside Down Room, where all the furniture is suspended from the ceiling and you sleep and sit in boxes beneath the floorboards? Or how about the Symbol Room (above), made from 300 square, wooden plates decorated with black-and-white symbols? What about the Coffin Room or the Padded Cell Room? Propeller Island City Lodge Hotel in Berlin, Germany, has 30 rooms, each with a unique, wacky theme.

▶ Backwards Biking

Some people aren't satisfied with riding a bicycle the conventional way—they prefer to ride it backwards. In this curious sport, the rider sits on the handlebars instead of the seat, facing backwards, and peddling and steering in reverse! The bikes are not fitted with mirrors or any special adaptations. In 2002, Dutchman and expert backward-cyclist Pieter de Hart cycled an amazing 16.7 mi (26.9 km) in one hour.

Car Spike

The parking lot at the Cermak Plaza Shopping Centre, Berwyn, Illinois, looks like the scene of a horrific accident—shoppers turn a corner to discover eight cars impaled on a 40-ft (12-m) spike! Luckily, it is only a sculpture, named "The Spindle," created by Californian artist Dustin Shuler, from Los Angeles, in 1989.

Monkey Mayor

When the residents of Hartlepool, England, voted for a new mayor in 2002, they elected a man in a monkey costume! H'Angus the Monkey, mascot of the town's soccer team, campaigned successfully with the slogan "free bananas for schoolchildren."

Frog Race

Since 1946, Rayne, Louisiana, has hosted a Frog Derby. Girls from the town dress up frogs in jockey uniforms and encourage them to hop along a course.

Tree Tunnel

You can drive through trees at Leggett, California. The bases of giant redwoods have been tunneled out so that cars can pass through.

> **TWO HARBORS**, Minnesota, must be the only place in the world that has a **museum** devoted solely to **sandpaper**. The collection is located in the house of **John Dwan**, one of the founders of the 3M Company. As a special treat, visitors are given *free* sandpaper samples.

Fireproof City

The Bolivian capital, La Paz, is very nearly fireproof. Located 12,000 ft (3,660 m) above sea level, there is barely enough oxygen in the air to support combustion.

Magnetic Hill

Bizarrely, cars seem to roll uphill at Magnetic Hill, near Moncton, New Brunswick. The phenomenon was first noticed in the 19th century when farmers observed their horses straining to pull wagons down the hill, but when going uphill the wagons would bunch up at the horses' feet. Today, tourists drive their cars to the foot of the hill, stop, put them into neutral and then coast backward, uphill.

The Goat King

For three days a year, Ireland is ruled by a goat! Before the Puck Fair, held in Killorglin, Kerry, every August, chief goat-catcher Frank Joy heads into the hills and captures a wild mountain goat. The goat is duly crowned King Puck and placed on an elevated platform in the center of the town square where, from a height of 50 ft (15 m), he looks down on his subjects for the three-day duration of the fair.

ARTIST MARCO FIGGEN PAINTS in his studio in Pattaya City, Thailand, with his own beard. It measures 3 ft 7 in (1.1 m) long, and Figgen describes his unique paintbrush as an extension of his soul. He has been growing his beard for 13 years.

WEIRD

For a dignified last ride, bikers can have their coffins drawn by a Harley Davidson motorbike
page 63

A multi-pierced and tattooed man had his tongue split to resemble a snake's, and also installed fang caps on his teeth
page 64

Contestants eat a variety of creepy crawlies, such as crickets, mealworms, hornets, and locusts at the Bug Eating Championships
page 66

& WONDERFUL

BREaD HEaD

KITTIWAT UNARROM makes edible human heads and torsos out of dough! His workplace looks like a mortuary or a serial killer's dungeon, but it is in fact a bakery.

Visitors to Unarrom's workshop near Bangkok are alarmed to see the heads and torsos lined up on shelves, and rows of arms and hands hanging from meat hooks. The Thai art student, whose family runs a bakery, uses anatomy books and his memories of visiting a forensics museum to create the human body parts. In addition to heads crafted from bread, chocolate, raisins, and cashews, he makes human arms and feet, and chicken and pig parts, incorporating red food coloring for extra bloody effect. "When people see the bread, they don't want to eat it," he says. "But when they taste it, it's just normal bread. The lesson is, don't judge by appearances."

His macabre project started out as the centerpiece of his of Arts degree, but as word spread about his novelty-shaped bread, regular orders began coming in from the curious or from pranksters who want to surprise their friends.

Basing the models on pictures from anatomy books, Thai art student Kittiwat Unarrom lovingly creates lifelike human heads from bread. Not surprisingly, most people think twice before eating the heads.

Some of Kittiwat's creations are really gruesome and would not look out of place in a chamber of horrors. And if they're not bloody enough, he adds red food coloring to increase the effect.

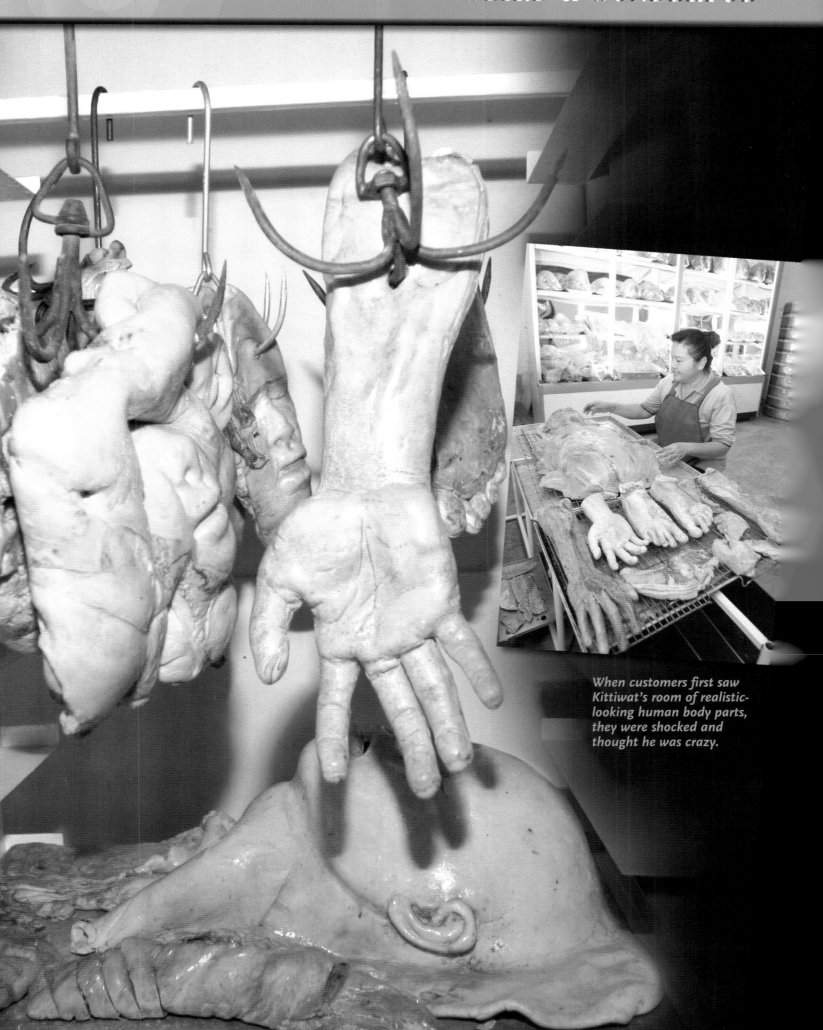

When customers first saw Kittiwat's room of realistic-looking human body parts, they were shocked and thought he was crazy.

Let it Be

This toilet paper, auctioned at a starting price of £40,000 ($71,000), was removed from the toilets in the EMI studios at Abbey Road, London, England, when the Beatles refused to use it, objecting to its hardness and shininess. They were also said to have disliked the fact that EMI was stamped on every sheet.

The toilet paper, still on its original 1960s roll, was framed in a glass box.

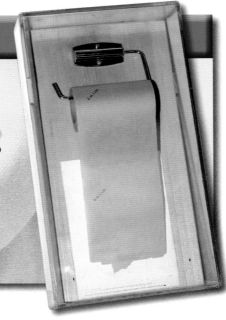

Bearded Lady

Vivian Wheeler has a weird claim to fame—she is the woman with the world's longest beard. Wheeler, who comes from Wood River, Illinois, was born with facial hair, having inherited a genetic hormonal disorder from her mother. Her father refused to accept her beard and forced her to shave it off from the age of seven, but she later traveled with sideshow acts under the stage name of Melinda Maxie, dying her natural red hair black for greater impact. Her full beard has now reached a length of 11 in (28 cm), although she usually wears it tied up.

Self-liposuction

Believe it or not, Yugoslav-born plastic surgeon Dimitrije Panfilov performed liposuction on himself to remove a double chin!

Tiny Letters

In 2004, physicists at Boston College, Massachussetts, managed to carve miniscule letters into a single strand of human hair. Using a laser, they created letters that were 15 micrometers tall. The technique can form items a thousand times smaller than the diameter of a human hair.

Miracle Birth

Nhlahla Cwayita was born healthy at Cape Town, South Africa, in 2003, despite developing in her mother's liver. She was only the fourth baby in the world to survive such a pregnancy.

● On a Shoestring

Big Bear City, California, is home to The Shoe Tree—no one quite knows how it started, but the tree continues to accumulate shoe upon shoe. Local police tried to prevent the tree being used in this way by removing all the shoes and fencing off the area, but by the next morning it was covered once again.

Circus Club

At one of the world's strangest nightclubs, the California Institute of Abnormalarts, you can dance the night away in the company of the remains of a dead clown, the stuffed carcass of a piglet-Chihuahua hybrid, a mummified arm, and such weird exhibits as Octopus Girl! The museum and nightclub is run by Carl Crew and Robert Ferguson, who collect circus memorabilia.

Bead Art

Liza Lou of Topanga, California, used 40 million glass beads to create a kitchen and garden that was first displayed at the Kemper Museum of Contemporary Art in Kansas City in 1998. If the beads had been strung together, they would have stretched about 380 mi (610 km), the same distance as that between Los Angeles and San Francisco.

Two-faced Kitten

A kitten was born in Glide, Oregon, in June 2005, with two faces! Gemini astounded vets and owner Lee Bluetear with her two mouths, two tongues, two noses, and four eyes. Sadly, she died within a week.

Sentimental Value

Ezekiel Rubottom decided to keep his left foot after it was amputated in 2005! He stored it in the front porch of his Kansas home. After neigbors complained, he said "I'm not sick, I just wanted my foot."

Mark Hostetler, an ecologist at the UNIVERSITY OF FLORIDA, has written a book on how to identify **insect splats** left on your car. The book is titled *That Gunk On Your Car*.

Burning Passion

To demonstrate his love for his girlfriend, Todd Grannis set himself on fire before going down on one knee and asking her to marry him! Wearing a cape soaked in gasoline, Grannis, 38, climbed a 10-ft (3-m) scaffold at Grants Pass, Oregon, in July 2005. After being set on fire, he plunged into a swimming pool and told stunned sweetheart Malissa Kusiek: "Honey, you make me hot ... I'm on fire for you." After such a stunt, she had to say yes!

Bird Poop

Believe it or not, an American firm offers individually crafted models of birds made from genuine Californian horse dung!

Faking for Fun

Chaucey Shea of St. Catherine's, Ontario, has a potentially illegal hobby. He has mastered more than 2,000 forgeries of famous signatures, including English playwright William Shakespeare, and several presidents of the United States.

Seat of Learning

Bill Jarrett, a retired artist from Grand Rapids, Michigan, has been studying toilet paper for the past 30 years and now boasts a vast collection of tissue-related memorabilia.

Wacky Wedding

At a wedding in Calgary, Alberta, Canada, in 1998, the bride was a sword swallower, the groom tamed bees, and the maid of honor made a living eating live bugs and worms! Megan Evans married Jim Rogers (Calgary's "Bee Man") in front of 200 musicians and freak-show performers, including worm-loving bridesmaid Brenda Fox.

Half-size Jeanie

Born without any legs, Jeanie Tomaini achieved fame in U.S. sideshows as "The Half Girl." While on tour, Jeanie, who is 2 ft 6 in (0.76 m), married Al, who stood 8 ft 4 in (2.54 m) tall and wore size 22 shoes. They went on to form a successful act as "The World's Strangest Couple."

Ash Art

Bettye Jane Brokl incorporates the ashes of dead people into abstract paintings. The Biloxi, Mississippi, artist sprinkles the cremation ashes on the artwork to create a pictorial memorial for a loved one.

There's no **fast food** at **June**, a new restaurant in LAKEWOOD RANCH, FLORIDA. The **nine-course** meals take **four hours** to eat.

Gerbil Installation

An artist from Newcastle, England, made her pet gerbil the star of a 2005 exhibition. "The Gerbil's Guide to the Galaxy" showed Sally Madge's rodent chewing its way through a 1933 edition of the *New Illustrated Universal Reference Book*, "choosing" certain words to eat.

Fiberglass Shell

A mud turtle that had its shell broken into eight pieces by cars in Lutz, Florida, was given a new fiberglass one in 1982.

All Fingers and Thumbs

Filipinos Albert M. Perculeza and his son Karl Cedric each have 12 digits on their hands and 12 digits on their feet (see below). All 48 digits are fully functional.

Junk Exhibition

In 2005, an exhibition in London, England, by Japanese artist Tomoko Takahashi featured 7,600 pieces of junk. The exhibits included old washing machines, broken toys, a rusty muck-spreader, and three stuffed blackbirds.

Love Shack

In April 2005, a building was covered in 6,000 love letters, some penned by international celebrities, as part of the annual Auckland Festival in New Zealand.

Mind Reader

Matthew Nagle, of Weymouth, Massachusetts, has a brain chip that reads his mind. Severely paralyzed after being stabbed in the neck in 2001, he has a revolutionary implant that enables him to control everyday objects simply by thinking about them. After drilling a hole into his head, surgeons implanted the chip a millimeter deep into his brain. Wafer-thin electrodes attached to the chip detect the electrical signals generated by his thoughts and relay them through wires into a computer. The brain signals are analyzed by the computer and translated into cursor movements. As well as operating a computer, software linked to other items in the room allows him to think his TV on and off and change channels.

Soaring Success

For her 1999 work "100 Ideas in the Atmosphere," Canadian performance artist Marie-Suzanne Désilets launched 100 helium balloons from the rooftop of a Montreal shopping mall with self-addressed notecards and an invitation to reply.

Elastic MaN

DUBBED "MR ELASTIC," Moses Lanham can turn his feet around 180 degrees, completely backwards, and then walk in the opposite direction!

Lanham puts his unique talent down to being born with extra ligaments and cartilage within the joints of his ankles, knees, and hips, which enable him to rotate his bones freely within the sockets of his joints.

Amazingly, he didn't realize he had this ability until he suffered a fall in gym class at the age of 14 and landed awkwardly. Jumping to his feet, he suddenly found that he could easily twist both of his feet around backward. Lanham, from Monroe, Michigan, has discovered that his son Trey also appears to have inherited the extra joint tissue. At 11, he can turn his feet backward just like his dad! "He can't walk backwards yet," says Moses, "but he is learning."

Moses Lanham's body contains extra joint tissue that enables him to turn his feet backwards. Moses can even walk backwards too!

Moses enjoys putting his best foot backwards, and often performs at local fund-raising events.

Wrist-breaker
That K.S. Raghavendra, from India, is capable of breaking 13 eggs in 30 seconds doesn't sound amazing in itself, except he doesn't break them by clenching his fist, but by bending his hand back over his wrist.

Hardy Eater
"Hungry" Charles Hardy, of Brooklyn, New York, describes himself as "the Michael Jordan of competitive eating." In 2001, he ate 23 hot dogs in 12 minutes, and also became Matzo Ball Eating world champion. But his talent has drawbacks. Hardy explains: "I found a place in Manhattan with all-you-can-eat sushi for $19.95. When the lady sees me coming, she hits the clock and gives me one and a half hours."

Button King
Dalton Stevens of Hartsville, South Carolina, has fixed an incredible 600,000 buttons to his Pontiac hearse. Another 60,000 buttons cover the coffin inside! Besides the hearse, he has shoes, musical instruments, and even a toilet covered with buttons.

Human Soap
A bar of soap that was said to have been made from body fat pumped from the Italian Prime Minister Silvio Berlusconi sold for almost $20,000 in 2005. Artist Gianni Motti said that he acquired the fat from a private Swiss clinic where Berlusconi reportedly underwent liposuction. Motti said the fat was "jelly-like and stunk horribly."

Heart Beat
Jeweler Didier Verhill, of Antwerp, Belgium, creates wedding rings engraved with the couple's heartbeat pattern taken from a cardiograph!

Ham Actors
Father and son, Olivier and Yohann Roussel, won one of Europe's most coveted prizes in 2005—the French Pig-squealing Championships. Dressed in pig outfits, the Roussels impressed the judges and spectators with squeals, grunts, and snuffles to represent the four key stages of a pig's life—birth, suckling, mating, and death under the knife.

Doctor, Doctor!

★ Dr. James T. Clack, of Wadley, Alabama, treated patients in the 1940s even though he was blind.

★ Allergist Dr. Edwin Dombrowski, of Stamford, Connecticut, had the automobile licence plate "AH-CHOO."

★ Dr. Anna Perkins, of Westerloo, New York, charged the same rates in 1993 that she had set in 1928: $4 for an office visit, $5 for a house call, and $25 to deliver a baby.

★ When Dr. William Price, of Llantrisant, south Wales, died in 1893, more than 6,000 tickets were sold for his public cremation, as specified in his will.

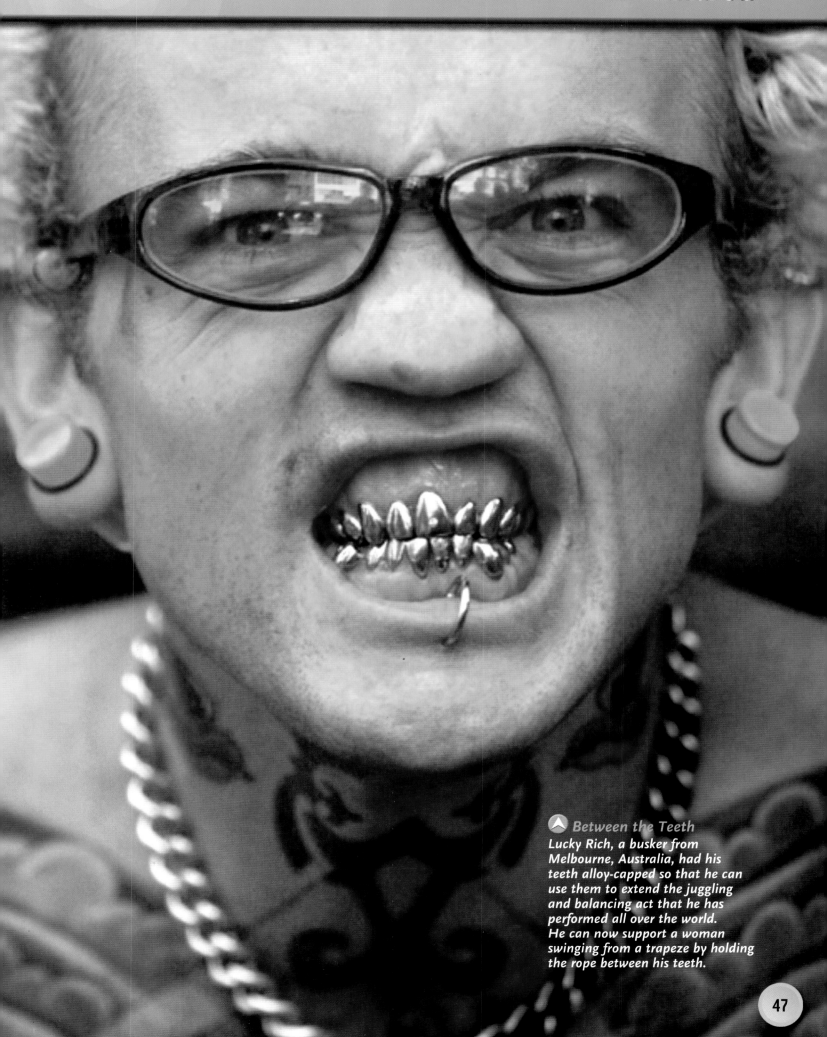

Between the Teeth
Lucky Rich, a busker from Melbourne, Australia, had his teeth alloy-capped so that he can use them to extend the juggling and balancing act that he has performed all over the world. He can now support a woman swinging from a trapeze by holding the rope between his teeth.

HAIRS AND GRACES
Jo Jo "the Dog-faced Boy" was a circus performer in the 1880s. He suffered from a rare condition called hypertrichosis, which meant hair grew all over his face.

GOGGLE-EYED
Avelino Perez Matos, of Baracoa, Cuba, had the ability to dislocate each of his eyes out of their sockets whenever he chose.

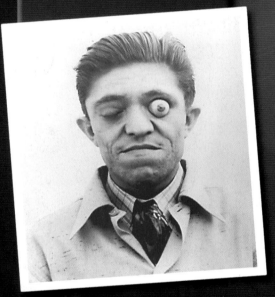

HALF AND HALF
John "half-and-half man" Pecinovsky, from Bonair, Iowa, dressed himself in a different color on each side of his body, as well as shaving and not shaving!

MINI MARRIAGE
In 1863, "General Tom Thumb," or Charles Stratton, married Lavinia Warren. Lavinia was heralded as a miniature of perfect proportions, and the marriage was a major event in New York society.

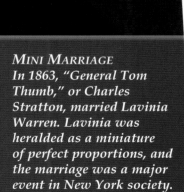

SMALL AND LARGE
Welsh giant George Auger and midget Tom Sordie both performed with the Barnum and Bailey Circus. Auger stood at 8 ft 6 in (2.6 m), while Sordie was a diminutive 2 ft 5 in (0.74 m).

SKINNY
Miss Agnes Schmidt, of Cincinnati, Ohio, pictured here in 1934, had rubber skin owing to a rare disease called Elos Dandros Syndrome.

LOBSTER FEET
The fingers of this unidentified man from upstate western New York have mutated to look like lobster claws. This was the result of inbreeding.

INSEPARABLE TWINS
The "Tocci" twins were born with one body but two heads and four arms. The photo was taken in 1892 when they were 12 years old.

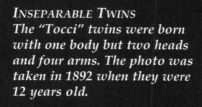

Looking Back

February 15th, 1890 Frank Damek stopped collecting stray cards from the street—he had at last made a full deck, after 20 years. **September 9, 1930 Thurber Brockband** took nine hours to find a needle in a haystack. **May 2, 1802 Timothy Dexter** published *A Pickle for the Knowing Ones*, a book that was full of intentionally misspelled words and without punctuation.

Species for Sale

A new species of rodent was discovered in 2005—for sale on a food stall in a market in Laos. The rock rat, or kha-nyou, was spotted by conservation biologist Robert Timmins who knew it was something he'd never seen before. The animal looks like a cross between a rat and a squirrel, but is not actually related to any other rodents.

Ledger Balancing

Balancing ledgers while balancing on ledges or deep-sea diving with a tax return are just some ways to perform Extreme Accounting. First established by Arnold Chiswick, the extreme sport incorporates everything involved in an accounting desk job with the thrill of sporting action.

Snake Diet

Neeranjan Bhaskar claims to have eaten more than 4,000 snakes, including deadly cobras. Bhaskar, who is a vegetarian otherwise, hunts for snakes every morning on the banks of the Ghagra River near his home in India. He first ate a snake at the age of seven.

Skin Horror

After being prescribed a common antibiotic to treat a routine sinus infection in 2003, Sarah Yeargain from San Diego, California, looked on in horror as her skin began peeling away in sheets. With Sarah's condition—caused by a severe allergic reaction to the drug—getting worse, more of her skin came off in her mother's hands as she was carried into a hospital. She eventually lost the skin from her entire body—including her internal organs and the membranes covering her mouth, throat, and eyes. Doctors gave her no chance of survival, but they covered her body in an artificial skin replacement and within a few days her own skin returned.

Dog Diver

When Dwane Folsom went scuba diving, his dog went too! Folsom, from Boynton Beach, Florida, designed the first scuba-diving outfit for dogs, comprising a lead-weighted jacket, a helmet, and a tube that allowed the animal to draw air from the human diver's tank. Folsom and his dog, named Shadow, regularly dived to depths of 13 ft (4 m).

Our Lady of the Underpass

Thousands of worshipers flocked to a Chicago underpass in April 2005 and created a shrine of candles and flowers, after a watery mark on the concrete wall was interpreted as an image of the Virgin Mary. Visitors touched and kissed the mark, which was thought to have been caused by salt running down from the Kennedy Expressway overhead. However, the devout insisted it was a miracle that had appeared in order to mark the death of Pope John Paul II.

IN DEPTH
Live by the Sword

New Yorker Natasha Veruschka, 32, claims to be the world's only belly-dancing sword swallower, and defies a strict religious upbringing to risk her life for her passion.

When did you first become fascinated by swords?

" My British mother died when I was two. I don't remember my Siberian father—I was adopted into a strict Mennonite family in southern Ukraine. I wasn't allowed to hear music, or look in a mirror, or cut my hair. When I was four I saw a knife in a church—I was mesmerized. I remember putting the tip of it on my tongue to feel it. **"**

How did your act begin?

" I grew up in countries including India, Egypt, and Iran, and later took belly dancing lessons in New York.

I learned sword balancing, but one night I ended a performance by kissing the sword—I realized then that I wanted to be a sword swallower. The first time I did it, nine years ago, it felt like home—it made me complete. **"**

What kinds of swords do you swallow?

" The longest is 27½ inches—which is a lot because I am only 5 ft 4 in tall and weigh just over 100 lb. I have 25 different swords—including a Sai sword, which is an eight-sided Japanese war weapon. I can swallow up to 13 swords at once. **"**

Which is the most dangerous?

" The neon sword, which is filled with poisonous gas and is so fragile that your stomach muscles can shatter it inside you. It is electric and heats up—one time, it started to burn and adhere to my insides. Since 1942, six people have died swallowing one. **"**

Have you ever cut yourself on a sword?

" Once I nearly died—I lost 53 per cent of my blood. I had three swords inside me and a man pushed me. The blades scissored and cut my lower esophagus. After the show, I was vomiting blood everywhere and even had a near-death experience. They told me at the hospital that I would be in the morgue by the following morning. I was back swallowing swords within a month. **"**

Where does the sword go?

" To the bottom of the stomach. I can swallow a chocolate cherry, put a sword down and bring it back up. You have to overcome much more than a gag reflex—the sword has to go past two muscle sphincters as well, on its way past the lungs and heart. **"**

Do you have any special techniques?

" I say a prayer before every performance, and use yoga to go into 'a zone.' I use no lubricant, no special tubes. You need a lot of upper body strength—the swords weigh close to 12½ lb when I swallow them all at once—and a lot of lung capacity. It's not magic. I have been X-rayed and you can see the sword in me. The neon one glows through my body for all to see. **"**

What drives you—and how long will you do this?

" My family have shunned me for what I do. To them, I am dead. I think this all stems from an 'I'll show you' attitude. As for how long, I won't be happy until I'm the oldest female belly-dancing sword swallower in the world! **"**

Free Pig

In an unusual bid to boost sales in 2005, an entrepreneurial British housing developer offered a free gift of a live pig to anyone who bought a property from him. Jeremy Paxton, who is based in Gloucestershire, England, promised that the rare breed Gloucester Old Spot pigs would be fully house-trained before delivery.

Giant Rodent

For a 2004 art festival, Dutchman Florentun Hofman built a sculpture of a beaver 100 ft (31 m) long and 25 ft (8 m) high, using just wood and reeds. The year before, he made a 37-ft (11-m) high rabbit.

▶ Pierced Glasses

An American artist has had permanent glasses pierced through the bridge of his nose. Twenty-three-year-old James Sooy, from Dallas, Texas, came up with the eye-catching invention to stop his spectacles from constantly slipping down his nose. The piercing features magnets, so that he can take the glasses off when he bathes and sleeps.

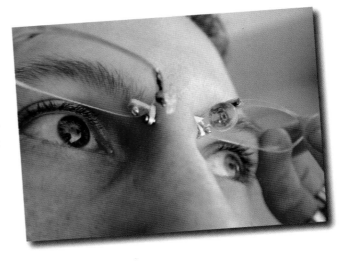

Nose Grown

Madina Yusuf had her face reconstructed by growing a new nose on her arm. The Nigerian woman was severely disfigured by a flesh-eating disease that left her without a nose and with very little mouth. But, in 2001, she flew to Aberdeen, Scotland, where Dr. Peter Ayliffe grafted her new nose from extra skin grown on her arm, plus bone and cartilage that had been taken from her right rib.

Balloon Sculpture

U.S. balloon sculptor Larry Moss used more than 40,000 balloons to construct a model of two football players at Mol, Belgium, in 2000. Each player was 40 ft (12 m) tall.

The Smell of Italy!

In 2003, Ducio Cresci, of Florence, Italy, created bathroom products—including soap, lotion, and bubble bath—that smelled just like pizza!

◀ Superhuman Suit

Japanese scientists have designed a robot suit that gives you superhuman strength. People wearing the HAL (Hybrid Assistive Limb) exoskeleton have been able to carry 88 lb (40 kg) more than they could normally. The equipment reads nerve signals sent from the brain to muscles in the wearer's arms or legs. Motors then start up to support the limbs as the wearer moves. It is hoped that the suit could help disabled people to walk.

Tiny Tackler

The ace defence tackler on the football team at Flint Southwestern Academy High School, Michigan, was only 3 ft (0.9 m) tall, having been left with no legs after a 1994 railroad accident. Willie McQueen earned his place on the team by courage and tenacity. He didn't play in a wheelchair or wear prostheses, but scooted around to create havoc in the opposing backfield.

SWISS ENGINEERS have designed a car that reacts to your mood. The **Rinspeed Senso** can introduce **relaxing smells** and will even *shake* the seat to wake you up if it thinks you've dozed off at the wheel.

Garbage Tour

In Chicago in 2005, people were paying $7 to see some of the city's less desirable spots on a three-hour bus tour of garbage sites, landfills, and smelly sludge sewage fields. The excursion showed residents and visitors what happens to garbage once it leaves their trash cans.

Astral Grooming

Astronauts in space shave using razors equipped with tiny vacuum cleaners inside!

Mini Cows

In a bid to combat his country's serious milk shortage of 1987, Fidel Castro urged his scientists to create a breed of mini cows. Castro wanted the most productive cows cloned and shrunk to the size of dogs so that families could keep one inside their apartments. There, the cows would feed on grass grown under fluorescent lights.

Peculiar Pastimes

In Rieti, Italy, there is an annual washtub race in which contestants race wooden washtubs along a course 875 yd (800 m) long.

Extreme Carving

In Port Elgin, Ontario, Canada, there is an annual pumpkin festival that includes such events as underwater pumpkin carving.

▶ Wrappers Reborn

Finnish artist Virpi Vesanen-Laukkanen exhibited this dress, in St. Petersburg, Russia, made entirely of candy wrappers. The artist said that her creation reminded her of sweets eaten during long journeys.

Busse Load

When the Busse family marked the 150th anniversary of the arrival of their ancestors in the U.S.A. from Germany, it was no ordinary reunion: 2,369 family members turned up at Grayslake, Illinois, in 1998, some from as far away as Africa.

◀ Huge Halloween

Belgian artist Michel Dircken sits in his carving, created during a competition for the fastest carving of a jack o'lantern in October 2005. The pumpkin weighed 637 lb (289 kg) and measured 131 in (333 cm) around.

Space Oddity

Canadian performance artist Julie Andrée T. sought to redefine space by walking blindfold in a confined space for six hours, marking the walls and singing a children's song.

Competitive Kite-flying

Kite fighting is common at the spring Festival of Basant in Lahore, Pakistan. Skilled kite-flyers from all around the country use bladed and chemical-lined strings to bring down or capture their opponents' kites.

Birth Art

As part of an exhibition in a German art gallery, a woman gave birth in front of dozens of spectators. Ramune Gele had the baby girl, named Audra, in 2005, at the DNA gallery in Berlin. The father, Winfried Witt, called the experience "an existential work of art."

Two Noses

Bill Durks was born in 1913 with two noses, each with a single nostril. Between the bridges of his noses, he painted a third eye, over what may have been a vestigial eye socket, and became known in U.S. sideshows as "The Man with Three Eyes." He married Milly Durks, "The Alligator-skinned Woman From New Jersey."

FyRe EaTeR

EATING FIRE, swallowing swords, juggling machetes, hammering nails up his own nose—they're all in a day's work for the Amazing Blazing Tyler Fyre!

Fyre (real name Tyler Fleet), born in Georgia, was a one-off even as a kid, when he found that he could squirt milk, water, and even spaghetti and meatballs out of his nose. He learned trapeze, juggling, balancing, the high wire, and fire-eating, before progressing to a routine as a Human Blockhead. In ten years, Fyre, who also eats glass, razor blades, live crickets, and lit cigarettes, and has been known to pound a nail through a hole in his tongue, has done more than 7,500 live shows, sometimes performing 15 a day. He admits: "It's

grueling on the body. At the Coney Island Circus Sideshow I was the Human Blockhead, the sword swallower, I ate fire, and I did the inverted escape act, cranked up by my ankles until my head was 6 ft (1.8 m) above the stage."

Tyler learned his fire-eating from a fellow student while training to be a circus performer. Of all his sideshow skills, it remains

Tyler used to hammer a nail through the hole in his tongue. He still enjoys putting toothpicks in it.

In a daring escapology routine, Tyler is tied in a straitjacket and hung upside down by his ankles 6 ft (1.8 m) above the stage.

When it comes to swallowing swords, Tyler's act puts him at the cutting edge of show business.

Killer Tree

In 1860, nearly 200 years after his death, the Rhode Island Historical Society exhumed the body of Roger Williams—only to find that he had been eaten by an apple tree! The coffin was empty apart from the invading tree roots. A large root curved where his head should have been and entered the chest cavity before growing down the spine. It then branched at the two legs and upturned into feet.

Ice Sculptor

Richard Bubin, aged 44, from Wilkins, Pennsylvania, has been sculpting ice for over 20 years and once carved 61 blocks in under 4½ hours. For Pittsburgh's First Night celebration in January 2005, he turned ten giant blocks of ice into a sculpture of the Roberto Clemente Bridge.

Jumbo Junk

British artist Anthony Heywood made a full-size elephant sculpture in 2004 entirely from household junk, including TV sets, heaters, fans, radios, and a toilet.

Stair Ride

In the 2005 urban Down the Hill bike race, held in the town of Taxco, Mexico, competitors rode their mountain bikes through a house! They went in through a door, down a flight of stairs and exited through another door. They also sped through narrow alleys and jumped heights of 13 ft (4 m) on the 2-mi (3.2-km) course.

▲ Through the Nose
Jin Guolong, from China, can drink through his nose—he consumes both milk and alcohol using this method.

Legged It!

A man testing an artificial leg worth $17,000 ran off without paying the bill. The theft occurred after the man called in to collect a prosthetic from a specialist in Des Moines, Iowa, in 2005, and was allowed to take it away for a couple of hours to ensure that it fitted him properly.

Chicken Protest

Ottawa performance artist Rob Thompson caged a man and a woman in 1997 to protest about the conditions of commercially bred chickens. Eric Wolf and Pam Meldrum spent a week together in the small wooden cage to make the point. Their drinking water came from a dripping hose and they ate vegetarian mash.

Love Birds

During the Middle Ages, people in Europe are said to have believed that birds chose their mates every year on Valentine's Day!

X-ray Eyes

A teenage Russian girl appears to have X-ray vision, which enables her to see inside human bodies. Natalia Demkina has baffled scientists across the world by describing the insides of bodies in detail and using her talent to correctly diagnose the medical conditions of complete strangers. She says that she possesses dual vision when looking at others, but that she can't see inside her own body.

Natalia can switch from normal to X-ray vision by focusing on a person for two minutes.

Pet Pillows

In 2005, Nevada taxidermist Jeanette Hall offered to make fur pillows from dead pets. Each Pet Pillow was handmade for prices ranging from $65 for a cat to $150 for a horse. Hall described the idea as a "unique way of keeping your pets close to you even after they pass away."

Shopping Break

Tired shoppers in Minnesota's Mall of America can rest their weary legs for 70 cents a minute. In the Bloomington shopping center there is a store called MinneNAPolis aimed at bored spouses of shoppers and also at travelers, who need a nap after a lengthy flight, but aren't staying long enough to book a hotel.

Circus Sideshow

★ Prince Randian, known as "The Living Torso," had no arms or legs. However, he amazingly learned to roll, light, and smoke a cigarette by moving his mouth.

★ Myrtle Corbin, the four-legged woman from Texas, had a malformed Siamese twin, which resulted in Myrtle having two pairs of legs. She used to gallop across the stage like a horse.

★ Edward Mordrake was born a united twin, and had another face on the reverse of his—that of a beautiful girl whose eyes used to follow you around the room.

Pavement Picasso

Ben Wilson roams the streets of London, England, looking for used chewing gum, which he turns into works of art. He burns the gum with a blowtorch, adds a clear enamel as a base, then colors in acrylic enamels, and finishes with a coat of varnish. His gum gallery includes human portraits, animals, and buildings.

Cricket Lover

Danny Capps of Madison, Wisconsin, spits dead crickets from his mouth over distances of up to 30 ft (9 m). Capps, who has been fascinated by insects since he was a small boy, says that dead crickets have no flavor.

Winter Woollies

In 2001, a group of volunteers in Tasmania, Australia, knitted turtleneck sweaters for a colony of rare Australian penguins to protect the birds against oil spills!

Robot Riders

In 2005, Qatar, in the Middle East, staged a spectacular camel race using robot jockeys. Seven robots were placed on top of seven camels at Al Shahaniyya racecourse, near the country's capital Doha, after there had been widespread protests about the use of children as jockeys in the popular sport.

Pretty as a Picture

A participant in the 13th International Tattoo Convention, held in Frankfurt, Germany, in 2005, sports a tattoo on the back of his head.

Sensitive Shirt

Italian designer Francesca Rosella has come up with the perfect gift for people involved in long-distance relationships—a hugging T-shirt. Fitted with sensors, the T-shirt simulates the missing partner's caress by recreating breath, touch, and heartbeat based on information transmitted via their cell phone.

Time Capsule

At the 1957 Tulsarama Festival in Tulsa, Oklahoma, a brand-new Chrysler car was buried in a time capsule, to be unearthed in 2007. People were asked to guess Tulsa's population in 2007. Whoever is closest wins the car; if that person is dead, the heirs get the car.

CUTLERY ART
A figure made from ordinary knives, forks, and spoons.

ONE OF RIPLEY'S BIGGEST, this museum in Mexico City can be found in an eye-catching replica medieval castle. Open since 1992, it features a full-size humpback whale skeleton and a giant solid jade Buddha with 1,000 hands.

TOAST ART
The *Mona Lisa* created in a toaster from 64 pieces of white bread.

THEATER MASK
A rare Indonesian Topeng mask of a bulging-eyed demon.

DON'T MISS!

▶ Painting on a rice grain

▶ Flag flown in space aboard *Apollo 7*

▶ Human faces painted on a human hair

▶ Spiked collar-torture device

▶ Leo Sewell junk art figures

▶ Collection of metal objects removed from a human stomach

▶ Egyptian mummified head

▶ Smallest working camera

CROCODILE NECKLACE
This necklace from New Guinea is made from crocodile teeth, and was worn for luck.

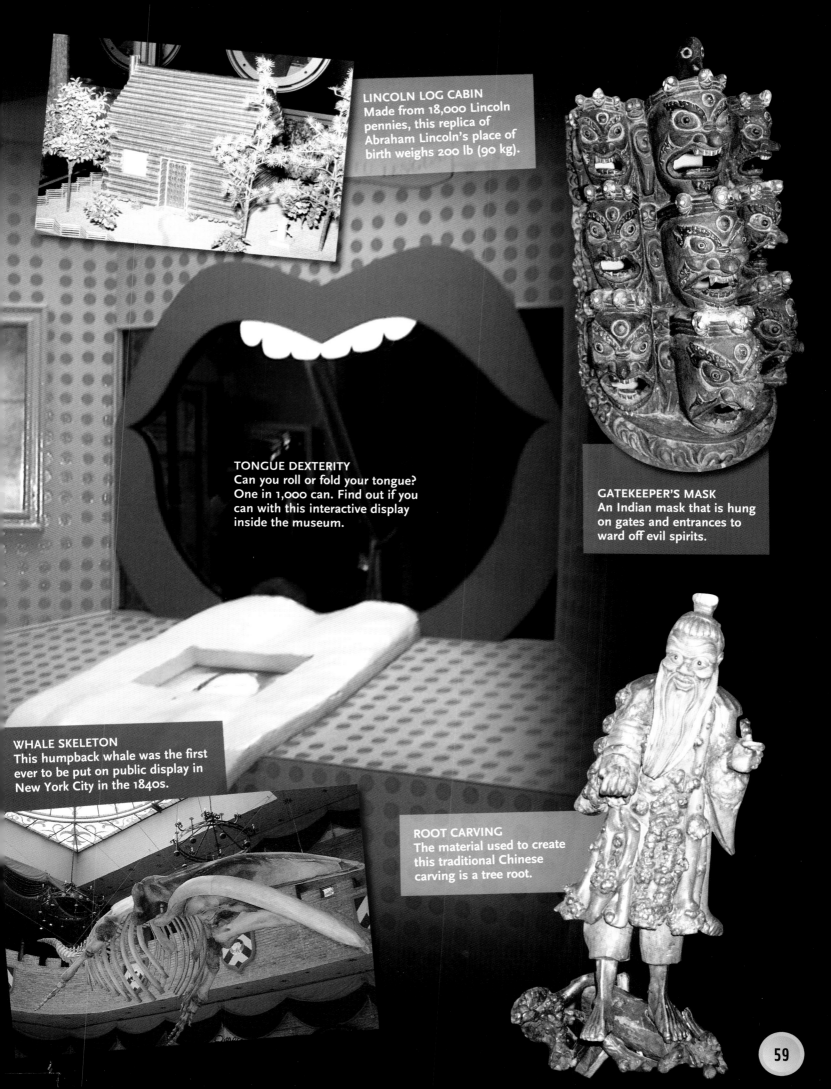

LINCOLN LOG CABIN
Made from 18,000 Lincoln pennies, this replica of Abraham Lincoln's place of birth weighs 200 lb (90 kg).

TONGUE DEXTERITY
Can you roll or fold your tongue? One in 1,000 can. Find out if you can with this interactive display inside the museum.

GATEKEEPER'S MASK
An Indian mask that is hung on gates and entrances to ward off evil spirits.

WHALE SKELETON
This humpback whale was the first ever to be put on public display in New York City in the 1840s.

ROOT CARVING
The material used to create this traditional Chinese carving is a tree root.

Pregnant Boy

When seven-year-old Alamjan Nematilaev's tummy began to bulge, his parents thought he had rickets, a common childhood disease in his native Kazakhstan. But, in 2003, a concerned schoolteacher took him to hospital, where doctors removed a 4-lb (1.8-kg) baby boy from Alamjan's stomach! Alamjan had been born with the fetus of his twin brother growing inside him. For seven years it had lived like a parasite, growing a head, a body, hair, and nails. Doctors were able to save Alamjan but not the 8-in (20-cm) fetus.

Medical Marvels

★ When teenager Doug Pritchard, of Lenoir, North Carolina, went to his doctor in 1978 with a sore foot, a tooth was found growing in the bottom of his instep!

★ Jens Jenson, of Denmark, fell into a pile of spiky barberries in 1990 and had to visit his doctor 248 times to have a total of 32,131 thorns removed from his punctured body.

★ After Peter Morris from Kingswinford, England, lost his thumb in a 1993 accident, doctors replaced it with his big toe.

★ Trampled by a bull in 1993, Jim McManus, of Calgary, Canada, had his left ear reattached by doctors—aided by 75 leeches to control the bleeding.

In Fond Memory

Swedish artist and sculptor Lars Widenfalk has created a violin with a difference. He sculpted the working instrument from the tombstone of his late grandfather, Gustav. The violin's fingerboard, pegs, tailpiece, and chin rest are all made of ebony, and by lining the interior with real gold, it produces the finest possible tone. The instrument is considered to be worth in the region of $1.7 million.

Small Wonder
Ma Chaoqin from China is 22 years old, but still looks like a baby. She suffers from an incurable disease called Rachitic, or rickets, and as a result has failed to grow at a normal rate.

Wall Eater

In 2005, Emily Katrencik ate through the wall of her Brooklyn gallery until she could put her head through it—all in the name of art. She said: "The wall has a mild flavor. The texture is more prominent than the taste—it's chalky with tiny sharp pieces in it." Visitors could eat bread made with minerals extracted from the wall.

Frog Birth

A woman from Iran was reported to have given birth to a gray frog-like creature in 2004. It apparently grew from a larva that had entered the woman as she swam in a dirty pool. A doctor described the creature as resembling a frog in appearance, particularly the shape of the fingers, and the size and shape of the tongue.

Talon Contest

Louise Hollis of Compton, California, has let her toenails grow to a staggering 6 in (15 cm) long. She has to wear open-toed shoes with at least 3-in (7.6-cm) soles to stop her nails dragging along the ground, and she needs 2½ bottles of nail polish to paint the nails on both her hands and feet.

Pan Christ

As Juan Pastrano, of Prairie Lea, Texas, was hanging up his frying pan after washing it in 2005, he spotted an uncanny image where the anti-stick coating on the pan had worn thin. There before him was the face of Jesus Christ in a crown of thorns. He promptly sealed the pan in a plastic bag to protect the image from curious visitors.

HEaRiNG CoLoRs

COLOR-BLIND art student Neil Harbisson wears a special device that enables him to "hear" colors.

Neil, from Spain, uses a device called the Eye-Borg, that was invented by Adam Montandon, a digital multimedia expert from Plymouth, England. It works by converting light waves into sounds, and consists of a digital camera and a backpack that contains the computer and headset for Neil to listen to the colors. A low-pitched sound indicates reds, a high-pitched sound indicates violet, while shades of blue and green fall somewhere in between.

Now Neil, who takes off the invention only when he sleeps, is able to buy clothes that he

Neil now paints in vibrant colors.

"likes the sound of." He can also order his favorite foods, whereas previously he struggled to differentiate between apple juice and orange juice.

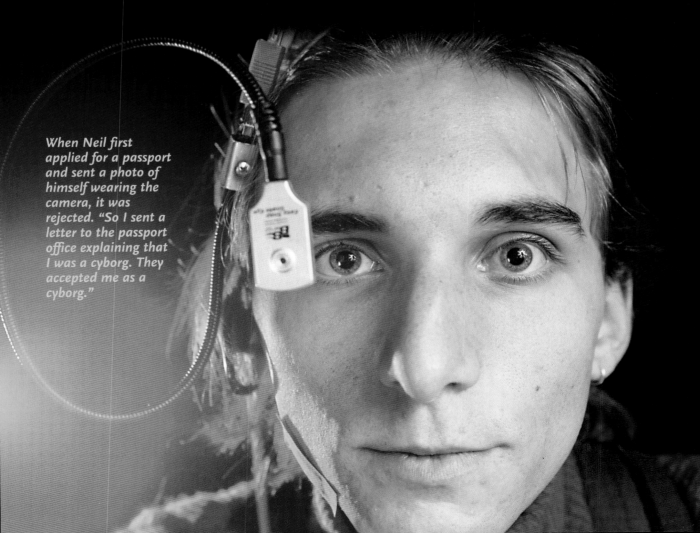

When Neil first applied for a passport and sent a photo of himself wearing the camera, it was rejected. "So I sent a letter to the passport office explaining that I was a cyborg. They accepted me as a cyborg."

Snake Man

For more than 50 years, Bill Haast injected himself with deadly snake venom. He built up such powerful antibodies in his system that his blood was used as a snakebite antidote. Haast, who ran a Florida serpentarium, began in 1948 with tiny amounts of rattlesnake venom and built up the dosage until, by the time he was 90, he was injecting himself once a week with venom from 32 species. Although he was bitten more than 180 times by snakes from which a few drops of venom could kill any ordinary human, Haast managed to survive every single time.

Two Hearts

A boy in Tbilisi, Georgia, was born with two hearts. In 2004, doctors discovered that one-year-old Goga Diasamidze had been born with a second perfectly functioning heart near his stomach.

Steve Relles makes a living by scooping up **dog poop**! The *Delmar Dog Butler*, as he calls himself, has over **100 clients** in NEW YORK STATE who pay **$10**, each for a **weekly clean** of their yard.

Snail Trail

In Januray 2005, Chilean artist Paola Podesta promoted her new exhibition by gluing 2,000 plastic snails to a Santiago church. The snail trail led from the Church of Santo Expedito to the nearby Codar art gallery.

Omelette Surprise

When Ursula Beckley of Long Island, New York, was preparing an omelette in 1989, she cracked open an egg—only to see a 6-in (15-cm) black snake slither out. She sued her local supermarket for $3.6 million on the grounds that she was so traumatized by the incident that she could never look at an egg again.

Last Ride of your Life!
Gordon Fitch took his passion for motorcycles to a new level when he started his Blackhawk Hearse business. For a fitting and dignified last ride, bikers can have their coffins drawn by a Harley Davidson motorbike.

Head Reattached
Marcos Parra must be one of the luckiest guys alive. He survived a horrific car crash in 2002, in which his head was technically severed from the rest of his body. His skull was torn from his cervical spine, leaving his head detached from his neck. Only skin and his spinal cord kept the two body parts connected. Amazingly, however, surgeons in Phoenix, Arizona, managed to reattach his head. The bones were pulled into the right position by two screws placed at the back of his neck, enabling Parra to live.

Miracle Heart
Nikolai Mikhalnichuk leads a healthy life even though his heart stopped beating several years ago. He suffered a heart attack when his wife said she was leaving him, but doctors in Saratov, Russia, found that although his heart has stopped, its blood vessels are able to keep on pumping blood around his body.

Bushy Brows
In 2004, Frank Ames of Saranac, New York State, had his eyebrow hair measured at an incredible 3.1 in (7.8 cm). Ames said "I don't know why it grows like that. It just always has."

Hot Stuff
New Mexico State University has developed a special Halloween chili pepper, a miniature ornamental specimen that changes from black to orange. However, Paul Bosland, head of the university's chili-breeding program, warns that these hot peppers are actually too hot to eat.

Turtle Recall
In 2005, a Chinese man pretended to be a hunchback in order to smuggle his pet turtle onto a plane. The elderly man strapped the turtle, which was 8 in (20 cm) in diameter, to his back before boarding a flight to Chongqing, but after getting through security, he was stopped by a guard who thought his hump looked strange.

Snowball Flag
In 1998, Vasili Mochanou, of Ottawa, Ontario, created a replica of the Canadian Flag using 27,000 snowballs!

Bizarre Menu
The Balaw Balaw restaurant in Angono, the Philippines, offers dishes that are more than simply unusual. The menu includes monitor lizard, cow testicles, giant eel, snake eggs, and giant python.

Fish Bones

Chinese artist Liu Huirong recreates famous works of art in fish bones! She took two years and used more than 100,000 fish bones to complete a copy of "Spring's Back," a 300-year-old painting by Yuan Jiang. She has been making fish-bone pictures for more than 20 years. Every day she collects fish bones from roadside garbage bins and degreases, marinates, and chemically treats them before sticking them on to canvas.

Branching Out

For more than 25 years, performance artist David "The Bushman" Johnson has been alarming people on Fisherman's Wharf, San Francisco, by jumping out from behind branches as they pass by. He has been arrested over 1,000 times as a result of people not getting the joke.

Bone Sculpture

In 2001, U.S. artist Sarah Perry created "Beast of Burden," a 9-ft (2.7-m) rocketship made from horse and cattle bones! She has created other sculptures from hundreds of tiny rodent bones, which she has painstakingly extracted from owl pellets. She also makes art using junk that has been discarded in the Nevada Desert and once made a 700-lb (318-kg) gorilla from old rubber truck-tires.

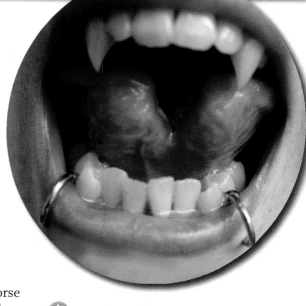

Speak with Forked Tongue
A multi-pierced and tattooed 25-year-old man, who wanted to be known only as "Ian," had his tongue split in May 2003 to resemble that of a snake. He also installed fang caps on his teeth.

Raw Talent

Gabriela Rivera horrified visitors to an art gallery in Santiago, Chile, in 2005, by showing a video of herself with her face covered in raw meat. She said it showed the relationship people have with themselves each day when they look in the mirror.

In 2001, an **insurance company** in **Great Britain** offered a "**Spooksafe**" policy for *death, injury, or damage* caused by a **ghost** or **poltergeist**.

Hair Force

Indian police have been trying to improve their public image by paying officers to grow mustaches. In 2004, chiefs in Madhya Pradesh announced a monthly mustache bonus of 30 rupees (about 50 cents) after research showed that officers with smart facial hair were taken more seriously. Mustaches are a sign of authority in India.

Over Your Head
Shanghai, in China, saw the premiere of what was billed as the first acrobatic ballet—a combination of Western dance and ancient Chinese acrobatics. In this scene from "Swan Lake the Acrobatic," a ballerina balanced on her toes on the head of a male dancer.

IN DEPTH
In a Twist

Los Angeles contortionist Daniel Browning Smith, 26, is otherwise known as The Rubberboy—he is so flexible he can cram his whole body into a box the size of a microwave oven.

When did you first discover your flexibility?

"I was four years old when I jumped off my bunk bed and landed in a perfect saddle split. I showed my father and he went to the library and brought me home pictures of contortionists—I tried to copy them, and I could. As a kid playing hide and seek I could hide in the sock drawer!"

How did you turn that into a career?

"When I was 18 the circus came through town where I grew up in Mississippi. I told my family I was joining it and would be back in three weeks—that was eight years ago."

What exactly can you do?

"I believe I am the most flexible person alive. Most contortionists can only bend one way—I can bend so far backwards the top of my head touches the seat of my pants, and so far forward I can kiss my own behind! I can also disconnect both arms, both legs, and turn my torso 180 degrees."

What is your favorite stunt?

"De-Escape—it is the complete opposite of Houdini's straitjacket routine. I have to dislocate my arms and squeeze into a locked straitjacket, then chain myself up with my mouth and flip myself into a box."

What else can you do?

"I can make my ribcage go up and my abdomen go down so you can see my heart beating through my skin! And I can get into a box about the size of a microwave. I get my shins in first, because I can't bend them, then my back, then my head and arms fill the holes. I have to slow down my breathing because my arms and legs put pressure on my lungs."

Does it hurt?

"I practice a stretch until just before it becomes painful, then hold it a bit until it feels normal, then stretch a bit further. The connective tissue between my bones is different genetically, inherited from both sides of my family. My father's father was in the military and it helped him to dislocate his hips when it was time to march. The stretches I do enhance that for me."

Have you ever got stuck?

"I can get through an unstrung tennis racquet or a toilet seat, but once a toilet seat got stuck around my torso with my thigh in the hole as well. I was home alone, and had to crawl into the kitchen and get a bottle of vegetable oil and pour it all over me. The seat finally came off—I just made a huge mess."

Are you working on future stunts?

"I'm trying to turn my head 180 degrees. I can get to about 175 degrees already. It's the only thing I've tried that's made me gasp—it's weird looking down and seeing your own butt!"

Rock Around the Clock

Thirty-six-year-old Suresh Joachim, from Mississauga, Ontario, spent 3 days 3 hours 3 minutes 3 seconds rocking in a rocking chair nonstop in August 2005. In the course of his challenge at the Hilton Garden Inn, Toronto, Ontario, he ate just one plain white bun, some noodle soup, three hard-boiled eggs, and one and a half potatoes. He also drank water and energy drinks, but not enough so that he would have to go to the toilet. His greatest fear was falling asleep because of the continuous rocking back and forth.

Chomping Champ

Australian "Bushtucker Freddy" devours a locust during the 2005 Bug Eating Championships. He went on to win the competition that involved challengers from all over the world eating a variety of creepy crawlies, such as crickets, mealworms, hornets, and locusts.

Blood Stains

Mexican artist Teresa Margolles staged a 2005 exhibition in Metz, France, featuring clothing stained with human blood. She worked in a morgue for ten years and her display comprised clothes worn by corpses.

Heads turn when **Paul Miller**, from **Alta Loma**, California, walks down the street. That's because his **mustache** is **10 ft (3 m)** long! It takes him *an hour* to groom it each day.

Hair Wear

Nina Sparre, of Vamhuf, Sweden, practices the art of Haarkulla, or "Hair Farming," creating art and clothing out of human hair!

Living Billboard

Forty models lived in a 3-D billboard on the side of a building for two days in July 2005, creating New York City's first-ever live billboard. They were advertising a new fragrance from Calvin Klein. The models were told to create an illusion of a big party, 24 hours a day.

Car Polish

You can't miss Yvonne Millner when she drives down the streets of Hopkins, South Carolina—hers is the car decorated in nail polish. She started by painting on a smiling face, but now she has designs and slogans all over her car, including a palm tree and the words "Hang Loose." She spends three to four hours a day on the creation and has used over 100 bottles of nail polish.

Hidden Monkeys

When Californian Robert Cusack was asked if he had anything to declare on arrival at Los Angeles Airport in 2002, customs officers could hardly have expected what they would find. They discovered a pair of pygmy monkeys in his pants and a bird of paradise in his suitcase. Cusack was subsequently sentenced to 57 days in jail for smuggling the monkeys, as well as four exotic birds, and 50 rare orchids into the U.S.A. from Thailand.

Fancy Dress

The first prize in the youth division of the July 4 Parade in Haines, Oregon, in 2005, went to three children dressed as dung beetles! Wearing tubes covered by garbage bags, they pushed huge rubber balls coated in sand, dirt, and dead grass.

Ambidextrous Bilinguist

In 2004, Amanullah, a 53-year-old man from India, learned to write different sentences simultaneously with both hands. Most amazing of all, he could write one sentence in English, and the other in Tamil.

⬤ Pulling Power

The Great Nippulini can tow a car from the piercings attached to his nipples, as well as lift a phenomenal 55 lb (25 kg).

Holy Shower

In 2005, Jeffrey Rigo of Pittsburgh, Pennsylvania, sold a water stain on his bathroom wall for nearly $2,000 because he considered that it bore a resemblance to Jesus. Following the publicity for the "Shower Jesus," Rigo had requests from people who wanted to pray in his bathtub.

Emergency Repairs

Jonas Scott, from Salt Lake City, Utah, was left with no esophagus after industrial cleaning fluid at his workplace ate away his insides in 1988. With no stomach, he had to be fed intravenously. He went three years without eating solids until surgeons connected the remaining 7 ft (2.1 m) of his small intestine directly to the base of his throat so that he could eat almost normally again.

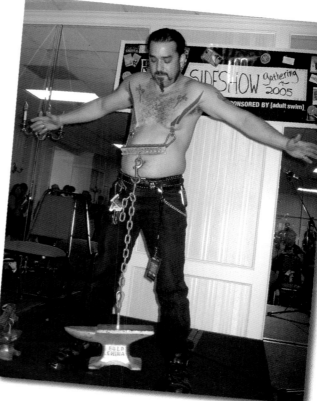

⬤ Great Balls of Fire!

Stonehenge in Wiltshire, England, was the location for a massive synchronized fire-eating spectacular. Seventy fire-eaters came together to create a landscape of flames at the event in September 2004.

SIX BRITONS AND ONE AUSTRALIAN took dining to new heights when they prepared and ate a five-course meal 22,000 ft (6,705 m) up a mountain in Tibet. The diners dressed for the occasion with white ties and top hats and carried the tables, chairs, silver cutlery, floral centerpieces, candelabra, wine, and food all the way to the top.

BREAKING

Hurtling down a ramp at speeds of around 50 mph (80 km/h), a skateboarder leapt over the Great Wall of China
page 92

A rocketman took to the skies above England, reaching the height of a 12-storey building
page 96

A woman who wore a corset continually for over 20 years has reduced her waist to a tiny 15 in (38 cm)
page 97

BOUNDARIES

Building Ace

FOR THE PAST 14 years, Bryan Berg has been creating some of the world's most famous buildings from playing cards. At the 2005 Canada National Exhibition in Toronto, the celebrated cardstacker amazed audiences with his detailed replicas of the Taj Mahal, the Colosseum, and the Pyramids.

Berg bases his card towers on carefully constructed grids. He says that the combined weight of the cards actually adds to the stability of the structure.

Thirty-one-year-old Berg, who comes from Spirit Lake, Iowa, was introduced to cardstacking by his grandfather at the age of eight. By the time he was 17, Berg was building towers of cards over 14 ft (4.3 m) tall. In 1999, he built a 133-storey tower that was 25 ft (7.6 m) high from 2,000 packs of cards. He needed scaffolding so that he could reach the very top. In February 2005, as part of the Asian tsunami relief effort, Berg worked for 18 hours a day, ten days straight, to construct a skyline of New York City. He used 178,000 playing cards, each of which represented a victim of the disaster. The Empire State Building, the Chrysler Building, and Yankee Stadium were all there in breathtaking accuracy.

Berg puts the finishing touches to a Gothic cathedral.

The Taj Mahal stands in the foreground with Rome's Colosseum behind. Berg never uses adhesives. "There are no tricks," he adds. "It's all in the balancing."

Berg demonstrated a refreshing anarchy toward his art on the final night of his Canadian spectacle by enthusiastically destroying his patiently created work with a gas-powered leaf blower!

Air Guitar

At the 2005 Guilfest music festival in Guildford, England, 4,083 people gathered to play air guitars at the same time. With air-guitar "experts" on hand to dispense advice, the wannabee rockers mimed to "Sweet Child of Mine" by Guns 'n' Roses.

Eggs Galore

At the annual Easter egg hunt at Rockford, Illinois, on March 26, 2005, an incredible 292,686 eggs were hunted for and found by 1,500 children in just 15 minutes. The event involved 200 volunteers, 156 bales of straw, and 1,000 hours of stuffing plastic eggs.

⊙ Eggstraordinary

Brian Spott from Colorado balanced 439 eggs on the floor at Melbourne's Australian Centre for Contemporary Art in 2005. He said the secret was to find the sweet spot on the base of an egg, adding: "You need a steady hand and a lot of patience."

Modern Houdini

Canadian escape artist Dean Gunnarson specializes in freeing himself from handcuffs and locked coffins. One of his most famous routines is the "Car Crusher," which he performed in Los Angeles, California, in 1990. First he was handcuffed and then chained into a 1970 Cadillac by the South Pasadena Chief of Police. Gunnarson's neck was chained to the steering wheel, his legs were bound to the brake pedal, and his arms fastened to the doors. The Cadillac was then lifted into a car crusher, which was set into motion, its steel jaws closing menacingly. A mere 2 minutes 7 seconds later, Gunnarson amazingly leapt to freedom from his automobile prison, just a few seconds before the vehicle was completely destroyed by the merciless crusher.

Plane Sailing

Canada's Ken Blackburn is no regular aviator—he deals strictly in paper airplanes. He has been making paper planes since the age of ten and broke his first record in 1983, when he managed to keep his creation airborne for 16.89 seconds. But he bettered that at the Georgia Dome, Atlanta, in 1998 with an unbeatable 27.6 seconds.

At Seattle's 2005 Northwest Folklife Festival, Andy Mackie led no fewer than 1,706 harmonica players in a 13 min 22 sec rendition of "Twinkle, Twinkle Little Star."

Voice Broke

Terry Coleman of Denver, Colorado, sang continuously for 40 hours 17 minutes in July 2005. His target was 49 hours, but his voice gave out after 40. "The hardest thing was staying awake," he said afterward.

Wheelchair Star

In July 2005, neuroscientist William Tan from Singapore covered 151 mi (243 km) in a wheelchair in just 24 hours by completing a staggering 607 laps of an athletics track. Two months earlier, the redoubtable Tan had completed 6½ marathons on seven continents in the space of only 70 days.

Lip Stick

Joseph Cervantez of Gurnee, Illinois, makes contact, puckering his lips up for an uninterrupted kiss lasting 7 hours 43 minutes on February 14, 2005. He beat rival Juan Hyde and won a new truck worth $32,235 for his achievement.

Unicycle Feats

Between 1976 and 1978, Wally Watts of Edmonton, Canada, rode a unicycle 12,000 mi (19,300 km) in various countries around the world. And through 1983 to 1984, Pierre Biondo of Montreal, Canada, rode a unicycle around the entire perimeter of North America, just over 12,000 mi (19,300 km).

Hula Heroine

Australian circus performer Kareena Oates created history in June 2005 by managing to spin 100 hula hoops around her waist for three full revolutions.

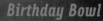

Pulling Teeth

In June 1999, 36-year-old Krishna Gopal Shrivestava pulled a 270-ton boat a distance of 49 ft (15 m) in Calcutta harbor using only his teeth.

Birthday Bowl

Seventy-year-old Jean Beal bowled 70 games in one day (one game for each year of her life), on June 29, 2005, to celebrate her birthday. It took her nearly 14 hours. Jean, from Hickory, North Carolina, said of the challenge: "I was just doing it to see if I could."

The One that Got Away

In May 2005, Tim Pruitt of Alton, Illinois, caught a record 124-lb (56-kg) blue catfish in the Mississippi River. The monster-sized fish measured a staggering 58 in (147 cm) long and 44 in (112 cm) around. Alas, the fish, which was thought to be at least 30 years old, died the following week while being transported to a Kansas City aquarium where it was to go on public display.

Happy Birthday!

An incredible 27,413 birthday candles lit up New York City on August 27, 2005. Taking 1½ minutes, 50 people rapidly lit candles on top of a cake that measured 47 x 3 ft (14 x 0.9 m).

Backward Bowler

Jim Cripps isn't content with bowling scores of over 250—he does it backwards! It all started as a joke. Jim, from Nashville, Tennessee, was clowning around at the lanes one afternoon when he suddenly made a decision to bowl backwards. He turned his back on the pins, took a few steps, hurled the ball and got a strike! One of his friends bet him he couldn't bowl a 150 in reverse, but after six weeks of practice, Jim managed it. Bowling backwards, he rolled a 279 in a game that included 11 consecutive strikes.

Blind Date

In July 2005, Singapore's Nanyang Technological University staged a romantic event as part of its 50th anniversary celebrations, whereby 536 first-year undergraduates (268 couples) got together to stage a mass blind date.

Large Deposit

In June 2005, Edmond Knowles walked up to a Coinstar machine at a bank in Flomaton, Alabama, and cashed in 1,308,459 pennies, which amounted to $13,084.59. He had started saving pennies in 1967, keeping the coins in a 5-gal (19-l) can. But, by the time of his huge deposit, he had collected so many that they were being stored in four large 55-gal (208-l) drums and three 20-gal (76-l) drums.

Hockey Marathon

In June 2005, Canadian radio host Mike Nabuurs played air hockey for 48 hours straight, at a table in the lobby of McMaster University Medical Center, Hamilton, Ontario.

Ice Statue

Russian Karim Diab stood motionless in the freezing Moscow River for one whole hour. He had prepared for two years to accustom his body to surviving in the icy water for an hour without moving. He recovered with a hot bath, but was still too cold to talk.

Fastest Fingers

Dean Gould of Felixstowe, England, can lay claim to being amazingly dexterous. Over the past 20 years the 42-year-old father-of-three has shown that he has the fastest fingers and the handiest hands by setting new standards in such reaction-testing skills as beer-mat flipping, winkle picking, pancake tossing, coin snatching, and needle threading.

Tongue-tied

Using only his tongue, Florida firefighter Al Gliniecki tied 39 cherry stems into knots in three minutes in 1999. On another occasion, he tied an incredible 833 stems in one hour. Yet Al nearly wasn't around to put his talented tongue to use. While working as a lifeguard at Pensacola in 1982, he was struck by a bolt of lightning that threw him 38 ft (12 m) and blew the fillings out of his teeth.

Ballpark Marathon

In 2005, Mike Wenz and Jake Lindhorst saw 30 baseball games in 29 days—each in a different major-league ballpark. The 22-year-old buddies from Chicago began their ballpark marathon in New York's Shea Stadium on June 12 and finished at Miami's Dolphin Stadium on July 10.

Wrap Artist

ON MARCH 11, 1965, a 14-year-old Canadian boy stuck a wad of Wrigley's gum in his mouth and carefully folded the wrappers into links. That night he scribbled an entry in his diary: "I started my gum-wrapper chain with 20 spearmint gum wrappers today."

Forty years later, Gary Duschl's gum-wrapper chain is made up of over one million wrappers and stretches for more than 47,000 ft (14,325 m)—9 mi (14.5 km)—at his home in Virginia Beach, Virginia. To travel the length of the chain would take 9 minutes in a car traveling at 60 mph (97 km/h)! What started out as a desire to have the longest chain in class, then in school, then in the area, has become a 630-lb (285-kg) monster. There is more than $50,000-worth of gum in Duschl's incredible chain.

Many of the wrappers are sent in by well-wishers. Duschl admits that even he couldn't have chewed that amount of gum during the past four decades!

Sky High

To celebrate her 99th birthday on February 17, 1996, Hildegarde Ferrera made a parachute jump over Hawaii. She came through the jump with nothing worse than a sore neck, but sadly died two weeks later from pneumonia.

Most people would use a **14-oz** (400-g) bottle of ketchup sparingly. Not **Dustin Phillips** from Los Angeles, California. In 1999, he drank **90 per cent** of a bottle through a straw in just **33 seconds** (and wasn't sick)!

Handstand Display

A total of 1,072 people turned up at Indianapolis in 2005 to perform an astonishing display of simultaneous handstands. Participants in the challenge came from as far afield as Kansas, Texas, and Oregon.

⊻ Get the Picture

Australian artist Ando has created a huge painting of the outback, which measures an amazing 328 x 39 ft (100 x 12 m). Painted on a curved canvas, "The Big Picture" is complemented by more than 300 tons of red landscaped earth (see right), which adds to the image's 3-D effect. Only from certain angles are visitors able to see where 2-D meets 3-D.

Short Story

Adeel Ahmed, a 24-year-old Pakistani seen here being interviewed, is only 37 in (94 cm) high. He was born a normal child, but by the age of five had stopped growing.

Giant Skis

In February 2005, in Jacques Cartier Park in Ottawa, Ontario, 100 skiers traveled 330 ft (100 m) on a gigantic pair of skis, 330 ft (100 m) long.

Check Mates

An incredible 12,388 players turned out to take part in simultaneous chess matches at a public park in Pachuca, near Mexico City, one day in June 2005. Around 80 per cent of the competitors were children.

Long Train

When Hege Lorence married Rolf Rotset in Norway in June 1996, her bridal train was 670 ft (204 m) long, and had to be carried by 186 bridesmaids and pageboys.

Delicious Worms

"Snake" Manohoran, a 23-year-old hotelier from Madras, India, ate 200 earthworms in 30 seconds in 2004. He said that he overcame any reservations about eating them by simply thinking of them as meat. He acquired the nickname from his trick of putting his pet snake up his nose and pulling it out through his mouth!

Icy Voyage

After chasing a coyote on the ice near Canada's Prince Edward Island in 2001, foxhound Scooter was carried out to sea in a blizzard. She was rescued five days later after traveling 43 mi (70 km) on an ice floe across the Northumberland Strait.

Whip-cracker

Illinois entertainer Chris Camp cracked a 6 ft (1.8 m) bullwhip 222 times in one minute on the Mike Wilson Show in April 2005!

Child Prodigy

Michael Kearney did not sleep as much as other babies. Instead, he just wanted to talk. By the age of just five months, he was using four-word sentences, and at six months he calmly told a pediatrician: "I have a left-ear infection." He enrolled at Santa Rosa Junior College when he was just six years old and graduated two years later with an Associate of Science in Geology. In 1994, aged ten, he received a bachelor's degree in Anthropology from the University of South Alabama. He achieved a master's degree in Chemistry at 14 and was teaching in college at the tender age of 17.

High Flyers

A team from Edmonds Community College, Washington State, flew a kite continuously for more than 180 hours (7½ days) at nearby Long Beach in August 1982.

▶ More than a Mouthful

This appetite-buster hamburger, made by Denny's Beer Barrel Pub in Clearfield, Pennsylvania, on June 1, 2004, weighed about 11 lb (4.9 kg).

Twisted Walk

Inspired by an item on the *Ripley's Believe It or Not!* TV show, an Indian teenager has perfected the art of walking with his heels twisted backward. Despite misgivings from his mother that he might injure his legs, Bitu Gandhi from Rajkot in the state of Gujarat practiced until he was able to walk 300 steps forward and 300 steps backward by twisting his ankles nearly 180 degrees.

TV Addicts

Believe it or not, Chris Dean, 16, and Mike Dudek, 17, from Grand Rapids, Michigan, watched television for 52 hours nonstop in August 2004!

TIGHTROPE WALKER
*Clifford Calverley, of
Toronto, Canada,
crossed Niagara Falls
on a steel cable in 1892,
taking just 6 minutes
32 seconds.*

STRONG CHEST
*In 1938, Rasmus
Nielsen, a tattooed
weightlifter from
California, lifted
115 lb (52 kg) with
his nipple.*

GIANT CHAIR
*Built in 1934 by W.E.
Houston of Orlando,
Florida, this chair
measured 26 ft (8 m)
high by 12 ft (3.7 m)
wide by 8 ft (2.5 m)
deep, and weighed
1,400 lb (635 kg).*

EYE-OPENER
*Ever wanted a beer but couldn't find
the opener? Bob Oldham of South
Carolina was able to remove bottle
tops with his eyes!*

MISSISSIPPI MARATHON
Long-distance swimmer Fred Newton of Clinton, Oklahoma, swam an incredible 2,300 mi (3,700 km) down the Mississippi River in 1931.

ALL THUMBS
This 1920s photo shows Robert Jones of Pine Bluff, Arkansas, practicing "thumb-stands" on juggling pins!

HEAD TO TOE
Myra Jeanne of Buffalo, New York, specialized in tap dancing on her own head.

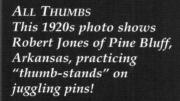

PRICKLY MATTRESS
This photograph of a young boy lying on a bed of nails was taken by missionary W.E. Morton in Benares, India, in 1926.

Looking Back

August 14, 1934 **Lee Chisman**, from Danville, Kentucky, was known as the "Big Bellow Man" because his voice could be heard from 8 mi (13 km) away. **October 11, 1942** **Warren Moore** from Jennings Lodge, Oregon, played 240 notes in one breath on the tuba. **May 20, 1952** **Myrtle Bliven**, aged 70, crocheted five tiny hats that could rest side by side on a single dime.

Sweet Treat

Jim Hager, a dental-plan manager from Oakland, California, ate 115 M&M's® with a pair of chopsticks in just 3 minutes in September 2003.

Endurance Test

Cathie Llewellyn of Wintersville, Ohio, won a new car in 2005 after living in the vehicle for 20 days. She triumphed when her last remaining opponent gave up because she needed to use the bathroom. All contestants had been allowed a five-minute break every six hours during the challenge, which took place in a Steubenville, Ohio, shopping mall.

Fast Fingers

Barbara Blackburn, of Salem, Oregon, can type 150 words per minute for 50 minutes (37,500 key strokes), and has a top speed of 212 words per minute and an error frequency of just 0.002 per 100 words. Her secret is a special keyboard, which has vowels on one side and consonants on the other.

Ear We Go

Lash Pataraya, 23, from Georgia, lifted 115 lb (52 kg) with his ears in Tbilisi in October 2003. He also used his ears to pull a minibus weighing 1½ tons a distance of 158 ft (48 m), by attaching it to his ears with string.

Using Your Loaf

In August 2005, in the small town of Mottola, Italy, a monster focaccia was baked. Measuring 78 x 41 ft (23.7 x 12.5 m), the traditional flat bread covered an area of 3,200 sq ft (297 sq m). It was baked in a special wood-and-coal burning oven 4,840 sq ft (450 sq m) wide. The cooked focaccia weighed an estimated 62,000 lb (28,000 kg) and was consumed by 40,000 spectators.

A Knife's Edge

The Great Throwdini is a world-champion knife-throwing minister from Freeport, New York, who takes the world of "impalement arts" to the extreme with his death-defying Maximum Risk act.

When and why did you become a knife thrower?

❝My real name is the Rev. Dr. David Adamovich and for 18 years I was a professor of exercise physiology. When I was 50, I opened a pool hall and one of my customers brought in a small throwing knife. I threw it into a tree outside and struck it perfectly. Nine months later I came second in the world knife-throwing championship. ❞

What is Maximum Risk?

❝I'm one of the world's best in competition throwing, and I've converted that skill into a stage act called Maximum Risk. The name is a line from the French movie 'Girl on the Bridge,' about a knife thrower who persuades suicidal girls to be his assistants. ❞

Do you just throw knives at your assistants?

❝I throw knives, tomahawks, axes, and machetes—but I never throw 'at,' I throw 'around!' My assistant stands in front of a board, or is strapped on to the Wheel of Death while I throw two knives per revolution, one on each side of her. I also catch knives mid-air, and throw both right- and left-handed, blindfolded, and with my back to the board. I don't know why they call it 'impalement arts' because the last thing we want to do is impale our assistants. ❞

How fast can you throw?

❝Throwing a single knife at a time, I can throw 75 in one minute. Throwing three knives at a time, my personal best is 144 knives around my partner in one minute. ❞

Do you have any special techniques?

❝I video what I do and watch it back—I study my hands very carefully. When I throw blind, I use sound to judge where to throw. My assistant sets me up facing the board, and I know exactly where she's standing. ❞

Have you ever injured yourself or an assistant?

❝I once had to stop because I stuck myself with the point of a knife and started bleeding from my fingers. Knives have bounced from the Wheel of Death and scraped the girl, but I've never impaled a girl. ❞

Is it difficult to find willing assistants?

❝Very! I don't just want a girl to stand there as my target—it's about the way she flirts with me and the audience, while facing danger. ❞

Do you come from a performing family?

❝Through my high school years I was a gymnast. I competed in the junior Olympics. One of my daughters is a surgeon who is very good with a knife in a different way! My wife Barbara was a knife thrower herself but retired—she has no wish to be my assistant. ❞

Mini Chain
These toothpicks have 28 chainlinks carved into each of them. They were made by Mallikarjun Reddy from Bangalore, India, in 2005.

ACTUAL SIZE!

Just for Laughs
In 1992, American comedian Mike Heeman set out to tell as many jokes as possible in 24 hours. By the end of his marathon gag-fest, he had cracked no fewer than 12,682 jokes.

Riding High
In June 2004, Terry Goertzen, a pastor from Winnipeg, Canada, completed a 328-yd (300-m) ride on a bicycle constructed like a ladder that stood 18 ft 2½ in (5.5 m) high and was powered by a chain measuring 35 ft 8 in (11 m) in length.

Mass Pillow Fight
No fewer than 766 people knocked the stuffing out of each other at Oregon State University in 2003 in a mammoth pillow fight. The event was organized by student Lige Armstrong as part of a class project.

Math Marvel
A 59-year-old man from Chiba, Japan, recited pi—or the ratio of the circumference of a circle to its diameter—to over 80,000 decimal places during a 12-hour challenge in 2005. Akira Haraguchi started the attempt shortly after noon on July 1 and stopped at 83,431 decimal places early the following day. In doing so, he comfortably beat his previous best of 54,000 decimal places.

Balloon Bonanza
In a bizarre challenge, students from Temasek Secondary School in Singapore set out to produce as many objects shaped from balloons as possible. In July 2005, a huge gathering of 1,471 students exercised their lungs to create 16,380 balloons in shapes that ranged from flowers to giraffes.

Super Bowl
Suresh Joachim created bowling history in Toronto, Ontario, in June 2005, by bowling nonstop without sleep for 100 hours. To meet his challenge, he endured 360 games of bowling in which he achieved a fantastic 120 strikes. However, he also managed to break nine bowling balls!

In Peak Condition

On May 21, 2004, Pemba Dorjie Sherpa, a 27-year-old Nepali, climbed the upper reaches of the world's highest mountain, Mount Everest, in just 8 hours 10 minutes. Everest is 29,039 ft (8,851 m) high and Pemba's climb—from base camp at 17,380 ft (5,297 m) to the summit—usually takes experienced mountaineers three to four days.

In September 1998, **1,000 students** from the University of *Guelph* in Ontario, Canada, formed an enormous human **conveyor belt**— passing a surfboard along the belt's entire length.

Wild Bill's Bike

When William "Wild Bill" Gelbke decided to build a giant motorcycle at a Chicago workshop, he had no plans or blueprints. It took him eight long years, but when the Roadog finally appeared in 1965, it created quite a stir. The mammoth bike measured 17 ft (5.2 m) in length, weighed 3,280 lb (1,488 kg), had a frame built from aircraft tubing, and had a cruising speed of a cool 90 mph (145 km/h).

Lawnmower Ride

As part of the Keep America Beautiful campaign, Brad Hauter, from Indiana, rode a lawnmower coast to coast across the U.S.A. He set off from San Francisco in April 2003 and arrived in New York 79 days later after a journey of more than 5,600 mi (9,012 km). The specially adapted mower had a top speed of 25 mph (40 km/h).

Full House

Believe it or not, 15,756 players took part in a single game of bingo at the Canadian National Exhibition in August 1983.

Human Ramp

Tim Cridland's feats are inspired by the mystics of the Far East. Through using "mind-over-matter" philosophy, he has taught his brain not to register the feeling of pain. He can swallow swords and dance on broken glass, but it is his car feat that he counts as his greatest achievement. While lying on a bed of nails with spikes 5 in (13 cm) long, he is able to endure the weight of a 1-ton car driving over him. His skin is not even punctured.

Basketball Marathon

At New England's Beatrice High School gym between July 28 and July 30, 2005, players staged a 52-hour marathon basketball game. "Everyone was exhausted by the end of the game," said organizer Jim Weeks. Some players struggled through the early hours of the mornings and were ready to give up when they reached 40 hours, but they bravely battled on. The final score was 7,935 points to 6,963.

Monster Board

In 1996, Todd Swank from San Diego, California, built a skateboard for himself and his friends that was 10 ft (3 m) long, 4 ft (1.2 m) wide, and 3 ft (1 m) high. It weighed 500 lb (227 kg) and used tires from a sports car. He said he wanted to create a skateboard that no one would ever forget.

Reading Aloud

In March 2005, 1,544 students from Pleasant Valley Middle School, Pocono, Pennsylvania, simultaneously read aloud *Oh the Places You'll Go* by Dr. Seuss.

Inflated Lizard

If attacked, the chuckwalla, one of the largest lizards in the U.S., will crawl into a space between two rocks and puff itself up with air so that it can't be pulled out. It can inflate its lungs to increase its body size by as much as 50 per cent.

49-DaY FasT

CHEN JIANMIN, a 50-year-old doctor of Traditional Chinese Medicine, went 49 days without food in 2004, drinking only water.

An exponent of the practice of fasting, Chen entered the sealed glass cabin, measuring 160 sq ft (15 sq m), on March 20, 2004. The box was fixed 30 ft (9 m) high above the ground on a mountainside near Ya'an City. More than 10,000 visitors who turned out to watch the fast could see into Mr. Chen's house, except for two areas where he showered and used the toilet. While doing so he had to keep his head above a curtain to prove that he wasn't eating. Chen entered the box weighing 123 lb (56 kg) and emerged from the box at least 33 lb (15 kg) lighter. He claimed to have once gone 81 days without food.

Chen takes a call. He claimed to have answered more than 8,000 telephone calls from all over China while in his box.

Suspended 30 ft (9 m) above the ground, Chen sits in his glass box watched over by his team below.

Chen pours himself a drink of water inside his box, which was equipped with items such as a fan, table, chairs, and electric power.

Clever Kids

★ Born in 1982, Anthony McQuone from Weybridge, England, could speak Latin and quote Shakespeare when he was just two years old.

★ David Farragut, who later served as a naval officer during the American Civil War, was given command of his first ship when just 12 years old.

★ American singer Tori Amos began to play the piano at 2½ years of age and wrote her first song when she was just five years old.

★ Romanian painter Alexandra Nechita had her first solo exhibition in 1993 at the age of eight at a library in Los Angeles, California.

Ding-Dong Merrily

Canadian choir leader Joe Defries had music ringing in his ears after playing the handbells for nearly 28 hours straight. Joe, from Abbotsford, British Columbia, has been playing the handbells for more than 25 years and drew up a list of 1,300 tunes for his marathon solo venture in July 2005. Although he had never previously gone beyond 8 hours of solo ringing, Joe rose to the challenge, even finding time to crack jokes in the 30-second breaks he took after each tune.

Horror Crawl

Colorado Springs students Leo Chau and Sean Duffy crawled on their hands and knees for an agonizing 32 mi (51.5 km) through hailstorms and lightning in June 2005 to raise money for charity. The tortuous 44-hour crawl took its toll. Duffy suffered hallucinations and motion sickness while Chau was struck by severe dehydration.

On a Roll

In May 2005, to raise money for the Asian tsunami relief fund, students at the Cornell School of Hotel Administration, New York State, created a huge spring roll 1,315 ft (400 m) long. The monster hors d'oeuvre contained 3,500 spring-roll wrappers, 400 lb (180 kg) of vermicelli noodles, 250 lb (113 kg) each of carrots and cucumbers, and 80 lb (36 kg) of lettuce.

Speed Juggling

Shawn McCue from Sedalia, Missouri, was surfing the Internet when he came across a site for speed juggling. In high school he had been able to bounce a soccer ball on his foot as many as 600 times in three minutes, so he resolved to recreate past glories. In July 2005, in Jefferson City, he performed 155 juggles in 30 seconds, maintaining perfect balance throughout, while the ball never once rose more than 1 in (2.5 cm) off his foot.

▶ **Super Boy**
Eleven-year-old Bruce Khlebnikov tows an airplane with a rope attached to his hair on May 24, 2001, in Moscow, Russia. He has also pulled cars, lifted Russia's heaviest bodybuilder, torn thick books in half, and used his fists to break 15 ceramic plates that were attached together.

Waist Spinner
Ashrita Furman successfully hula hoops with a hoop that is 14 ft 7½ in (4.46 m) in diameter in New York's Flushing Meadow Park on July 15, 2005.

Elvis Lives!
They were all shook up in July 2005 in Cleveland, Ohio, when a total of 106 Elvis impersonators gathered on a high-school football field and performed a three-minute rendition of "Viva Las Vegas." Men, women, and children alike all donned gold shades and black plastic wigs for the occasion.

Bumper Bagel
For the 2004 New York State Fair, Bruegger's Bakeries created a bagel that weighed 868 lb (394 kg) and measured 6 ft (1.8 m) in diameter.

Whole Lotta Shakin'
While campaigning in Albuquerque for election as New Mexico's governor in September 2002, Bill Richardson, a former U.S. Ambassador to the United Nations, shook 13,392 hands in 8 hours, smashing President Theodore Roosevelt's previously esteemed total of 8,513. At the end of the gruelling session, Richardson immediately sunk his hand into ice.

High Tea
Dressed in formal evening wear, three explorers climbed into a hot-air balloon in June 2005 for an airborne dinner party. David Hempleman-Adams, Bear Grylls, and Alan Veal soared to a height of 24,262 ft (7,395 m) above Bath, England. Then, Grylls and Veal climbed 40 ft (12 m) down to a platform where, at a neatly laid dinner table, they ate asparagus spears followed by poached salmon and a terrine of summer fruits, all served in specially designed warm boxes to combat the freezing temperatures at altitude.

Jumping for Joy
Gary Stewart, of Ohio, made 177,737 consecutive jumps on a pogo stick in 20 hours in May 1990.

Chocolate Delight

Pastry cook Ugo Mignone is seen here working on a Christmas display made entirely of chocolate at a cake workshop in Naples, Italy, in November 2004. Twenty Neapolitan pastry chefs, using a huge 6,600 lb (3,000 kg) of chocolate, worked to create this tasty nativity scene.

The mouthwatering chocolate nativity receives its finishing touches.

MUSEUMS Gatlinburg

OPENED IN 1970, the first Gatlinburg museum was destroyed by fire in 1992. Reopened the following year, the new museum was built as if crumbling during a severe earthquake. Gatlinburg has many exhibits, including a Mastodon skeleton, Yeti hair, and a giraffe made out of coat hangers.

DANCE RATTLE
A Maori crocodile hand rattle from New Zealand.

BOTTLED ARROW
These wooden arrows were inserted through the bottle without any cutting or gluing!

FUTURISTIC ROBOT
Created by Simon Blades, this robot is made entirely from used automobile parts.

DON'T MISS!

- ► Extinct elephant bird egg
- ► World's largest gum wrapper chain
- ► Elephant jaw
- ► Fiji mermaid
- ► Berlin Wall
- ► Wood carved Vespa motorcycle
- ► Egyptian mummy
- ► Giant punt gun
- ► Car parts robot soldier

TALLEST MAN
When Robert Wadlow died in 1940, at the age of 22, he was 8 ft 11 in (2.7 m) tall, weighed 440 lb (200 kg), wore a size 37AA shoe, and had a 25 ring size.

MASTODON SKELETON
Robert Ripley watches over this mastodon, a prehistoric relative of the elephant discovered beneath a golf course in Ohio.

Robert L. Ripley 1893–1949

KUGEL BALL
Weighing 10,518 lb (4,770 kg), this ball can amazingly be moved by the touch of a finger.

SHRUNKEN HEAD
The Jivaro tribe of Ecuador claimed their enemies' heads as war trophies.

TWO-HEADED GOAT
Each head has a trachea and esophagus, but each leads to only one lung.

Snow Boat

An amazing sculpture of an ancient warship was carved out of snow and ice in the city of Jilin, China, in January 2005. It was 82 ft (25 m) long, 20 ft (6 m) wide, and 30 ft (9.1 m) high.

Night Skiing

Canadians Ralph Hildebrand and Dave Phillips water-skied for 56 hours 35 minutes around Rocky Point, British Columbia, in June 1994. They used spotlights and infrared binoculars during the night-time periods of the marathon.

Fish Swallower

In just one hour in July 2005, Indian yoga teacher G.P. Vijaya Kumar swallowed 509 small fish through his mouth and blew them out of his nose! Kumar was inspired by American Kevin Cole, who blows spaghetti strands out of a nostril in a single blow. After successfully ejecting peas and corn through his nose in earlier exhibitions, Kumar turned to live fish.

Property Giant

The game of Monopoly was played on this huge board in Berlin in June 2005. To make a move, the pieces had to be lifted by two players!

VICTORY TO RELISH

FOR THE FIFTH straight year, it was a moment for Takeru Kobayashi to relish when he consumed 49 hot dogs in just 12 minutes!

In 2005, the 27-year-old speed eater from Nagano, Japan, retained his crown at Nathan's Famous Fourth of July International Hot Dog Eating Contest at Coney Island, New York. Kobayashi, who stands 5 ft 7 in (1.7 m) tall and weighs just 144 lb (65 kg), beat runner-up Sonya Thomas of Alexandria, Virginia, by 12 hot dogs, enabling the coveted Mustard Yellow Belt to return to Japan for the ninth year out of the past ten. Kobayashi's personal best is a staggering 53½ hot dogs in 12 minutes!

A brief moment before Takeru Kobayashi's success, he is seen struggling to keep his mouth closed as he valiantly attempts to chew and swallow his 49th hot dog.

Nailed Down

Lee Graber of Tallmadge, Ohio, was sandwiched between two beds of nails with a weight of 1,659 lb (752.5 kg) pressing on top of him for 10 seconds in June 2000. The weight was lowered into position by a crane.

Tree Planter

Ken Chaplin planted 15,170 trees in a single day near Prince Albert, Saskatchewan, on June 30, 2001.

Highly Strung

In June 2000, a team of 11 students from the Academy of Science and Technology at Woodlands, Texas, and their physics teacher, Scott Rippetoe, unveiled a fully playable Flying V guitar that measured 43 ft 7½ in (13.2 m) long and 16ft 5½ in (5 m) wide. It weighed 2,244 lb (1,018 kg) and used strings that were 8 in (20 cm) thick and 25 ft (7.6 m) in length.

⊽ Danny's Way

Daredevil American skateboarder Danny Way created history in 2005 by clearing the Great Wall of China without motorized assistance. He hurtled down a 120-ft (36.5-m) specially constructed vertical ramp at a speed of approximately 50 mph (80 km/h) and leapt a 61-ft (19-m) gap to land safely on a ramp erected on the other side of the wall. The 31-year-old from Encinitas, California, spent eight months planning the two-second jump.

Mime Master

Bulgarian mime artist Alexander Iliev performed a 24-hour mime in July 2001 at the Golden Sands resort near Varna, Bulgaria, pausing for only a one-minute break every hour. His marathon effort featured more than 400 different pantomime pieces and saw him cover around 140 mi (225 km) on stage.

Jai Narain Bhati, a barber from *Bhopal,* India, cut the hair of **1,451** people over a **108-hour** period in January 2002. His only breaks were for **10 minutes** every hour.

Toga Parade

In August 2003, in the town of Cottage Grove, Oregon, 2,166 people dressed in togas paraded down Main Street re-enacting the parade scene from the movie *National Lampoon's Animal House,* which had been filmed in the town in 1977.

Maggot Bath

Christine Martin of Horsham, England, sat in a bathtub of maggots for 1 hour 30 minutes in 2002.

▲ Brick It Up
Terry Cole balances 75 bricks weighing a staggering 328 lb (148.8 kg) on his head. Among other things, he has also carried a single brick held downward for 72 mi (116 km) and balanced 16 bricks on his chin!

Dog Tired
Andrew Larkey tried to walk 19 dogs simultaneously in Sydney, Australia, in May 2005. He began by being pulled in 19 directions before controlling 11 of the dogs single-handedly over the ⅔-mi (1-km) walk.

Coffin Ordeal
In May 2005 in Louisville, Kentucky, escapologist Aron Houdini (his legal name) spent an amazing 79 minutes inside a sealed coffin with no air. He was handcuffed, leg-cuffed, and chained inside the coffin. "I freaked out at first," admitted Houdini, who was able to communicate with his crew by way of a radio from inside the wooden box. "However, once I got my mind under control, I started what I had been practicing for almost a year. I slowed my metabolism down and then I concentrated on resting."

Stone Skipper
For years the leading exponent of the art of skipping a stone across the water was an American called Jerdone Coleman-McGhee. In 1994, he achieved 38 skips from a bridge on the Blanco River in Texas.

Wurst is Best
In June 2005, 80 cooks from Leipzig, Germany, created a sausage that was 108 ft (33 m) long and required 294 broilers (grills) to cook it. The attempt to broil the sausage had to be called off when gusts of wind scattered the burning charcoal.

▶ Eye-watering
Brian Duffield from Newent, U.K., chewed and consumed a whole onion weighing 7.5 oz (212 g) in 1 minute 32 seconds. He said: "The hardest thing is actually swallowing it. You just have to get it down." A keen gardener, Brian grows his own onions and uses them for practice.

Group Hug
In April 2004, a staggering total of 5,117 students, staff, and friends from St. Matthew Catholic High School, Orleans, Ontario, joined forces—and arms!—to have an enormous group hug.

Tightrope Crossing

Age was no bar to American acrobat, balloonist, and tightrope-walker William Ivy Baldwin. During his lifetime, he made 87 tightrope crossings of the South Boulder Canyon, Colorado—the first when he was 14 and the last on July 31, 1948, his 82nd birthday! The wire was 320 ft (97.5 m) long and the drop was a terrifying 125 ft (38 m).

Believe it or not, in **May 2004**, **927** students and staff at Taylor University, Indiana, *leaped* over each other in a mammoth exhibition of **leapfrogging!**

Handcycle Tour

In 2005, paraplegic Andreas Dagelet set out from Coochiemudlo Island, Brisbane, to circumnavigate Australia on a handcycle—a sort of bicycle that is powered by arms and hands instead of legs and feet. The entire journey measured approximately 10,600 mi (17,000 km).

Self-taught Cowboy

There aren't too many cowboys in Maryland, but Andy Rotz is an exception. The self-taught cowboy from Hagerstown—who learned his art from watching John Wayne and Clint Eastwood movies—can do over 11,000 Texas skips, a maneuver that entails whipping a vertical loop of rope from side to side while jumping through the middle. He had to keep the rope spinning for 3 hours 10 minutes and perform a skip roughly every second.

Chorus Line

In 2005, 15,785 workers in Tangshan City, China, all sang "Workers are Strong" simultaneously

Aerial Wedding

Nobody in the world has done more skydives than Don Kellner. Don from Hazleton, Pennsylvania, has over 36,000 skydives to his name and his wife Darlene is no slouch either, having made around 13,000. Naturally enough, their wedding in 1990 was conducted in mid-air, the ceremony being performed by fellow skydiver, the Rev. Dave Sangley.

Inside Job

In April 2005, a British couple drove the length of Europe without getting out of their car. Dr. James Shippen and Barbara May, from Bromsgrove, England, made the 2,000-mi (3,200-km) journey from John O'Groats, on the northern coast of Scotland, to the southern tip of Italy to demonstrate their invention, the Indipod, an in-car toilet.

▶ Baby Bike

Bobby Hunt (aka Circus Boy) reckons he has spent over $1,500 on building and fixing his bike—and it's only 3 in (7.6 cm) long, axel to axel, and 7¾ in (20 cm) tall. The bike's size might be a problem, but Bobby rides it with ease, and can even perform wheelies.

Open Wide

Jim Mouth, 51, is a comedy entertainer based in Las Vegas who has been performing incredible stunts for more than 20 years. These often involve putting absolutely *anything* in his mouth!

When did you get started— and why do you keep going?

❝ My first stunt, when I was about 29, was playing drums for two weeks non stop. I had to drink lots of coffee to stay awake! I'm 51 now, and my comedy shows are more of a full-time thing, but my biggest drive is to use stunts to raise money for charity. ❞

What is your most famous stunt?

❝ I like doing the "most cigarettes in the mouth" stunt. I'm up to 159 cigarettes now. I've performed this on TV many times. I put all the cigarettes in apart from one which the host of the show puts in. Then they light them with two propane torches, I cough and wheeze for about three minutes, then spit them out. I'm dizzy for about half an hour afterwards. One time I coughed out about 100 cigarettes— the crazy thing is I'm actually a non-smoker. I've actually done this stunt on non-smoking days to support people giving up cigarettes. ❞

Do you have a special technique?

❝ Before a stunt I wedge corks into my mouth to stretch my lips, but my real secret is that I can dislocate my jaw. I didn't know I was doing it until they X-rayed me on a TV show last year. All I knew was that it was painful and made my eyes water! ❞

What other stunts do you do?

❝ Mouth stunts include smoking 41 cigars at once, and 41 pipes. We once had a whole band playing music under the water in a pool, and another time I sat on every seat in the University of Michigan football stadium, the biggest in the United States. There were 101,701 seats— it took me 96 hours and 12 minutes, and four pairs of pants! ❞

How dangerous are your stunts?

❝ Apparently when my jaw dislocates it rests on my larynx, which could suffocate me. No one will insure me! ❞

Is there anything you would not do?

❝ Because I play drums I really don't want to break a finger or an arm. But I will put up with anything in my mouth—I might try keeping a tarantula spider in my mouth for half an hour. ❞

How long will you carry on?

❝ My goal is to do one stunt every year for at least the next ten years. One I've got in the pipeline is "most hats on the head"—I'm aiming for a stack of 300, which will be about 8½ ft tall and weigh about 110 lb. I'll probably retire when I'm in my sixties— I'll do 170 cigarettes and then call it a day. ❞

★ Czech climber Martin Tlusty survived a terrifying 1,000-ft (305-m) fall down the side of a mountain in Slovakia in 2005.

★ Swiss authorities wrap some mountain glaciers with aluminum foil in the summertime to stop them from melting.

★ Frenchman Christian Taillefer cycled down a glacier at 132 mph (212 km/h) in Vars, France, in 1998.

★ When Mount St. Helens in Washington State, the highest peak in the U.S.A., erupted spectacularly in 1980, the avalanche on the north slope reached incredible speeds of 250 mph (400 km/h).

Rocketman
Texan Eric Scott took to the skies in England in April 2004, rocketing upward to 152 ft (46 m)—the height of a 12-storey building. Eric remained airborne for 26 seconds. His "rocketbelt" was mounted on a fiberglass corset with two rocket nozzles and a belt that had basic controls for steering.

Biker Duo
American couple Chris and Erin Ratay covered 101,322 mi (163,058 km) on separate motorcycles during a journey that took them through 50 countries on six different continents. They set off from Morocco in May 1999 and arrived home in New York in August 2003.

Lengthy Lecture
Errol Muzawazi, a 20-year-old lecturer from Zimbabwe, delivered a lecture lasting for 88 hours in 2005, talking nonstop for more than three days. His audience at Jagellonian University in Krakow, Poland, fell asleep!

Internet Marathon
In November 1997, Canada's Daniel Messier spent 103 hours nonstop surfing the internet—that's more than four days!

Giant Noodle
Believe it or not, participants at Canada's Corso Italia Toronto Fiesta in 2003 created a spaghetti noodle that was an amazing 525 ft (160 m) long.

Sore Hands
Peter Schoenfeld of Ontario, Canada, chopped 209 wooden blocks by hand in just two minutes in October 2001.

Making Whoopee
In July 2005, following a baseball game in Bowie, Maryland, an incredible 4,439 Bowie Baysox fans sat on whoopee cushions simultaneously to create a gargantuan flatulence sound!

Quick Solution

If you need help with math, ask Gert Mittring. The 38-year-old needed just 11.8 seconds to calculate the 13th root of a 100-digit number in his head during a special challenge near Frankfurt, Germany, in 2004. He even solved the problem faster than onlookers with electric calculators.

In Flight

Australian professional golfer Stuart Appleby drives off on one of the runways at Sydney Airport, Australia, on November 22, 2004. Appleby was competing against fellow golfers in a golf driving distance contest, which he won with a massive shot that reached an incredible distance of 2,069 ft 3 in (630.58 m)— over one-third of a mile.

On a Sydney Airport runway, Appleby makes his golf ball fly.

Sundae Best

On July 24, 1988, a giant ice-cream sundae was made by Palm Dairies of Alberta, Canada. It featured an amazing 44,689 lb (20,270 kg) of ice cream, 9,688 lb 2 oz (4,394 kg) of syrup, and 537 lb 3 oz (244 kg) of toppings!

Balancing Act

At the age of 12, Tim Johnston, of Piedmont, California, balanced 15 spoons on his face for 30 seconds in May 2004.

◀ Corset Cathie

Cathie Jung, now aged 68, has been wearing a corset, even when asleep, for over 20 years. At 5 ft 6 in (1.68 m) tall and weighing 135 lb (61 kg), her waist measures a tiny 15 in (38 cm). The only time Cathie removes the corset is when she showers. Cathie's corset training started with a 26-in (66-cm) corset in 1983, when she had a 28-in (71-cm) waist. She gradually reduced the size of the corsets as they became comfortable.

Freestyle Rap

Toronto rapper D.O. performed a freestyle rap that went on for 8 hours 45 minutes in July 2003.

In what was an **enormous gathering** of Christmas carolers, **519** hardy souls braved the New York cold for a mass sing-along on the steps of Manhattan's General Post Office in December 2003.

Having a Ball

David Ogron has a ball every day of his life. In fact, in an average year he has 400,000 balls. The Californian hit on his unusual career some years ago when he was practicing with friends on the golf range. "We were seeing who could hit the ball the fastest. That's when I realized I had a talent." With the help of ball-setter Scott "Speedy" McKinney, who puts each ball on the tee, Ogron hit 1,388 balls in 30 minutes in May 2005 at Louisville, Kentucky. And in July 2005, he hit 82 in one minute in Miami. On another occasion, he hit 10,392 balls in 24 hours.

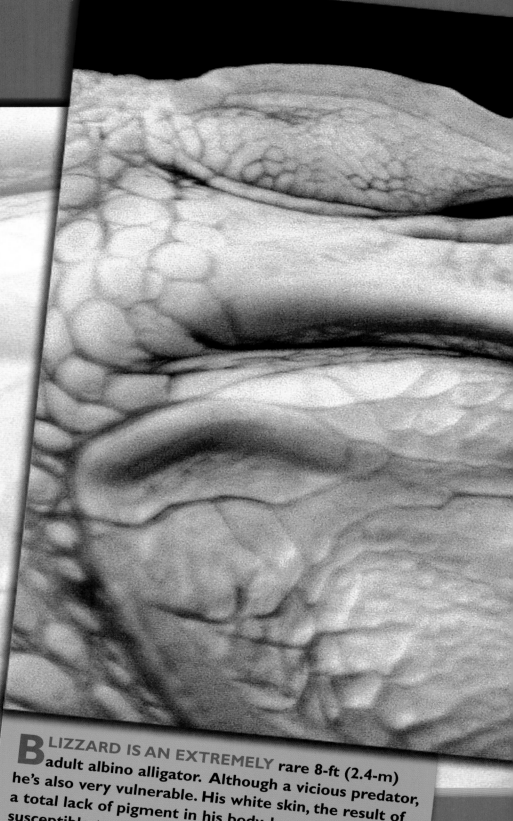

BLIZZARD IS AN EXTREMELY rare 8-ft (2.4-m) adult albino alligator. Although a vicious predator, he's also very vulnerable. His white skin, the result of a total lack of pigment in his body, leaves him very susceptible to sunburn. Because of this he was kept under cover in a specially designed tent while at the Maritime Aquarium in South Norwalk, Connecticut.

AMAZING

A herd of miniature pigs compete in the Pig Olympics
page 121

Miniature horses, 24 in (61 cm) tall, wearing sneakers and warm blankets were spotted in a busy shopping mall
page 123

Bruce, an Oranda goldfish, measures a staggering 17.129 in (43.507 cm) from snout to tail fin
page 124

ANIMALS

Web of Intrigue

INSTEAD OF USING traditional canvases, Enrique Ramos of Mexico City, known as "The Fly Guy," creates tiny portraits of famous people on flies, feathers, beans, animal bones, and even bats!

George Washington, Marlon Brando, "The Lighthouse Man," and Alfred Hitchcock painted on quails' eggs, measuring only 1 in (2.5 cm) high.

Without the help of any kind of magnification, Ramos has handpainted Da Vinci's "Mona Lisa" on a bird feather, a bean, and a stuffed bat. Often his pictures take under two minutes. He has even painted seven faces on a single human hair!

Sometimes Ramos uses no paint at all. He made a portrait of The Beatles from more than 60 dung beetles and hundreds of butterfly wings, and a bust of Abraham Lincoln from the hair of his son and daughter.

Ramos likes to paint subjects on real cobwebs too. He is unable to correct mistakes and also considers himself lucky if one-third of the gathered webs survive to form one of his cobweb paintings.

ACTUAL SIZE!

This bat was created to celebrate Halloween and the Mexican Day of the Dead festival and depicts Bela Lugosi as Dracula, and Lon Chaney as the Wolfman.

These butterflies are part of a 35-piece Mexican history series. The first shows the Spanish conquistador, Hernando Cortez, and the second depicts the tragic Aztec-Mayan love story of Popoca and Miztla.

To gather enough spiderweb for his re-creation of "The Last Supper," Ramos spent two weeks scouring the most remote areas of Mexico with the help of his family. In an old abandoned village he came across thousands of spiderwebs, and managed to gather the 22 lb (10 kg) needed for his picture. After carefully removing all living creatures from a web, Ramos placed it in a bucket of soapy water to clean it, before flattening it by placing it on a plastic canvas on the ground and wringing out the water with his hands and feet. As the web dried, it began to take shape with Ramos gently massaging it to stretch it as thinly as possible. Within a day the web had dried completely and was ready for use.

A depiction of Spiderman— one of Ramos's most recent works—is made from nearly 20 lb (9 kg) of large wolf spiderwebs, and stands over 2 ft (60 cm) in height.

This miniature painting of Moses kneeling before the burning bush, painted on spiderweb, measures 2 x 1 in (5 x 2.5 cm) and was done without the use of magnification.

Nation in Mourning
China went into mourning for Mei Mei, the world's oldest captive giant panda, raised at Guilin Zoo. She died in July 2005 at the age of 36. An elaborate funeral was held during which visitors filed past, paying their respects to the much-loved animal.

Golf-ball Guzzler
Doctors in England removed 28 golf balls from the stomach of a German shepherd who frequently takes walks along a golf course with his owner.

Vanishing Act
Seven years after mysteriously disappearing, Ewok, a nine-year-old Shih Tzu, suddenly returned to Crofton, British Columbia, home of Jim and Barbara Reed in 2001.

Barking Math
Alissa Nelson of Urbandale, Iowa, has a mongrel named Oscar who can do math addition problems. He answers a variety of mathematical sums by barking. For example, when asked the sum of two and two, he responds with four barks.

The Yap of Luxury
Dudley's bakery is a dog's dream come true. Created by Vickie Emmanuele, the bakery offers specially made fancy gourmet treats and dog cakes.

Duck Dialects
It sounds quackers, but an English scientist has discovered that ducks have regional accents. Ducks in London are noisier than those in rural Cornwall as they have to raise their voices to compete with traffic.

Canine Candidate

In a bid to add color to the 2002 French presidential campaign, and to warn politicians against complacency, Serge Scotto tried to enter the name of his dog Saucisse as a rival candidate. But despite picking up over four per cent of the vote in municipal elections in Marseille, Saucisse failed to obtain the necessary backing to oppose Jacques Chirac in the final stages of the presidential election.

Expert Witness

A police dog took the stand in a Pittsburgh, Pennsylvania, courtroom in 1994. The defense attorney tried to prove that the dog, not his client, was the aggressor in a fight.

Punch-drunk

A black bear in Baker Lake, Washington, was found passed out on a resort lawn. He got that way after stealing and drinking 36 cans of campers' beer!

Gone in a Flash

A single lightning strike on a farm in northern Israel killed an incredible 10,000 chickens.

High Marking

Giant pandas mark their territory by performing a handstand and urinating as high as possible up the side of a tree!

Frog Festival
A live frog is dressed in lavish finery as a "King" for a competition during the frog festival in the city of San Fernando in the Philippines.

Lost and Found

A dog that had been reported missing from his home in Columbus, Ohio, in 2002 turned up inside a 10-ft (3-m) long python that was found lurking under a neighbor's house. The neighbor called the police when she spotted the large snake with an ominous bulge in its middle.

Holy Cat

Mike McGregor, from Edinburgh, Scotland, had never spotted anything unusual about the markings of his pet cat Brandy, until he saw Christ's face, just as it appears on the Turin Shroud, staring out at him. He said: "It's not every day that you see the face of Jesus in your cat's fur."

Cow Hide

It takes an incredible 3,000 cows to supply the National Football League with enough leather for just one season's worth of footballs!

Inheritance Kitty

In the 1960s, San Diego doctor William Grier left his entire fortune of $415,000 to his two 15-year-old cats, Brownie and Hellcat.

Survived Fall

Andy, a cat owned by Florida senator Ken Myer, fell 16 floors (200 ft/61 m) from a building in the 1970s—and survived!

First-class Hamster

Emptying a mail box in Cambridge, England, one day, mailman Robert Maher was stunned to see a hamster peeping out from an envelope marked "Do Not Bend." He took it to veterinary surgeon Patrick von Heimendahl, who said that the animal—nicknamed First Class—was lucky to be alive. The hamster, thought to be about a year old, had miraculously survived a journey through the postal system.

First Class emerges from his envelope unscathed.

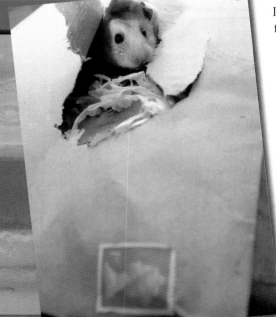

Unusual Passenger

When a man rides a bike, it's nothing special, but when a dog rides a man who rides a bike, that is special! The dog is Spike, a Jack Russell terrier, who can be seen perched on the shoulders of his owner, Denton Walthall, as the latter cycles around the streets of Henrico, Virginia. Mr. Walthall explained how the unusual pose started: "One day I was calling him and he came running at a fast pace. I was squatting down to catch him but he flew up, landed on my leg and then scrambled up on my shoulder. And he was at home. Sometimes I try to get him down, but he simply positions himself further on my back so that he can stay there."

Central Heating
This amazing X ray of a snake clearly shows the electric heating pad that the snake has swallowed!

Human Zoo
In August 2005, visitors to England's London Zoo were in for a big surprise at the bear enclosure. Instead of black bears, prowling around on the rocky landscape were eight human beings wearing little more than fig leaves. The volunteers spent three days on Bear Mountain, entertaining themselves with games and music. The zoo explained that the exhibition was designed to show the basic nature of humans.

Cattle Wedding

In July 2005, a pair of dwarf Brahman cattle were married in a lavish Thai wedding ceremony. Krachang Kanokprasert, the owner of the bull, originally wanted to buy the bride, but when her owner refused to sell, the two farmers agreed to join the miniature breeding stock in matrimony.

Mighty Plunge

Sam, a German shepherd with California's Lodi Police Department, jumped 50 ft (15 m) into a river from a bridge while pursuing a suspect in 2001. Once in the water, Sam swam after the suspect and proceeded to herd him to his human colleagues on the bank.

An **ant colony** built beneath **Melbourne**, Australia, in 2004 measured a **staggering** **60 mi** (**97 km**) wide. The ARGENTINE ants formed a giant **supercolony** as a result of co-operative behavior.

GrEat EScApE

Who let the dogs out? That's exactly what staff at Battersea Dogs' Home in London, England, wanted to know.

In 2004, several mornings in a row, staff arrived at Battersea Dogs' Home to find that as many as nine dogs had escaped from their compounds and were causing chaos in the kitchen. In a bid to solve the mystery of how the dogs managed to get free, the dogs' home installed video surveillance cameras. These revealed that a three-year-old Lurcher called Red had learned how not only to unbolt his own kennel door using his nose and teeth, but also how to to free his fellow hounds to join in the adventure, helping themselves to food in the kitchen.

Having studied how staff moved the bolt to unlock the kennel door, Red the Lurcher used his teeth to do the same.

Red (right) and his friends make good their escape, heading toward the kitchen to forage for food.

Scary Creepy Crawly

This enormous cockroach is an amazing 3 in (80 mm) long and weighs 1¼ oz (35 g). Found in Brisbane, Australia, in 1997, it now holds permanent residence at the Queensland Museum.

ACTUAL **SIZE!**

Green Bears

In 2004, the usually white coats of Sheba and her son Inuka, Singapore Zoo's two polar bears, turned green! The color change was caused by harmless algae growing in the bears' hollow hair shafts, and was the result of Singapore's tropical climate. Both bears were successfully bleached with hydrogen peroxide.

Large Litter

Tia, a Neopolitan blue mastiff from the village of Manea in the U.K., gave birth to an amazing 24 puppies in January 2005. Four puppies died shortly after birth, but the remaining 20 were more than a handful—the puppies had to be bottle-fed every four hours! Fully grown the dogs will stand 2 ft (0.6 m) high.

Walking Octopus

Scientists in California have discovered an octopus that appears to walk on two legs! A species of the tiny tropical octopus has developed a technique whereby it wraps itself up into a ball and then releases just two of its eight tentacles so that it can "walk" backward along the ocean floor.

Crazy Gator

An albino alligator at Blank Park Zoo in Des Moines, Iowa, turned pink when it became excited!

Rooster Booster

Melvin the giant rooster just can't stop growing. At 18 months old, he stood 2 ft (60 cm) tall and weighed more than 15 lb (6.8 kg), twice as much as other Buff Orpingtons. His owner, Jeremy Goldsmith of Stansted, U.K., said: "We're staggered. No one's heard of a cockerel this big."

Toad Marriage

A female toad is painted with vermilion during a traditional Hindu wedding ceremony between two giant toads at Khochakandar, India. The ceremony was held by villagers in the hope that the raingods would end a dry spell.

Mixed Parentage

Nikita the foal earned her stripes soon after her birth in Morgenzon, South Africa, in 2004. Her mother, Linda, was a Shetland pony and her father, Jonny, was a zebra!

Animal Crackers

★ A giraffe has the same number of bones in its neck as a human.

★ When feeding, an anteater sticks its tongue in and out up to 160 times a minute and can eat 30,000 ants a day.

★ The mouth of a hyena is so tough that it can chew a glass bottle without cutting itself.

As a **REWARD** for the dog saving her from a 2001 house fire, actress **Drew Barrymore** placed her $3-million Beverly Hills home *in trust* with her golden labrador *Flossie* so that it would always have a roof over its head.

Happy Shopper

We've all heard of dogs that fetch newspapers or slippers. Well, J.C., a golden retriever from Penn Hills, Pennsylvania, goes a step further. He regularly fetches prescriptions for his owners, Chuck and Betty Pusateri, from a nearby drugstore.

Well-groomed

A Denton, Texas, firm called Groom Doggy offers tuxedos, bow ties, and wedding dresses for our canine friends. In fact the company has everything a dog could ever want to fulfill its formal-wear needs.

My Little Pony

Even miniature horses expect to reach a height of 3 ft (1 m) or more, but Peanut, the miniature dwarf stallion, stands just 20 in (50 cm) tall. He owes his diminutive stature to his mother, who was only 26 in (66 cm) tall.

Flying Dog

Star of the 2002 Great American Mutt Show, held in Central Park, New York, was Rhoadi, a small brown dog who flew through the air on a bungee cord, reaching heights of over 6 ft (2 m). Another contest at the show, which was open to only mongrels and strays, was for the dog that was the best kisser!

Sniffer Rat

Gambian giant pouch rats are used to sniff out deadly landmines in Mozambique. The rats are trained to associate the smell of explosives with a food reward and indicate the potential danger to their handlers by frantically scratching the earth.

Muddy Swim

For his act "Becoming Earthworm," performance artist Paul Hurley of the U.K. spent nine days in the mud and rain wearing only swimming trunks and goggles.

Big Mouth

The North American opossum can open its mouth wider than 90 degrees when trying to scare away an attacker.

Flying Snake

Believe it or not, there is a snake that flies! The little-known U.S. Navajo flying snake has lateral wing-like membranes running down its body, enabling it to glide through the air.

Two-nosed Dog

There is a rare breed of dog in the Amazon basin that has two noses. The double-nosed Andean tiger hound was first described a century ago but, in 2005, an expedition led by British adventurer John Blashford-Snell came nose to noses with a specimen. Not surprisingly, the dogs are valued for their excellent sense of smell, which they use to hunt jaguars that prey on villagers' cattle.

MATHEMATICAL GENIUS!
Clever Hans, a horse, lived during the early 1900s. His owner, a math professor named Wilhelm von Osten, taught him how to solve math problems by stomping his feet to count out numbers.

WOOLLY COAT
In 1932, an Angora goat, 30 in (76 cm) tall, owned by Lester Pierce of Eureka, California, had hair 5 ft (1.5 m) long!

TREE-CLIMBER
Ted, a four-year-old terrier, could climb 10 ft (3 m) up a tree and retrieve his ball. He was owned by Bill Vandever from Tulsa, Oklahoma.

STRETCHY
This dog, owned by Pat Murphy, had skin that stretched at least 18 in (46 cm) in any direction.

FROG-LIFTER
Bill Steed, professor of Frog Psychology at Croaker College, Emeryville, California, trained frogs to lift barbells.

INDIAN MARKING
This horse, owned by J.F. Daniel and R.L. Anderson of Craigsville, Virginia, had a marking on its neck in the shape of an American Indian head.

BEE BEARD
When Fred Wilcutt of Falkville, Alabama, captured a queen bee and placed it under his chin, the colony of bees arranged itself around his neck like a beard.

HAIRY HORSE
An extraordinary horse from California had a 14-ft (4.3-m) mane and 13-ft (4-m) tail.

Looking Back

October 2, 1930 **Buddy**, a cat from Roxbury, Massachusetts, ate corn and carrots, and drank tea and coffee. **October 24, 1935** Little **Margaret Rigon** of Corozal, Panama, aged 2½, chewed the head off a deadly coral snake but was unharmed. **March 20, 1946** **A milkmaid** discovered that a cow had swallowed a watch when she heard the watch ticking.

Winged Wizards

★ A North American osprey once built a nest that consisted of three shirts, a bath towel, an arrow, and a garden rake.

★ The wandering albatross can glide for six days without beating its wings and can even sleep in mid-air.

★ An African gray parrot named Prudie had a vocabulary of almost 800 words.

★ When awake, hummingbirds have to eat almost constantly to prevent themselves from starving to death.

Regular Customer

One of the best customers at The Chocolate Moose restaurant in Farmland, Indiana, is Missy Jo, a 60-lb (27-kg) bulldog. Even though she never actually sets foot inside the place, Missy Jo sits outside on the patio with owner Tony Mills for a daily treat of plain cheeseburgers and vanilla milkshakes!

Bamboo Cast

Malai, a 98-year-old female elephant in Thailand, broke her leg in June 2005. Her trainers put a bamboo splint on her front leg in the hope that she would fully recover.

Diving Pig

Meet Miss Piggy, the amazing diving pig! Miss Piggy jumped into the record books in July 2005 when she dived 11 ft (3.3 m) into a pool from a platform 16 ft (5 m) high at Australia's Royal Darwin Show. Owner Tom Vandeleur, who had been training Miss Piggy for a month leading up to the show, said: "She does everything herself. She goes up the 16-ft (5-m) ramp herself, she dives herself."

Marcy Poplett of PEORIA, *Illinois*, was injured and knocked off a personal watercraft on the Illinois River after a **silver carp** leaped out of the water and smacked her in the face!

Legal Rooster

Charged with raising poultry without a permit, David Ashley appeared in court in Seneca Falls, New York, carrying a rooster. When the judge ordered the bird to be removed, Ashley replied that it was his attorney!

Ugliest Dog

In June 2005, a 14-year-old Chinese crested pedigree dog named Sam, won the title that no dog wants—World's Ugliest Dog. And this was the third year running that Sam had won the title. Until his death in November 2005, Sam was famous for his ugliness. He was pale-eyed, wrinkled, had a withered neck, and appeared to have almost no hair.

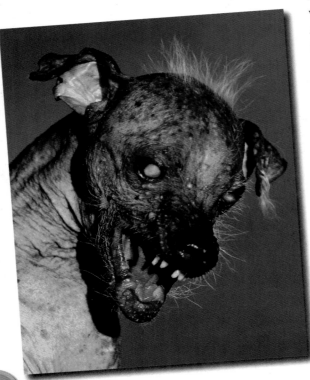

Dual-sex Crab

In May 2005, a fisherman caught a blue crab in Chesapeake Bay, Virginia, that was female on one side and male on the other. Females have red-tipped claws, while males have blue—but this crab had one of each. Experts at the Virginia Institute of Marine Science said the crab was an extremely rare creature called a bilateral gynandromorph, meaning it is split between two genders. They said that the crab's condition probably resulted from a chromosomal mishap shortly after its conception.

Snapped Back

Cooper, a five-year-old golden retriever, managed to fight off a 14 ft (4.3 m), 700 lb (318 kg) alligator in a canal near Lake Moultrie, South Carolina, in June 2005. The dog was swimming across the canal when the reptile—three times Cooper's size—pounced. Cooper lost a few teeth and some skin, but the alligator retreated after being bitten repeatedly on the snout. Cooper's owner, Tom Kierspe, said afterward: "We've changed the dog's name to Lucky."

IN DEPTH

Still Life

Californian taxidermist Tia Resleure, 47, stuffs animals to create fairytale worlds where pigeons wear ball gowns, chickens tell fortunes—and even kittens are framed!

Little shrill voices

How did you get the idea to create art from dead animals?

❝As a child I felt closer to our pets and farm animals than to my own family. I read 'Alice in Wonderland' and wanted to morph into an animal. I inherited my grandfather's collection of taxidermy from Australia, where he grew up, and my father was always picking up bones—he once made a headdress out of a zebra head. ❞

How did you learn how to create the animal art?

❝I started using animal remains in my sculptures in the early eighties, but in 1998 I went on a two-week taxidermy course just to see if I had the nerve to work with fresh specimens. ❞

What was the first piece you ever did, and do you have a favorite now?

❝On that course, I did the Mallard on a Circus Ball and the Fortune Telling Chicken. The director of the school mocked me and said it was unnatural. I didn't think there was anything natural about a conventional duck flying against a piece of driftwood! My favorite piece is 'Little Shrill Voices,' which uses fetal kittens from a cat that had to undergo an emergency pregnancy spay. ❞

What inspires your work?

❝Old European curiosity cabinets, and French, German, and Russian fairy tales. When I'm working on my pieces, I imagine little stories for them. ❞

Where do you get the animals you use?

❝Because of my work in the animal welfare community, I have a lot of contacts with hobby and livestock breeders. Nothing is killed for my work—I just recycle animals that have already died. ❞

Have you ever taxidermied your own pets?

❝Yes. Part of the process of dealing with the loss of my pets is doing something with their remains. The first one I did was my first Italian greyhound, Aissi. I had to keep her in the freezer for about three years before I could start. The first time I pulled her out of the bag to let her thaw, my heart just clenched up. But then it all just went away and became very peaceful. ❞

Do you have a future project you'd love to do?

❝I have a huge old doll's house that I want to fill with animals. I want to fill the lowest level with moles, then ground-level animals on the next floor up, and little birds in the attic. ❞

Fishy Kiss

In 1998, Dan Heath of Medford, Oregon, could barely believe his eyes when he saw Chino, his golden retriever, standing over a fishpond, nose to nose with Falstaff, an orange-and-black carp. Each day, Chino sprints out to the backyard, peers into the water and waits. Within seconds, Falstaff pops up and the two gently touch noses. Heath doesn't know how or why Chino and Falstaff became friends, but it's obvious to everyone that their friendship is watertight.

Resourceful Hamster

Two house moves and some years after thinking they had lost their pet hamster, the Cummins family, from Edmonton, Alberta, were amazed when it reappeared. It turned out that the hamster had never actually left home but had burrowed into the sofa, using it as a nest. The animal had survived by sneaking out at night and taking food and water from the bowls of the family's other pets.

▼ Swimming for Deer Life!

At a wildlife refuge in Georgia, Rangers saw a 13-ft (4-m) alligator that had attacked an adult deer and carried it off, swimming with the animal in its mouth!

Cat on a Hot Tin Roof

Torri Hutchinson was driving along the highway near Inkom, Idaho, in 2005 when a fellow motorist alerted her to the fact that her cat was on the car roof. Hutchinson, Torri's orange tabby, had been clinging to the roof for 10 mi (16 km). Torri hadn't even noticed the cat when she stopped for gas!

Jumbo Artist

The biggest draw at Taman Safari Park in Bogor, Indonesia, is Windi the artistic elephant. By holding on to the brush with her trunk, she dabs the paint on the canvas to form her own forest of colors. In her first six months at the park, the 18-year-old female created 50 paintings, many of which sold at over 20,000 Indonesian rupiahs ($2) each. Others were exhibited outside the park's restaurant.

Bear's Breath

In May 2005, vets at Seneca Park Zoo, Rochester, New York, used a hammer and chisel to remove an infected tooth from the mouth of an 805-lb (350-kg) polar bear named Yukon. The tooth had been giving the bear bad breath.

Invisible Bears

Polar bears are so well insulated they are almost invisible to infrared cameras.

Five-legged Dog

Believe it or not, a five-legged dog was found near a state park near Raleigh, North Carolina, in November 2003. Although it was previously unheard of for such an animal to live much past birth, this dog—a Maltese–terrier mix named Popcorn—was at least nine months old. A vet removed the extra leg because it was hampering the dog's movement, as well as another rear leg that rotated at a 90-degree angle, making it useless. The dog with five legs became a dog with only three.

A talented *tabby cat* named **Bud D. Holly**, who lived with **SHARON FLOOD** at her art gallery in Mendocino, California, had a number of his paintings exhibited in 1992. Twenty of the works, created with **paws** and watercolors, were sold, some fetching over **$100**.

Kiss of Life

When one of Eugene Safken's young chickens appeared to have drowned in a tub in 2005, the Colorado farmer saved the bird by giving it mouth-to-beak resuscitation! After swinging the chicken by the feet in an attempt to revive it, he blew into its beak until the bird began to chirp. The farmer said: "I started yelling, 'You're too young to die!' And every time I'd yell, he'd chirp."

Déjà Vu

A Canadian sailor and his dog were rescued from the same island twice in a week in May 2002. Melvin Cote was hoping to spend the summer in the Queen Charlotte Islands, British Columbia, but severe weather capsized his boat. After the rescue, Cote and his dog sailed back to the shipwreck to salvage their things, but sank again in the same spot!

◀ More than a Mouthful

Auggie was a dog who liked to do tricks with tennis balls. His owner Lauren Miller demonstrated his trick of picking up five tennis balls in his mouth at the same time!

Buried Alive

Thoughtful elephants in Kenya frequently bury sleeping hunters under leaves and piles of branches, thinking that the humans are dead.

Deadly Struggle

A 73-year-old Kenyan grandfather reached into the mouth of an attacking leopard and tore out its tongue to kill it. Farmer Daniel M'Mburugu was tending to his crops near Mount Kenya in June 2005 when the leopard leaped on him from long grass. As the leopard mauled him, M'Mburugu thrust his fist down the animal's throat and gradually managed to pull out its tongue, leaving the beast in its death throes. Hearing the screams, a neighbor soon arrived to finish the leopard off.

Cat Call

After receiving an emergency call, police smashed down the door of a house in Auckland, New Zealand, in 2005—only to find that the call had been made by the homeowner's cat! The cat, named Tabby, had managed to contact the police while walking across the phone.

Opportunity Knocks

A bear in Croatia has learned how to trick householders into letting him into their homes by knocking at the door. Experts think that the 490-lb (222-kg) brown bear learned the ruse while nudging at a door in an attempt to get it open.

Young and Old

A baby hippo, weighing about 660 lb (300 kg), was orphaned when the Asian tsunami in December 2004 washed away his mother. Named Owen, he has been adopted by a 120-year-old tortoise, Mzee. Owen was spotted on the coast and taken to the Haller Park in Mombasa, Kenya. There are other hippos at the Park, but on his arrival he made straight for the ancient tortoise and the pair are now inseparable! Owen often lays his head on Mzee's shell to rest when he's tired.

The young hippo affectionately nuzzles Mzee's outstretched neck.

Un-BEE-LieVaBLe

MARIN TELLEZ created a buzz around the Colombian city of Bucaramanga in September 2005 when he covered his entire body in 500,000 bees!

Wearing just a cap and shorts, and no protective chemicals, the 35-year-old beekeeper allowed the aggressive Africanized bees to swarm all over him for two whole hours.

Once the queen bee had landed on Tellez, the rest of the colony followed on behind her, guided by her scent.

Spectators were kept 30 ft (9 m) from the platform to avoid being stung, while other beekeepers stood by wearing protective suits and carrying smoke canisters in case of emergency.

Tellez explained: "I have been working with beehives for 23 years and I know how bees behave. I have to be very calm to transmit that serenity to them and to prevent them from hurting me."

He claims to have been stung so many times that his body has built up some resistance to the potentially lethal formic acid. His worst experience was being attacked by more than 150 bees when he was just 17 years old. On that occasion he saved himself by jumping into a water tank.

Once the queen bee had landed on Tellez, the other 499,999 followed, coating the beekeeper's entire body with their swarm.

Tellez claims that the key to his success was, perhaps unsurprisingly, staying very calm! The bees, he says, picked up on this, and just went about their ordinary business.

Mini Marvel

Each fall, despite weighing just 0.2 oz (6 g), the ruby-throated hummingbird propels its tiny body, only 3½ in (9 cm) long, on a nonstop 500-mi (800-km) flight from North America across the Gulf of Mexico to South America.

Lap of Luxury

Under the terms of their owner's will, Chihuahua Frankie and cats Ani and Pepe Le Pew live in a $20 million San Diego mansion while their care-giver lives in a small apartment.

Birdie Two

In 2005, a pair of storks made a nest on a German golf green and filled it with stolen golf balls. The birds gathered so many balls that they built a second nest on the course, too. Amazingly, storks rarely build nests on the ground.

Chickenwalk

Twenty chickens strutted their stuff on a Japanese catwalk in the latest styles for the fashion-conscious hen. A range of clothing, by Austrian designer Edgar Honetschlaeger, caters for sizes small, medium, large, extra large, and turkey.

Flight of Fancy

Pigeon-lover John Elsworth of Houston, Texas, decided to propose to his girlfriend via a message delivered by homing pigeon. But the bird got lost and took the note instead to the home of Rita Williams. Rita invited John over and they fell in love and got married.

A Lot of Lobster

At the Weathervane Restaurant lobster-eating competition in 2004, Barry Giddings of Chester, Vermont, devoured 19 lobsters in 35 minutes!

Kangaroo Bar

Boomer, an 18-month-old orphaned kangaroo, is fed peanuts by Kathy Noble, owner of the Comet Inn in Hartley Vale, Australia. In 2005, the baby kangaroo was found inside the pouch of his dead mother on the side of the road. After rearing, Boomer decided he liked the bar so much that he is now a regular visitor.

Cat Flap

When Tabitha the tabby cat escaped from her cage during a flight to California in 1994, it was the start of an unscheduled 13-day, 30,000-mi (48,300-km) trip that took in Los Angeles, Miami, Puerto Rico, and New York. Eventually, passengers reported hearing a faint mewing sound, prompting the missing pet's owner, Carol Ann Timmel, to obtain a court injunction to ground the plane at JFK Airport in New York so that officials could carry out a search. Sure enough, they found Tabitha in a ceiling panel behind the passenger compartment. Undaunted by her ordeal, the cat went on to become a national celebrity and the subject of a bestselling book.

Monkey Business

U.S. showbiz chimp Mr. Jiggs (who was actually female) was not everybody's favorite ape. On her way to entertain at a Scout jamboree, and accompanied by her trainer Ronald Winters, Mr. Jiggs walked into a bar at Freehold, New Jersey, wearing full Boy Scout's uniform. The shock caused customer Joan Hemmer to drop her drink, fall against a wall, and injure her shoulder. She sued Winters, but lost.

Frisbee Champion

Dog Ashley Whippet was such an accomplished Frisbee catcher that he was invited to appear at the 1974 World Frisbee Championships, which had previously been for humans only. Captivated by his display, the WFC devised a Catch and Fetch competition for dogs, of which Ashley became the first world champion. He performed at the Super Bowl and at the White House, and upon his death in 1985 he received a tribute in *Sports Illustrated*.

Dog Giovanni

Australian opera singer Judith Dodsworth is never short of an accompaniment—even if it is provided by her pet greyhound, Pikelet. Ms. Dodsworth says the canine virtuoso began copying her during rehearsals and hasn't stopped singing since. "As soon as I opened my mouth, he started singing. He's not bad but he's pretty loud and pretty high." And Pikelet's favorite composer? Pooch-ini, of course!

Remarkable Reptiles

★ North American garter snakes can give birth to as many as 100 young at a time.

★ When two-headed snakes are born, the two heads often fight each other for food.

★ To prevent indigestion. crocodiles invariably carry about 5 lb (2 kg) of pebbles in their stomach.

Chasing a seagull near **Beachy Head, England,** in 2001 a retriever named HENRY fell over the edge of the cliff and **plunged 140 ft (43 m)** into the sea below. Owner **Louise Chavannes** thought he must be dead but was amazed to see him swimming back to shore with **merely** a broken leg. He had smashed his leg on a rock, but the water had broken his fall.

Strange Bedfellows

Rattlesnakes hibernate through winter in groups of up to 1,000. Amazingly, they often share a site with prairie dogs—their favorite prey when not in hibernation.

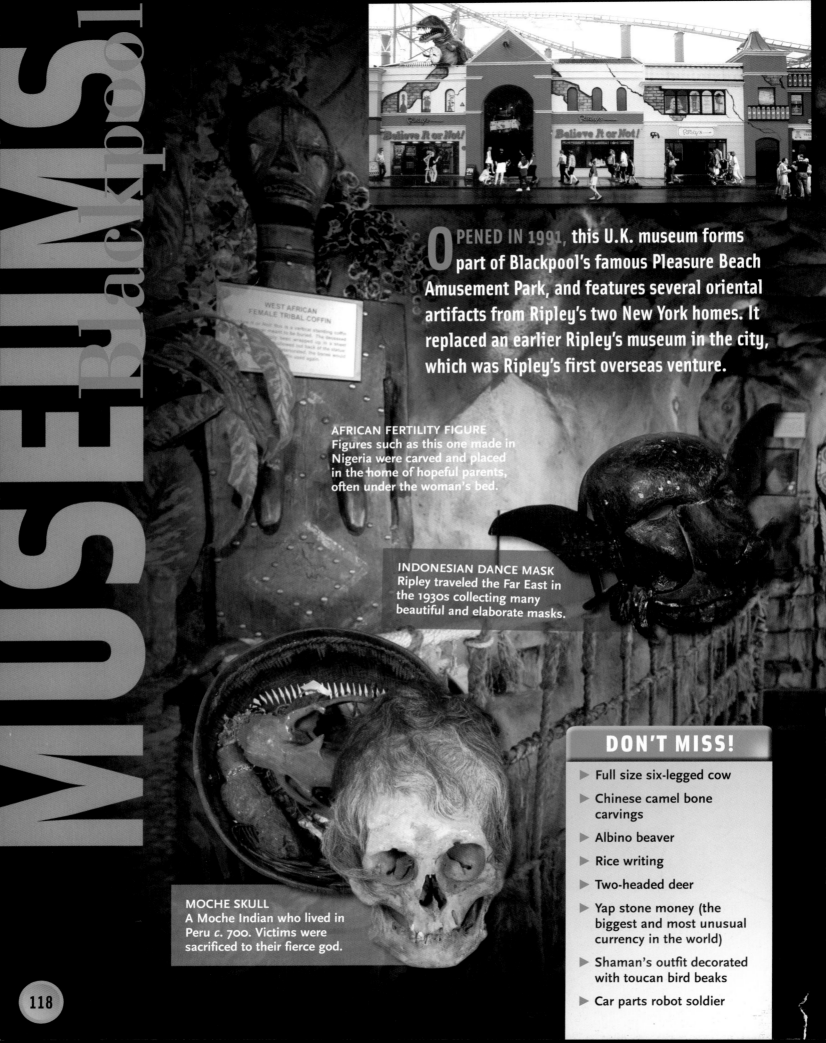

MUSEUMS
Blackpool

OPENED IN 1991, this U.K. museum forms part of Blackpool's famous Pleasure Beach Amusement Park, and features several oriental artifacts from Ripley's two New York homes. It replaced an earlier Ripley's museum in the city, which was Ripley's first overseas venture.

WEST AFRICAN
FEMALE TRIBAL COFFIN

AFRICAN FERTILITY FIGURE
Figures such as this one made in Nigeria were carved and placed in the home of hopeful parents, often under the woman's bed.

INDONESIAN DANCE MASK
Ripley traveled the Far East in the 1930s collecting many beautiful and elaborate masks.

MOCHE SKULL
A Moche Indian who lived in Peru c. 700. Victims were sacrificed to their fierce god.

DON'T MISS!

▶ Full size six-legged cow

▶ Chinese camel bone carvings

▶ Albino beaver

▶ Rice writing

▶ Two-headed deer

▶ Yap stone money (the biggest and most unusual currency in the world)

▶ Shaman's outfit decorated with toucan bird beaks

▶ Car parts robot soldier

BONE CARVING
Made from camel bone, this carving took 18 craftsmen over three months to complete.

STRAW GUITAR
A fully-working acoustic guitar made in the Caribbean.

WALTER HUDSON
Weighing 1,400 lb (635 kg) in 1987, Walter became famous for spending 27 years inside his bedroom.

STRING BALL
Taking nine years to make, this ball is 4 ft (1.2 m) in diameter and weighs over 600 lb (272 kg).

CROCODILE PUK PUK
The crocodile is feared by the New Guinea natives, but also revered as the father of all mankind.

119

Litter-Kwitter
No more unpleasant messy litter trays with the Litter-Kwitter, the ingenious invention that trains household cats to use the same toilet as their owners. Three disks slide into a seat-like device that can be positioned on the toilet bowl. The red, amber, and green disks have progressively larger bowls with smaller amounts of cat litter in them to help the cats adjust to using their owner's toilet.

Milli-magic
Capuchin monkeys use an unusual natural mosquito repellent—they rub themselves with millipedes.

Friends Reunited
Seven years after going missing from her Florida home, Cheyenne the cat was reunited with owner Pamela Edwards in 2004—after being found 2,800 mi (4,500 km) away in San Francisco.

Freak Fetus
A two-headed moose fetus, which measured about 1 ft (30 cm) long, was discovered in Alaska in 2002 after the animal's mother had been shot by a hunter.

Great Survivor
Talbot, a six-month-old stray cat, wandered into a car plant at Ryton, England, in 1999, and went to sleep in the body shell of a Peugeot 206 on the assembly line. With the cat still asleep inside, the shell then went into the paint-baking oven at a temperature of 145°F (63°C)! Amazingly, he survived, although his paw pads were completely burned off and his fur was singed.

Skateboarding Dog
Few sporting pets are more accomplished than Tyson the skateboarding bulldog. Tyson, from Huntington Beach, California, skates every day and is able to get on the board unaided. He runs with three paws on the tarmac and the fourth steering his skateboard. Then, as soon as he reaches a decent speed, he jumps aboard properly and skates for his life.

PiG OLymPics!

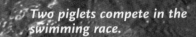
Two piglets compete in the swimming race.

IN APRIL 2005, thousands of Shanghai residents trotted out to a city park to watch a herd of miniature pigs compete in what organizers called the "Pig Olympics."

Piglets race down a track, jostling and jumping for key positions in the hurdle race.

The pigs, a midget species from Thailand, begin training soon after birth and can start performing when they are a year old. They learn to run over hurdles, jump through hoops, dive into water, and swim—in fact, these amazing sporting pigs can do almost anything... except fly.

Five-legged Frog

In August 2004, nine-year-old Cori Praska found a five-legged frog with 23 toes near Stewartville, Minnesota. Three of the frog's legs appeared normal, but the fourth had another leg as an offshoot, with its own three feet attached to it.

Healing Paws

In the 1980s, Jane Bailey of Lyme Regis, England, owned a cat named Rogan that was said to have healing powers. By "laying paws" on his patients' bodies, the cat was apparently able to cure sufferers of arthritis and back injuries. He became so famous that up to 90 people a week sought his help. His fur, which was combed daily, also possessed special properties and Jane would send parcels of it to those in need.

Long Trek

In 1923, Bobbie the collie became separated from his family on a visit to Indiana. Lost and alone, he returned to the family home in Silverton, Oregon, six months later, having walked 2,800 mi (4,500 km) across seven states!

In **Phoenix**, Arizona, the SWAT team announced plans in 2005 to train a **small monkey** as a spy. The CAPUCHIN monkey will wear a **bullet-proof vest**, *video camera*, and **two-way radio**, and, intelligence experts hope, be able to access areas that no officer or robot could go.

Back to Work

At the start of the 20th century, when sheep still grazed in New York's Central Park, a collie named Shep had the job of controlling the flock. When Shep was retired he was sent to a farm 40 mi (64 km) away in upstate New York. However, the determined dog quickly escaped and, even though he had never previously been beyond Manhattan, managed to find his way back to the Big Apple by first stowing away on a ferry that would take him to Manhattan Island, and then sniffing his way back from 42nd Street to Central Park!

Gorilla Talk

Born in 1971, Koko the gorilla has appeared in *The New York Times* and on the cover of several prestigious magazines. Three books have been written about her, and scientists hang on her every word. She has even had her life story told on TV. For Koko, who lives at the Gorilla Foundation in Woodside, California, can communicate with humans. The 35-year-old primate has been taught sign language since she was an infant by Dr. Francine (Penny) Patterson and has now mastered more than 1,000 words. In addition, she understands around 2,000 words of spoken English and has a tested IQ of between 70 and 90 on a human scale where 100 is considered normal. Koko has also learned to use a camera and loves the telephone.

Parrot Banned

In November 1994, a defense lawyer in San Francisco, California, wanted to call a parrot to the witness stand in the hope that the bird would speak the name of the man who killed its owner. However, the judge refused to allow it.

Pets' Send-off

In 1997, Patrick Pendville started the first Belgian pets funeral service. Animatrans, as it is known, offers transport, burial, individual or collective certified cremation, collection of ashes, taxidermy, facial masks, and urns. About 1,200 animals pass through the doors every year. His customers bring not only cats and dogs, but other animals such as birds, goats, horses, and sheep—and even exotic breeds, such as crocodiles, tigers, snakes, and monkeys.

Patrick Pendville holds a beloved pet in his taxidermy workshop.

Helping Hooves

Shoppers in Raleigh, North Carolina, have been witnessing some unusual sights around town—namely miniature horses, 24 in (61 cm) tall, wearing sneakers and warm blankets. These horses are the equine version of guide dogs and are being put through their paces in busy shopping malls. Janet and Don Burleson began training mini horses to help blind and visually impaired people in 1999.

Great Trek

In 1953, Sugar, a Persian cat, trekked 1,500 mi (2,414 km) from Anderson, California, to Gage, Oklahoma, after her owners had moved there. The family had left the cat with a friend because of her bad hip, but despite the injury Sugar made a 14-month journey to be reunited with them.

Trumpet Tunes

Thailand's elephant orchestra has 12 jumbo elephants playing oversized instruments! Their last CD sold 7,000 copies in the U.S.A. alone.

Computer Blip

In 1988, Mastercard sent a letter to Fustuce Ringgenburg of Hemet, California, with the offer of a $5,000 credit limit, unaware that Fustuce was in fact the family cat.

Mini Cat

A blue point Himalayan cat from the U.S.A. called Tinker Toy was just 2¾ in (7 cm) tall at the shoulder and 7½ in (19 cm) long—about the size of a check book.

Baby-dry Diaper

Dr. Kobi Assaf, of Jerusalem's Hadassah Hospital, once treated a 12-month-old baby boy who survived a venomous snake bite because the boy's diaper absorbed the venom.

Kennel of Love

The doggy love motel, complete with a heart-shaped mirror on the ceiling and a headboard resembling a dog bone, opened in August 2005 for loving doggy couples. Billy and Jully, two Yorkshire terriers, stayed at the pet motel in Sao Paulo, Brazil. The air-conditioned room has a paw-print decorative motif, special control panels to dim the lights, romantic music, and films that can be screened. The rooms cost 100 reais ($54) for two hours.

Language Problem

A customer at a pet shop in Napierville, Quebec, threatened to report the shop to the Canadian government's French-language monitoring office in 1996 after being shown a parrot that spoke only English.

Shark Escape

Dolphins rescued four swimmers off the New Zealand coast by encircling them for 40 minutes while a great white shark swam nearby!

Believe it or not, a **sunglasses**-wearing Dalmatian rides a **motorbike with sidecar** in the Chinese city of **NANJING!** Its owner says the dog can drive for about **656 ft (200 m)** at speeds of up to 5 mph (8 km/h).

Equine Allergy

Teddy the horse has to sleep on shredded newspaper, because he has an allergy to, of all things, hay! If exposed to hay or straw, he immediately starts coughing and sneezing in an equine version of hay fever. His owner, Samantha Ashby from Coventry, England, also has to damp down his feed to remove any dust spores.

Trendy Terrier

New York boutique-owner Heather Nicosia ensures that her Yorkshire terrier Woody is one of the most fashionable dogs in town. She makes him his own line of WoodyWear clothes and dresses him in a range of trendy outfits ranging from pajamas to Batman and Spiderman costumes.

▼ Fantastic Fish

Bruce, an Oranda goldfish, measures a staggering 17.129 in (43.507 cm) from snout to tail fin! Named after the late kung fu star Bruce Lee, Bruce swims with normal-sized goldfish at Shanghai Ocean Aquarium.

ACTUAL
SIZE!

Doggy Beach
Bau Beach, north of the Italian capital, Rome, is a beach with a difference. Opened in 2000, it has been designed specially for dogs. Most Italian beaches ban dogs, but here for 5 euros ($6) they are given an umbrella, a towel, and a dog bowl, and their owners are handed a shovel to clean up any mess. After frolicking happily in the waves, the dogs can also take a shower under a high-pressured hose.

Bull Chase
Despite six instances of human pile-ups, often injuring over a hundred people, during the annual Running of the Bulls in Pamplona, Spain, since 1900, only 15 people have lost their lives.

Mothers' Milk

A dog feeds two tiger cubs at a zoo in Hefei, China, in May 2005. The tigers' mother did not have enough milk to feed the cubs, so the zookeepers found a dog to act as wet nurse.

Jumping Jack

Jack, a six-year-old terrier, gained notoriety when he was banned from darts tournaments in a Welsh pub in 2001, because after each round he kept jumping up to the board, snatching the darts, and then running off with them. In his youth Jack could reach the height of the bull's eye (5 ft 8 in/1.73 m) with ease and would even snatch darts that had landed at the very top of the board.

Ferret Lover

C.J. Jones is mad about ferrets. After falling in love with an injured ferret that was brought to the animal hospital where she worked, C.J. opened her home to the furry little creatures, and in 1997 founded the "24 Carat Ferret Rescue and Shelter" in Las Vegas, Nevada. She looks after a maximun of 90 ferrets at a time and has rescued more than 1,500 so far in total.

Speaking Cat

Pala, a black-and-white tomcat that lived in the Turkish town of Konya in the 1960s, had a vocabulary equivalent to that of a one-year-old baby. His owner, Eyup Mutluturk, explained that the cat began talking after becoming jealous of the attention lavished upon the family's grandchildren and was able to speak freely in Turkish.

Eager Beavers

Police searching for stolen money in Greensburg, Los Angeles, discovered beavers had found the money in their creek and woven thousands of dollars into their dam!

Bark Park!

Dog Bark Park is home to Toby and Sweet Willy. Toby is a 12-ft (3.7-m) statue and Sweet Willy, officially known as Dog Bark Park Inn, is a bed-and-breakfast establishment where guests can enter the body of the beagle to sleep. Alternatively, they can enjoy curling up in the cosy reading place in the dog's muzzle.

Mayor Hee-Haw

The small town of Florissant, Colombia, elected Paco Bell as its mayor. Believe it or not, he is a donkey!

IN DEPTH
Lizard Loungers

Henry Lizardlover, 47, shares his Hollywood home with 35 lizards and takes amazing pictures of them in human poses. He loves them so much he even changed his name for them!

How long have you shared your house with lizards?

"Since 1981. I have a large house with separate rooms for the lizards—they don't live in cages so they get used to people. That's my secret."

Why the change of name?

"I changed my surname from Schiff to Lizardlover in the early eighties. I wanted to show my love and dedication to the lizards. I resented the stereotype that they are creepy-crawly and evil, and felt that by taking that name I was making myself a part of the lizard family."

How do you get the lizards to pose for pictures?

"If a lizard is calm and trusts you, it will demonstrate remarkably intelligent behavior, and will be happy to maintain these posed positions for up to an hour on furniture that is comfortable for him or her."

Do you have to train them?

"Not at all. I give them a comfortable room to hang out in, they see me come and go every day in a graceful and non-threatening way. They recognize that I am a friendly creature."

What are your favorite lizard pictures?

"A favorite is of Hasbro, an iguana I used to have, holding a guitar and singing into a microphone. There's also one of a big iguana cradling another in his arms—to portray that they can be loving to each other. My top models for postcards and calendars include iguanas Lovable and Prince Charming, and Chinese Water Dragons Larry Love, Laura Love, and Lana Love."

They pose like humans—do they behave that way too?

"I used to take some out to a parking lot to sunbathe—after 20 minutes they would walk back to my truck and get back in on their own. Hasbro used to scratch at night on my bedroom door, get into my bed and go to sleep. In the morning this lizard, weighing 20 lb, and measuring 6 ft in length, would lie on my chest or, if it was chilly, poke his nose underneath the blanket."

Does everyone love what you do?

"Some people can't believe the lizards are real, or they say I drug them, hypnotize them, put them in the refrigerator first, or paralyze them. They say they can't breathe when they're posing—it's all untrue. They're calm and relaxed—scared lizards run around and bounce off the walls."

Could anyone do what you do with lizards?

"Not all act the way mine do. Male adult iguanas can be dangerous if they are in breeding season moods, they can confuse humans for other male iguanas and become violent. They can attack, rip flesh, bite off a section of nose. You have to read their body language."

NISSAN TAMIR FROM OMER, Israel, has been growing organic vegetables for years. In 2006 he was amazed to discover two radishes that have been growing non-stop—each one weighed a staggering 22 lb (10 kg).

LARGER

THAN LIFE

CAR-nivoRous

Robosaurus, a mechanical dinosaur 40 ft (12 m) tall and weighing 30 tons, is a mean machine. Dwarfing its famous predecessor T-Rex, this awesome beast can lift, crush, burn, bite, and ultimately destroy cars—and even airplanes!

Robosaurus lifts 40,000-lb (18,145-kg) cars higher than a five-storey building. It crushes cars, splitting them in two, and incinerating paint and plastic. It bites and rips out roofs and doors with its fearsome stainless-steel teeth.

Whereas T-Rex had a jaw-crushing force of 3,000 lb (1,360 kg), Robosaurus—with teeth some 12 in (30 cm) long—is seven times stronger, and can also shoot 20-ft (6-m) flames from its giant nostrils. And while T-Rex's front claws were of little use, Robosaurus's are so strong that they can crush vehicles and 50-gal (190-l) metal drums at will.

Created by American inventor Doug Malewicki in 1988 at a cost of $2.2 million, Robosaurus is controlled by a human pilot strapped inside the monster's head. The pilot initiates the robot's movements by making similar movements himself and uses foot pedals to drive Robosaurus around.

Robosaurus has appeared in movies and on TV, and has amazed spectators at live events across the U.S.A., Canada, and Australia.

Robosaurus is a giant electro-hydromechanical machine. Seen here towering over a fighter jet, the giant robot seizes a Vandenberg missile, raises its mammoth head, and breathes flames through its nostrils.

Standing upright, Robosaurus is as high as a five-storey building, dwarfing the cars parked alongside its huge frame.

Battle of the Giants

	Height	Weight	Length of teeth	Jaw-crushing force
Robosaurus	40 ft (12 m)	58,000 lb (26,300 kg)	12 in (30 cm)	20,000 lb (9,070 kg)
T-Rex	16 ft (5 m)	14,000 lb (6,350 kg)	8 in (20 cm)	3,000 lb (1,360 kg)

Young Elvis

Sal Accaputo from Toronto, Ontario, became an Elvis impersonator at the tender age of eight. Better known as "Selvis," he has been paying tribute to the King for more than 27 years.

Baby Driver

When his three-year-old cousin was hurt in a fall in 2005, Tanishk Boyas drove him straight to hospital. Nothing unusual in that—except that Tanishk was only five at the time! The youngster had been learning to drive for three months at his home in India, but when he climbed into the family van it was the first time he had driven it without adult supervision. His father said, "He used to watch me drive and grasped the basics."

Plaid Car

Car artist Tim McNally of Upper Montclair, New Jersey, has covered his 1985 Buick Skyhawk in plaid. He hand-painted the plaid squares on the vehicle, which also boasts beads, rhinestones, tiles, marbles, and gargoyles.

⏷ Ice Cap

In February 2004, 69-year-old Josef Strobl finished another of his annual ice sculptures in Italy. Strobl has been building the sculptures every year for 42 years, with some of them soaring to more than 66 ft (20 m). Each sculpture takes 300 hours of work, and is made of around 265,000 gal (one million liters) of water!

Bunny Heaven

You know how rabbits multiply, but at a house in Pasadena, California, they've gone to ridiculous lengths! In 1992, there was just one rabbit; now there are over 12,000. The house is the Bunny Museum, home to Steve Lubanski and his wife Candace Frazee, and is the result of 14 years of dedicated collecting. Toy bunnies are everywhere and all the furniture, books, light fittings, kitchenware, toiletries, and games are bunny-themed. And among the collectibles there are five real rabbits making themselves at home.

Completely Bananas?

Becky Martz of Houston, Texas, has a collection of more than 5,000 banana labels! She began her collection in 1991 and has even traveled to Europe to meet fellow banana-label enthusiasts. But Becky doesn't only collect bananas, she has also collected 157 asparagus bands and 93 broccoli bands.

⊙ Bunny Pots

Ebony Andrews, a 22-year-old British student of Fine Art, displays her dead-animal works of art, which include not only rabbit plant pots, but a pen pot made from a decapitated owl.

Hermits of Harlem

Brothers Homer and Langley Collyer were popularly known as the Hermits of Harlem. They lived alone in a three-storey mansion at 2078 Fifth Avenue, New York City, along with 136 tons of junk. Homer was blind, paralyzed, and dependent on his brother who, in order to deter burglars, set a series of booby traps that would bring tons of garbage crashing down on any intruder. Langley had carved tunnels through the junk so that he could crawl to the spot where his brother sat day after day. In March 1947, Homer was found dead, but there was no sign of Langley. Three weeks later, Langley's body was found amid the garbage. He had, in fact, died first, having accidentally sprung one of his own traps and suffocated beneath the debris. With nobody to feed him, Homer had then starved to death.

◁ Lightweight Literature

This book measures a tiny ½ x ¼ in (13 x 6 mm) and contains an amazing 208 pages. Entitled Letter from Galileo to Madame Cristina di Lorena, *it is kept with 50,000 other priceless books at the Cappuccini Library in Palermo, Italy.*

Santa's Helper

Every day is Christmas for Jean-Guy Laquerre of Boucherville, Quebec, Canada. He has more than 13,000 items of Santa Claus memorabilia—including yo-yos, pens, candle holders, and music boxes—that he has collected since 1988. His festive hobby began when an aunt left him a papier-mâché Santa in her will.

Hopping Mad

★ The ears of a rabbit called Nipper's Geronimo, from Bakersfield, California, were measured at more than 31 in (79 cm) in 2003.

★ A French scientist created a glowing rabbit in 2000 by splicing the green fluorescent protein of a jellyfish into the genes of an albino rabbit.

★ In 2004, a Dutch rabbit named Roberto measured nearly 4 ft (1.2 m) long and weighed 47 lb (21 kg). He had to sleep on a dog's bed because he wouldn't fit in a hutch!

★ A rabbit owned by J. Filek of Cape Breton, Nova Scotia, Canada, gave birth to a litter of 24 bunnies in 1978.

Buttmobile

The Stink Bug is an unusual car with a serious message. Conceived and created by Carolyn Stapleton of Orlando, Florida, to highlight the dangers of smoking, the Volkswagen Beetle is covered in cigarette butts. The words "Kick Butt" appear above the windshield and there is a skull and crossbones on the hood.

Corny Appeal

When lovelorn farmer and divorcee Pieter DeHond decided to place a personal ad, he didn't put it in a paper or magazine, but in a field. His love message came in the form of 50-ft (15-m) letters made from corn stalks on his farm at Canandaigua, New York, in 2005. Beneath the message, which took him an hour to create, an arrow 1,000 ft (305 m) long pointed females toward his house. Although the plea, measuring 900 x 600 ft (274 x 183 m), was visible only from the air, the publicity it attracted led to 700 phone calls and e-mails.

Sports Fan

John Carpenter, of Firebrick, Kentucky, owns over 4,000 pieces of sports memorabilia, including autographed baseballs, basketballs, jerseys, plates, helmets, and letters. Best of all is the ball that Babe Ruth hit for his 552nd career home-run.

⊙ Serious Surfing!

Forty-seven surfers spent 4 minutes surfing their way along the Gold Coast in Australia on March 5, 2005, on a massive surfboard 40 ft (12 m) long and 10 ft (3 m) wide—possibly the largest board ever built!

Hoover Lovers

Founded in 1982, The Vacuum Cleaner Collectors' Club boasts around 40 American members with a passion for suction. They include Stan Kann of St. Louis, Missouri, who has a suit made of vintage vacuum-cleaner bags. He has more than 125 cleaners in his collection and can distinguish individual models by their whine and by the smell of their bags.

Stardate 6.21.97: **Star Trek fans** Jo Ann Curl and Vince Stone had a **Klingon wedding** at Evansville, Indiana, in front of some 300 costumed guests. The bride wore a dark wig, a **furrowed** latex brow, and spoke the vows in **Klingon**!

Plastic Wrap Ball

Andy Martell of Toronto, Ontario, Canada, created a ball of plastic wrap that in 2003 measured 54 in (137 cm) in circumference and weighed 45 lb (20.4 kg). He made it at the Scratch Daniels restaurant, where he worked as a day cook.

Duck Girl

Whenever Ruth Grace Moulon wandered through New Orleans' French Quarter, she would nearly always be followed by up to a dozen ducks. She trained the ducks to follow her everywhere and achieved local fame from the late 1950s as "The Duck Girl," charging tourists to take her photo. She called all her ducks variations on the name of Jimmy Cronin, her policeman friend.

Munster Mansion

Something spooky has sprung up on the outskirts of Waxahachie, Texas. Charles and Sandra McKee have spent $250,000 creating a replica of the house from *The Munsters* TV show. Designed from set photos and TV clips, the two-storey, 5,825 sq ft (540 sq m) house contains secret passages, Grandpa's dungeon, and a trap door leading to the quarters of Spot—the McKees' German shepherd dog, who was named after the fire-breathing dragon that the Munsters kept as a pet.

Citizen Cane

Robert McKay, of Manitoba, Canada, has a collection of more than 600 wooden walking canes, each one handmade.

Playing with Fire

In 2004, Steve performed over 50 full body burns—more than most stunt people do in an entire career.

Believe it or not, Steve Truglia encourages people to set him on fire! Britain's top fire stuntman has appeared in many films and TV shows burning from head to toe at temperatures of around 800°F (425°C).

Steve often performs these stunts without oxygen and can hold his breath for more than two minutes while on fire. "Breathing is not an option," he explains, adding that one gasp of air would almost certainly be his last. Steve is also planning to break his present record for the longest time spent totally on fire. His current best is 2 minutes, 5 seconds.

As a professional stuntman, he has been blown up, crushed, thrown down flights of steps, and "killed" more times than he can remember. To improve road safety, he also acts as a human crash test dummy, deliberately driving cars into aluminum highway signs at speeds of more than 60 mph (100 km/h)—and walking away unharmed.

Steve can hold his breath for 6 minutes, 10 seconds underwater, something that stands him in good stead for many of his burning stunts, but he is also able to control an air supply for longer stunts.

135

▶ Tall Tipple

This giant bottle of wine, auctioned at Sotheby's, holds the equivalent of 173 regular bottles, 1,200 glasses of wine, or 34 gal (130 l) of Beringer Cabernet Sauvignon Private Reserve 2001, and is protected by its own hard case.

Labor of Love

French postman Ferdinand Cheval spent 33 years building his Palais Idéal, or ideal castle. He began building it in 1879, collecting stones on his daily mail route, carrying them in his pockets, then in a basket, and eventually in a wheelbarrow. He often worked on the construction at night to the bemusement of his neighbors. When the authorities refused to allow him to be buried in his castle, he spent the following eight years building himself a mausoleum in the cemetery of Hautes-rives, southwest France. He finished it just in time: little over a year later, in August 1924, he died.

Chicken Robber

A man from Hillard, Ohio, robbed a grocery store while wearing a giant chicken costume!

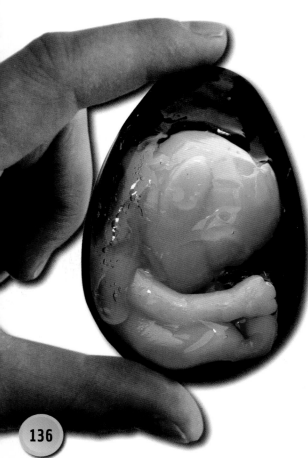

Lucky's Yo-yos

John Meisenheimer is an avid yo-yo collector. Nicknamed "Lucky," Meisenheimer began doing yo-yo tricks while on his rounds at medical school in Kentucky. His collection now stands at more than 4,250.

Menu Master

New Yorker Harley Spiller has his own "celebration of Chinese takeout food in America." His collection features 10,000 Chinese takeout menus, from every state in the U.S.A. and more than 80 countries. The oldest menu dates back to 1879. He also has an assortment of restaurant shopping bags and even a life-size, delivery-man doll. "It's one of the nicest things you can ask a friend to do," he says, "to bring you a menu from their trip: it's lightweight and it's free."

◀ Alien Landing!

A shocked homeowner in County Durham, England, sparked a major police alert with the discovery of a slimy egg-shaped container with an alien-like fetus inside it. Detectives, forensic specialists, and a police surgeon were called before the egg-like object was identified as a child's toy.

Ups and Downs

★ The town of Luck, Wisconsin, was the yo-yo capital of the world during the 1940s, producing an incredible 3,600 yo-yos an hour.

★ In 1962, the Duncan Company alone sold 45 million yo-yos in the U.S.A., which is a country with only 40 million children!

★ In 1990, the woodwork class of Shakamak High School, Jasonville, Indiana, constructed a yo-yo that was 6 ft (1.8 m) in diameter and weighed 820 lb (372 kg). The giant yo-yo was launched from a 160-ft (49-m) crane and managed to yo-yo 12 times.

★ American Hans Van Dan Helzen completed 51 different yo-yo tricks in just one minute in 2004.

Flying Granny

In September 2002, 84-year-old grandmother Mary Murphy made the 62-mi (100-km) trip from Long Beach, California, to Catalina Island by the extreme sport of hydrofoil water-skiing. She said she wanted to make the four-hour journey while she was still young enough.

Gum Blondes

It takes approximately 40 hours and 500 sticks of pre-chewed gum to complete one of Jason Kronenwald's Gum Blonde portraits. Kronenwald dislikes chewing gum himself, so has enlisted a team of chewers who chew a variety of flavors and colors for him—he uses no paint or dye. The portraits are made on plywood, and measure 24 x 32 in (60 x 80 cm). Kronenwald, from Toronto, Ontario, Canada, started his Gum Blonde series in 1996 and has made sticky portraits of such celebrities as Britney Spears, Paris Hilton, and Brigitte Bardot.

WALKING TALL
In 1958, Angelo Corsaro from Catania, Italy, walked 558 mi (898 km) to the Vatican City on wooden stilts.

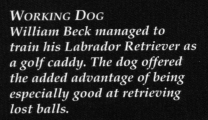

WORKING DOG
William Beck managed to train his Labrador Retriever as a golf caddy. The dog offered the added advantage of being especially good at retrieving lost balls.

FANTASTIC FIDDLE
Mr A.K. Ferris from Ironia, New Jersey, is pictured here playing a giant bass violin in 1934. The huge fiddle measured 14 ft (4.3 m) in height.

MARVELOUS MARTHA
Martha Morris was born without arms, but was still able to write, sew, knit, and type by using her feet instead of her hands.

TITANIC TRUMPET
This trumpet was so big that it required six boys to lift it! Only the mouthpiece and the valves were of normal size, so that the instrument could be played.

GREAT BALL OF TWINE
Started in the late 1950s by Francis Johnson of Darwin, Minnesota, this massive ball of string was 12 ft (3.7 m) in diameter and weighed 17,400 lb (7,892 kg) when Johnson died in 1989.

FLEA CIRCUS
These fleas, displayed inside a walnut shell, were dressed by Katherine Nugent of Los Angeles, who also made the tiny clothes.

TURNED TO STONE
George Kern of Columbus City, Iowa, is pictured with a giant ham on his knee: the amazing thing is that the ham has become petrified!

Looking **Back**

December 17, 1931 In Washington **a huge omelette** made of 7,200 eggs was fried in a pan 8 ft (2.4 m) across and weighed half a ton. **August 7, 1930** A massive **apple pie** was baked at the **Orleans County Fair** in New York—it contained 125 bushels of apples, 600 lb (270 kg) of flour, and 500 lb (230 kg) of sugar, and measured 12 ft (3.7 m) across.

Rhino Party

For 30 years, the Canadian political scene was enlivened by a party that claimed to be the spiritual descendants of a Brazilian rhinoceros! The Rhinoceros Party was founded in 1963 by writer Jacques Ferron and contested seven federal elections without ever winning a seat. In 1980, the party declared war on Belgium after the character Tintin blew up a female rhino in a cartoon adventure!

Scale Model

Models scaled the sides of the world's tallest building—the 1,667-ft (508-m) high Taipei 101 in Taiwan—for a fashion show that featured a vertical catwalk.

Body Toast

British artist Antony Gormley traced the shape of his own body within 8,000 slices of white bread. He ate the missing slices—the equivalent of his own body's volume.

Pet Project

In 1999, in a bizarre sponsorship deal, Australian Rules footballer Gary Hocking changed his name to a pet-food brand to help his cash-strapped club. Gary became "Whiskas" in return for a donation to the club.

Living Library

In 2005, instead of lending books, a library in Malmo, Sweden, lent out humans. In an attempt to overcome common prejudices, borrowers were able to take the human items, including a homosexual, a journalist, and a blind person, for a 45-minute chat in the library's outdoor café.

Branching Out

American tree surgeon Peter Jenkins has pioneered an exhilarating new sport—extreme tree climbing. Along with other devotees, Jenkins climbs trees and performs acrobatic stunts, including balancing on the branches and running across the canopy. "We also do tree surfing, where we go high into the canopy on a windy day and ride the branches. You can see the wind coming toward you in waves over the other trees."

A team of European researchers has put together a CREEPY-CRAWLY ROBOT called InsBot that *behaves and smells* like a **cockroach** and is accepted by the insects as **one of their own**.

Look Who's Tolkien

Believe it or not, American *Lord of the Rings* fan Melissa Duncan is so obsessed with the films that she takes cardboard cutouts of the characters out to dinner!

Bishop of Broadway

American playwright and producer David Belasco was known as the Bishop of Broadway, because he often roamed the streets of New York dressed up as a priest.

Love on a Roller Coaster

Angie Matthews and Steve Krist, from Puyallup, Washington, were married while riding a roller coaster!

Speedy Toilet

Paul Stender's jet-powered, portable toilet on wheels can reach speeds of 40 mph (64 km/h). He races it against his friend's jet-powered bar stool!

Pedal Power

Vancouver unicyclist Kris Holm, 32, takes off-road riding to the extreme, tackling volcano craters, molten lava, and cliff tops all on one wheel.

How did you discover the unicycle?

❝I saw a street performer when I was a child. He performed while playing the violin, and I had a violin too. I asked for a unicycle for my 12th birthday. I grew up doing adventure sports and rock climbing, so it was a natural progression to combine the two.❞

Where are the most unusual places you have ridden?

❝I rode an ancient trade route in the Himalayan kingdom of Bhutan, an area very few westerners have visited. I also rode the Great Wall of China—the security guards didn't know what to make of me. They were so surprised, they just left me alone.❞

Are the rides dangerous?

❝I have ridden on the rail of a 200-ft-high bridge, and on the edge of an 800-m-high cliff. I have also ridden on a lava flow in the Volcanoes National Park in Hawaii—the lava had crossed a road and solidified. It was too hot to touch but could hold my weight—I was riding within 10 m of actively flowing, red and bubbling lava.❞

What kind of unicycle do you use?

❝A 'muni'—a mountain unicycle— is stronger than a normal unicycle, with a fatter tire. I have developed my own range—they are sold all over the world. I realized I wasn't the only one doing it when I checked the internet by chance in the late nineties. Now there are tens of thousands of unicyclists— from Pro Skiers to Hollywood stars.❞

What are the hardest skills to master?

❝Riding on a narrow surface, and hopping over obstacles. I can hop up to 95 cm vertically. It's also hard on the legs because you have to pedal all the time, even downhill—you can't freewheel. You can learn to take your feet off the pedals, but it's a skill, not a chance to relax. And the endurance aspect is hard—riding along the edge of a volcano crater is not technically difficult, but it is at 18,500 ft and in below-zero temperatures.❞

How do you practice?

❝I try to ride every day. I take a unicycle to work and ride at lunchtime. My climbing background and my day job as a geomorphologist assessing landslide risks mean I'm good at judging where a fall could kill me. You learn to ride something narrow as a coin just a metre off the ground, so when you have to ride something a foot wide but several hundred metres off the ground it feels as easy as crossing the street.❞

What is "competitive trials unicycling?"

❝I organized the first formal trials competition for unicycles in the late nineties, and out of that grew the competitive trials. I have been a winner of the European, North American, and World trials.❞

Do you sustain bad injuries?

❝Just lots and lots of bruises, and stitches in my chin and elbow. You don't typically fall badly—with a bicycle you fall over the handlebars head-first, whereas with a unicycle you can usually get your feet beneath you.❞

Where else would you like to ride?

❝There's a couple of volcanoes in Bolivia I've got my eye on!❞

Bear Necessities

A German travel agent announced in 2005 that he was offering holidays for teddy bears! Christopher Böhm said the vacations are "a great opportunity for the real man's best friend see something different for a change." The teddies stayed in a luxury Munich apartment and spent the week sightseeing, playing games, and visiting a teddy bears' picnic and a beer house. And each bear received souvenir pictures to take home.

Two lucky teddies spend some time fishing and relaxing on a riverbank.

Newspaper Collector

Miao Shiming is never short of reading material at his home in China's Shanxi Province. He has collected more than 368,000 issues of over 30,000 different newspaper titles, 55,000 issues of 10,200 magazines, and 3,200 books.

▼ Big Read

This massive tome, Bhutan, A Visual Odyssey Across the Kingdom, *shown in Japan in December 2003, is 5 ft (1.5 m) high and 7 ft (2.1 m) wide. Only 500 copies were published.*

Solar Jacket

U.S. inventor Scott Jordan has developed a jacket that has integrated solar panels to recharge electronic gadgets in its pockets.

Play Mate

In 2002, computer-game fan Dan Holmes officially changed his name to PlayStation2. Holmes, from Banbury, England, played for four hours a day and had previously asked a few vicars to marry him to his console. "But none were keen," he said. "So I took its name instead."

Santa Plea

For the past four years Alan Mills, from Milford, Ohio, has been trying to change his name legally to Santa Claus—with little success. All judges have refused, just in case he uses the name for profit.

Everyman

In 2004, Andrew Wilson from Branson, Missouri, legally changed his name to "They." He says he made this unusual choice to address the common reference to "they." "They do this" or "They're to blame for that," he explained. "Who is this 'they' everyone talks about? 'They' accomplishes such great things. Somebody had to take responsibility."

Elvis Roots

Singer Elvis Presley's genealogical roots have been traced back to Lonmay, Scotland, where a new tartan was created in his honor.

Oldest Schoolboy

Kimani Maruge stands out from his classmates at Kapkenduiywa primary school in Kenya, for he is twice the height and 17 times the age of most of his fellow pupils. The 85-year-old student sits with his long legs folded under the tiny desk during classes. He is also the only pupil at the school to wear a hearing aid and carry a walking stick.

Sleepy Traveler

Tom Wilson of Los Angeles, California, is the first person to "sleep across America." He toured the country in a chauffered Winnebago that traveled only while he was fast asleep.

Young Doctor

In 1995, Balamurali Ambati graduated from the Mount Sinai School of Medicine, New York City, aged just 17. The average age for graduates from medical school is 26 or 27. Despite his young age, his first patients didn't realize they were being treated by a teenager— at 6 ft (1.8 m) tall, they thought he was much older.

Premium Bond

Matt Sherman thinks he's a real-life James Bond. He spends his spare time practicing survival techniques near his home in Gainesville, Florida, and turns routine shopping trips into pretend MI6 missions in which his two young children are given assignments to fetch certain groceries within a specified time. A collector of 007 memorabilia for more than 20 years, he has turned his den into a shrine to James Bond, complete with books, jewelry, and even cologne relating to his hero. He has also spent more than $10,000 on spy equipment that he uses for monitoring purposes.

Green-eyed

Ever since he was a child, Bob Green has been obsessed with the color from which his last name is derived. He lives on West Green Street, Greencastle, Indiana, invariably wears green clothes, drives a green car, and even named his three children after various shades of green—Forest, Olive, and Kelly.

Bumper Horse

This sculpture of a mustang horse was made by Sean Guerrero of Colorado from stainless-steel car bumpers. It stands nearly 14 ft (4.3 m) high and weighs several thousand pounds.

Roller-coaster Ride

During the 2005 summer vacation, a 14-year-old boy from Offenburg, Germany, built a roller coaster in his backyard that was 300 ft (91 m) long. He even designed his own carriage, which was able to reach speeds of up to 30 mph (48 km/h) on the 16-ft (4.9-m) high wooden construction.

Blowing BUBBLes

Fan Yang can do just about anything with bubbles. He has created bubbles within bubbles, smoking bubbles, and spinning, bouncing, floating bubbles of every imaginable size, shape, and color.

In 2004, Fan Yang managed to fit 15 people in a bubble at the Santa Ana Discovery Science Center, California.

In Seattle, Washington, in 1997, the Canadian bubble enthusiast created an amazing bubble wall that measured 156 ft (48 m) long and 13 ft (4 m) high—the equivalent of walking onto a football field and forming a giant bubble from the end zone to the 50-yard line. Three years later, he built a bubble so sturdy that his daughter was able to slide into a bubble hemisphere without bursting the film.

In 2001, Yang managed to arrange 12 bubbles inside each other; and in the same year, in Stockholm, Sweden, he interlinked nine bubbles to make one long chain that floated in mid-air.

Fan Yang has dedicated the past 20 years to developing the art of bubbles. His skill has been recognized by science centers all over the world, and was born out of a childhood fascination with bubbles.

Cereal Devotion

Roger Barr of Richmond, Virginia, has been dedicating his life to saving Boo Berry cereal from extinction. He is so devoted to the product that he has set up an Internet fan site and even hides rival brands on supermarket shelves in the hope of slowing their sales. And he's not alone. One woman once drove a staggering 26,000 mi (41,850 km) to get her hands on a packet of Boo Berry.

Walking Tall

Jeff Jay has taken the art of stilt walking to extremes—he is able to walk on stilts that are 60 ft (18 m) tall. They were specially designed and created by him, and require a crane in order to get on to them!

Last Request

Before his suicide in February 2005, popular American writer Hunter S. Thompson asked to be cremated and to have his ashes fired from a cannon. Accordingly, his remains shot into the sky six months later from a 153-ft (47-m) tower behind his home in Woody Creek, Colorado.

Crackpot King

In 2003, plain Nick Copeman changed his name officially to H.M. King Nicholas I. Calling himself "Britain's other monarch," he rode on horseback in full uniform through his home town of Sheringham, Norfolk, sold nobility titles over the Internet, and started the Copeman Empire from his royal palace, which was, in fact, a two-berth caravan.

Off His Trolley

An inventive designer has been turning Britain's unwanted supermarket carts into furniture. About 100,000 old carts are destroyed in Britain every year, but Colin Lovekin, from Exeter, Devon, has come up with a new use for them. He has been turning them into chairs and sofas, complete with cushioned seating, wheeled legs, and even a basket at the back.

Monster Ball

While working in the post room of a law firm near his home in Wilmington, Delaware, John Bain had to collect mail from the post office every day. At the post office he would routinely grab a handful of free rubber bands, which he then made into a ball. Five years and two months later, the monster ball, made up of 850,000 rubber bands, weighed 3,120 lb (1,415 kg), stood 5 ft (1.5 m) high, and had a circumference of 15 ft (4.6 m). Bain estimated that it would have cost him $25,000 to make.

Slingshot Lobes

Nicknamed "Slingshot Ears," Monte Pierce uses his amazingly long earlobes to launch coins distances of up to 10 ft (3 m)! Pierce, from Bowling Green, Kentucky, began tugging on his earlobes when he was young, not only increasing their length but also their ability to snap back. His lobes permanently hang down an inch (2.5 cm), but for his launches he can stretch them to 5 in (13 cm). He can also pull them up over his eyes and can even roll them up and stuff them into his ears.

Transformer!

Brazilian Olésio da Silva and his two sons Marcus Vinicius and Marco Aurelio have teamed up to create a life-size robocar. They transformed their Kia Besta van into a 12-ft (3.7-m) robot that plays loud music as it transforms. It cost them $122,000 and takes six minutes to transform.

Tattoo Tribute

Dan Summers, from Thompsonville, Illinois, is a living tribute to The Three Stooges. He has tattoos of Larry, Moe, and Curly covering his entire body, including his face.

Believe it or not, **animal behaviorist Jill Deringer,** from LANTANA, Florida, can mimic the distinctive barks of **261** different breeds of dog!

Crazy Craft

How about sailing down the river in an electric wheelchair or in a two-seater pedal-powered floating tricycle? Well, wacky inventor Lyndon Yorke, of Buckinghamshire, England, can make your dreams come true. Among his ingenious seaworthy designs are the tricycle (the PP Tritanic) and the Tritania, a 1920s wheelchair complete with wind-up gramophone, champagne cooler, and picnic basket.

American Patriot

Ski Demski was the ultimate patriot. He owned a Stars and Stripes flag that measured 505 x 225 ft (154 x 68.6 m), weighed 3,000 lb (1,360 kg), and took 600 people to unfurl. Each star was 17 ft (5 m) high. He also had a tattoo of Old Glory on his chest. Before his death in 2002, Demski ran unsuccessfully for mayor of Long Beach, California, whenever there was an election.

Kissing Cobras

Gordon Cates of Alachua, Florida, kisses cobras for fun. The owner of more than 200 reptiles, he says that he can anticipate the snakes' actions by reading their body language.

Heavyweight

Hercules is a three-year-old liger. An "accident," his father is a lion and his mother is a tiger. Standing 10 ft (3 m) tall on his back legs, he already weighs more than 900 lb (408 kg) and is still growing. Hercules consumes 20 lb (9 kg) of meat a day, usually chicken and beef, but can manage to eat 100 lb (45 kg) in one meal. This amazing animal is as strong as a lion and as fast as a tiger, reaching speeds of 50 mph (80 km/h)!

RIPLEY'S SECOND OLDEST MUSEUM, and the first outside the U.S., Niagara Falls, Ontario, was opened in 1963. Extensively renovated in 2003–2004, it features an exhibition on Niagara Fall's daredevilry, and portraits painted on the body of a housefly.

MAGPIE BIRD
Found in the 1990s in England, this bird has two heads and three legs.

STEGOSAURUS
This stegosaurus skeleton, found in China, is over 145 million years old.

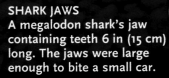

SHARK JAWS
A megalodon shark's jaw containing teeth 6 in (15 cm) long. The jaws were large enough to bite a small car.

HORSESHOE CRAB
More closely related to scorpians than crabs, these creatures have existed for over 200 million years.

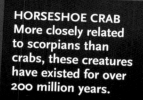

JUNK ART
These figures are made from kitchen utensils, plumbing supplies, auto parts, toys and rubbish.

SHRUNKEN HEAD
Fist-sized, this head is decorated with an ocelot fur headband and parrot feathers

UNICORN
A lamb was born in England with a single horn, 4 in (10 cm) long, growing out of its head.

DON'T MISS!

▶ Tibetan shaman's robe

▶ Matchstick model of the Statue of Liberty

▶ Two-headed turtle

▶ Ripley's personal giant beer stein

▶ Mustache collection

▶ Prehistoric giant beaver skull

▶ Large lint art mural

▶ Peerskill meteorite, a tiny meteorite famous for having hit a car

EIGHT-LEGGED BISON
Discovered in a wild herd in South Dakota, this bison has eight legs.

149

Mega Mushroom

Ty Whitmore, of Kansas City, Montana, discovered this 56-lb (25-kg) mushroom while cutting firewood. Desperate to get the fungus verified, he waded across creeks, protecting it from brushwood, until he reached a grocery store, where staff kindly obliged with their scales.

Ty proudly shows off his giant mushroom, measuring 30 in (76 cm) across.

Crawl to Work

A lifeguard from Essex, England, has hit upon the perfect way to avoid rush-hour traffic—by swimming to work. Each morning, 45-year-old Martin Spink walks down to the beach near his home, checks the tides, strips down to his shorts and flippers, and swims across Brightlingsea Creek. Ten minutes later, he emerges on the other side, pulls a clothes bag from his back, and dresses for work. He does it to save a 20-mi (32-km) round trip by road from home to his workplace.

On Top of the World

In May 2005, a Nepalese couple became the first to be wed on top of the world's highest mountain, Mount Everest. Moments after reaching the summit, Mona Mulepati and Pem Dorje Sherpa briefly took off their oxygen masks, donned plastic garlands, and exchanged marriage vows. The only witness was the third member of the party, Kami Sherpa.

Pac Mania

Tim Crist of Syracuse, New York, has a shrine to Pac Man in his home and calls himself Reverend of the First Church of Pac Man.

Waste Energy

The methane in cow dung collected at the Blue Spruce Farm in Bridport, Vermont, produces enough electricity to power 330 homes!

Super Saver

Roy Haynes from Huntington, Vermont, prides himself on being the cheapest man in the world. He splits his two-ply toilet paper into two rolls of one-ply, and dries out and reuses paper towels over and over again. He also saves money by taking ketchup packets from restaurants and squeezing them into his own ketchup bottle at home.

▶ Wicked Whiskers

There were some hair-raising creations at the 2005 World Beard and Moustache Championships in Berlin, Germany. Elmer Weisser (above, center) won the Full Beard Freestyle category with his Brandenburg Gate beard and moustache.

Surfing Mice

Australian surfing enthusiast Shane Willmott has been training three mice to surf small waves on tiny mouse-sized surfboards at beaches on the Gold Coast. The mice—Harry, Chopsticks, and Bunsen—live in miniature custom-made villas and own specially made jet skis. They train in a bathtub and then have their fur dyed when it's time to hit the beach. Willmott explains: "Because they're white, when they get in the whitewash of big waves, it's hard to find them."

Stair Climb

In September 2002, Canadian Paralympian Jeff Adams became the first person to climb the 1,776 stairs of Toronto's CN Tower in a wheelchair. It took him seven hours, moving backwards up the steps.

CockRoAch CElebriTies

Marilyn Monroach in her famous white dress.

Pestkiller Michael Bohdan has a love-hate relationship with his pests—he has killed thousands, but has also made a permanent feature out of his best catches in the Cockroach Hall of Fame.

After launching a stunt to find Dallas's largest cockroach, pest-control specialist Michael Bohdan was left with the problem of what to do with the dead bodies. Instead of throwing them out, he decided to dress them up as celebrities—and the Cockroach Hall of Fame Museum was born.

Each year, thousands of curious customers visit the museum in Plano, Texas, to catch a glimpse of such heroes in a half shell as H. Ross Peroach, David Letteroach, Marilyn Monroach, and, seated at a tiny piano and wearing a white cape, the inimitable Liberoachi.

"Liberoachi" poised for his performance.

Old Player

At 96, Henry Paynter was still a regular player at Kelowna Badminton Club, British Columbia, traveling to games across the region. He died in April 2005, aged 98.

State Names

The former editor of *The Wall Street Journal* was named Vermont Connecticut Royster. Indeed, his great-grandfather called his sons Iowa Michigan, Arkansas Delaware, Wisconsin Illinois, and Oregon Minnesota; while the girls were Louisiana Maryland, Virginia Carolina, and Georgia Indiana!

Secret Throne

Following the death of janitor James Hampton in 1964, it emerged that for the previous 14 years he had been building a secret throne from scavenged materials in a rented garage in Washington, D.C. The glittering throne was made from silver and gold foil, old furniture, pieces of cardboard, old light bulbs, shards of mirror, and old desk blotters. He had pinned the magnificent chair together with tacks, glue, pins, and tape. The throne, with its biblical messages, was later donated to the National Museum of American Art.

Giant Stocking

In 2004, J. Terry Osborne and friends, from King William County, Virginia, created a Christmas stocking over 35 ft (10.7 m) high and 16½ ft (5 m) wide. It was filled with presents for children in need.

Baseball Boy

Zach Spedden called an entire nine-inning baseball game on radio station WHAG 1410 AM, in Hagerstown, Maryland, in 2002, when he was ten years old. He also presented the pre-game show and the post-game analysis. It had been his ambition since the age of five.

And They're Off!

The first Office Chair World Championships took place in Olten, Switzerland, on June 11, 2005. The race, which was 200 m (650 ft) long, saw 64 competitors from Germany, France, and Switzerland take part.

Hemingway Days

The highlight of the annual Hemingway Days' festival in Key West, Florida, is the Ernest Hemingway look-alike contest. The event attracts national and international entrants, who dress themselves up in fishermen's wool turtlenecks and other sporting attire, and make their way to Sloppy Joe's Bar—Hemingway's favorite watering hole when he lived in Key West in the 1930s. Beating off 146 white-bearded, ruddy-faced rivals to snatch the coveted title in 2005 was 61-year-old Bob Doughty, a letter-carrier from Deerfield Beach, Florida.

High Church

In August 2003, ten couples took their wedding vows in mid-air aboard an airplane flying from Orlando, Florida, to Las Vegas, Nevada. Fittingly for such a bizarre occasion, the in-flight ceremony was conducted by a minister dressed as Elvis Presley.

Big Easter Buns

Baker Brian Collins proudly shows off his giant hot cross bun at Pegrum's Bakery in Rustington, England. His bun measured more than 48 in (122 cm) in diameter.

Ginger Ninja

From his nickname, you could guess that "Orange" Mike Lowrey of Milwaukee, Wisconsin, wears nothing but orange. He is usually seen out and about in an orange hat, orange shirt, orange belt, orange pants, orange sneakers, and orange wristwatch band. "It's no big deal," he insists. "I just like the color orange."

Underwater Wedding

Chandan Thakur and Dipti Pradhan's wedding took place underwater in June 2003 at the Vashi Marine Centre on Thailand's Kradan Island. First, diving instructor Ravi Kulkami conducted the engagement as the couple exchanged rings while suspended by ropes 50 ft (15 m) above the Vashi pool. Then, 11 days later, Kulkami, the bride and groom, and seven relatives dived under the water for the 30-minute ceremony. The couple had metal strips sewn into the hems of their wedding outfits so that they kept their shape in the water.

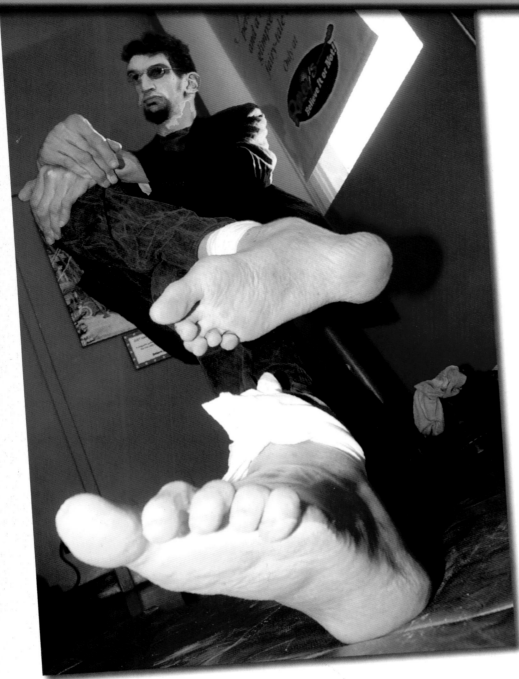

Rocket Mail

In the 1930s, German inventor Gerhard Zucker devised a plan to deliver mail and medical supplies from the Scottish island of Scarp to the nearby island of Harris by rocket! However, Zucker's test rocket scattered the mail all over the place, so the idea was scrapped.

Rob Poulos, of Kansas City, Missouri, and several others around the world, helped author **Shelley Jackson** write a short story by each having their bodies **tattooed** with a **single** word.

Rotating Home

Every room is a room with a view at Al Johnstone's unusual mountaintop residence in La Mesa, California. This is because Al lives in a rotating house, which completes a full circle every 30 minutes.

Boxing Dog

A former world champion kickboxer has trained his dog in the martial arts! Russ Williams, who runs a kickboxing school in North Wales, has trained Ringo, a Russian terrier, to jump up on command and kick with his two front legs. Williams said: "He can deliver a knock-out punch with his paws."

Flying Car

Imagine a vehicle that you can drive to the shops or fly in the sky. Molt Taylor did. In 1949, the inventor from Portland, Oregon, came up with the Aerocar, a four-wheeled car with a tail and wings, which was powered by an airplane engine: it was part car and part airplane. To demonstrate its dual purpose, Taylor would remove the wings and tail section and drive it into town—much to the amazement of his fellow motorists.

🔺 Big Foot

Matthew McGrory of Los Angeles had size 29½ feet, measuring an amazing 15⅝ in (39.7 cm), and had to pay as much as $22,745 for a pair of shoes. Matthew had always been large—at birth he measured 24 in (60 cm) in length, and he stood 5 ft (1.5 m) tall when he graduated from kindergarten!

Lucky Numbers

Kevin Cook, from Colorado Springs, has been collecting playing dice since 1977. His collection currently totals more than 15,500.

Bungee Bride

A pair of adrenaline junkies got married while on a bungee jump in 2005. Huang Guanghui and his bride Zhang Ruqiong had applied for a special licence to get married on the amusement park ride in the city of Wenzhou in Zhejiang province, China. After a short marriage ceremony at the top of the ride, the pair, already prepared in their safety harnesses, jumped from the platform. Huang hopes the excitement of their unusual wedding will maintain the bond between them for the rest of their lives.

IN DEPTH

All Taped Up

Wisconsin brothers-in-law Tim Nyberg and Jim Berg, are the Duct Tape Guys—they have collected well over 5,000 uses for the product and say there's virtually nothing it can't fix.

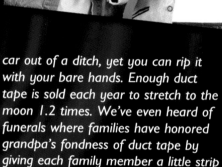

Tim, when did you first develop your passion for duct tape?

❝We were at Jim's sister's home for Christmas in 1993 and a storm caused a power outage. Jim said, 'If I knew where that power outage originated, I could probably fix it with duct tape.' His wife agreed, 'Jim fixes everything with duct tape!' They rattled off a few of his recent fixes, and I thought, 'There's a book here!' So we all sat around in the candlelight brainstorming uses for duct tape. By the end of the day, we had 365 uses listed. ❞

How did you become the Duct Tape Guys?

❝Back home, I illustrated and designed a book and sent it off to a few publishers. One acquisitions editor who happened to be familiar with duct tape humor from his college years pulled it out of the reject pile and convinced his editor by duct taping him into his chair until he agreed to publish it. That was seven books and close to three million copies ago. I have a background in stand-up comedy, and Jim is naturally funny, so we created the Duct Tape Guys to provide interviewable characters to accompany our books. ❞

What are some of the strangest uses for duct tape?

❝A dermatologist wrote us about nine years ago saying he successfully treated warts by simply adhering a strip of duct tape over the wart until it died. No chemicals needed. Five or six years later, there was a medical white paper written about the same treatment. Now people send us their wart testimonials. Jim's personal favorite use is duct taping his television remote control to his arm so he doesn't lose it (and doesn't have to relinquish remote use to his wife and kids). ❞

Why is it so well-loved?

❝It's a quick fix. It needs no directions, so there is no limit to one's creativity. It's extremely versatile. By folding it over onto intself two or three times it's strong enough to pull a car out of a ditch, yet you can rip it with your bare hands. Enough duct tape is sold each year to stretch to the moon 1.2 times. We've even heard of funerals where families have honored grandpa's fondness of duct tape by giving each family member a little strip of tape to seal the coffin. ❞

Does anything else come close?

❝We have two tools in our tool box. A roll of duct tape and a can of WD-40®. There are two rules that get you through life: If it's not stuck and it's supposed to be, duct tape it. If it's stuck and it's not supposed to be, WD-40 it. ❞

Is there anything you can't do with duct tape?

❝That's the leading question in our seventh book, 'Stump the Duct Tape Guys.' The question that finally stumped us was, 'How do you stop somebody who loves duct tape from using only duct tape?' We have no idea. Give someone more duct tape and they love it all the more, finding more and more uses for the stuff. Take it away and the heart only grows fonder. ❞

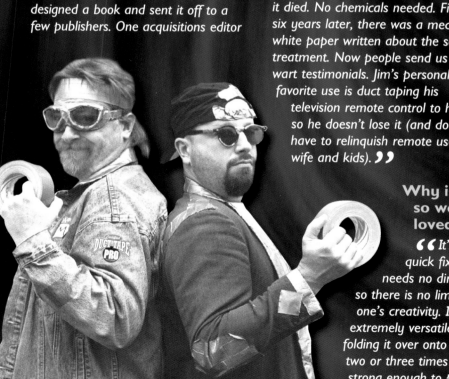

Party Animal

American financier George A. Kessler loved parties. In 1905, he threw a birthday party at London's Savoy Hotel with a Venetian theme. He had the hotel courtyard flooded with blue-dyed water to simulate a canal and, against a painted backdrop, his two dozen guests sat inside a vast silk-lined gondola, served by waiters dressed as gondoliers and serenaded by opera singer Enrico Caruso. Kessler's birthday cake was 5 ft (1.5 m) high and arrived strapped to the back of a baby elephant, which was led across a gangplank to the gondola.

Joel Freeborn, from Wauwatosa, Wisconsin, is a human bottle opener. He can open bottles of beer with his belly button!

Four-year Fast

In May 2005, German scientist Dr. Michael Werner announced that he had eaten nothing for the previous four years. He said he drank only water mixed with a little fruit juice and claimed to get all his energy from sunlight.

◗ Scorcher

Dr. Bunhead, aka Tom Pringle, is a teacher with a difference. He tries to bring science alive to both old and young by making it exciting—mainly with big bangs. His feats include firing eight potatoes from a potato launcher in three minutes and setting light to his head.

Quirky Castle

While both his parents were out at work one day, 17-year-old Howard Solomon ripped the back wall off their new suburban home and started adding on a porch. Now his parents live in a back room of their son's home—a castle in a central Florida swamp. That early brush with homebuilding inspired Solomon's love for grand creations. He began his castle at Ona in 1972 and it now covers 12,000 sq ft (1,115 sq m) and stands three storeys high. The exterior is covered in shiny aluminum printing plates, discarded by the local weekly newspaper, and the interior is home to his quirky sculptures, including a gun that shoots toilet plungers.

Inflatable Alarm

Chilean inventors Miguel Angel Peres and Pedro Galvez created the "Good Awakening Pillow," a device originally intended as an alarm clock for the deaf. The pillow very gently shakes the owner's head by slowly inflating and deflating.

◖ Howzat!

A cricket ball, made in Sri Lanka, boasts 2,704 diamonds, and is claimed to be the first life-size diamond-and-gold cricket ball.

ACTUAL SIZE!

Elvis Impersonator

New Yorker Mike Memphis will go to any lengths to look like his hero Elvis Presley. An Elvis impersonator since the age of 16, Mike underwent several facial procedures on Elvis's birthday in 1994 so that he could look more like the King. The multiple operations comprised liposuction of the face, cheek implants, a lower-lip implant, a chin implant, liposuction of the neck and chin, and implants on both sides of his jaw.

Klingon Pizza

American Star Trek fan Shane Dison is obsessed with being a Klingon! He makes sure that his daily diet includes Mexican-style pizzas, because they're the closest things to Klingon food on Earth.

Game's Up

Devoted baseball fan Joe Vitelli, of Westborough, Massachusetts, was so desperate to watch game seven of the New York Yankees–Boston Red Sox American League Championship series in 2003 that he faked a broken leg in order to get out of attending his girlfriend's sorority formal on the same day. He even wore a fake cast for six weeks, used a wheelchair, and "attended" various bogus doctor's appointments before he was spotted walking—and the game was up!

Brooklyn Miser

Henrietta Howland Green was one of the world's richest women. She had more than $31 million in one bank account alone, yet she lived a frugal life in a seedy Brooklyn apartment where the heating remained firmly switched off—even in the depths of winter. Her lunch was a tin of dry oatmeal, which she heated on the radiator at her bank. She never bothered to wash and usually wore the same frayed old black dress. Tied around her waist with string was a battered handbag containing cheap broken biscuits. When she died in 1916, she left an estate worth $100 million.

Mug Maestro

Since 1972, mug collector Harold Swauger from New Philadelphia, Ohio, has collected more than 4,500 examples from all over the world.

Riding High

New Jersey mountain biker, Jeff Lenosky can ride down stairs, over cars, and even along the top of a rail 2⅓ in (6 cm) wide. He also made a vertical leap of 45½ in (116 cm).

Chimp Marriage

After flirting through the bars of their respective enclosures for four months, two chimpanzees were married at a Brazilian zoo in 2003 in an attempt to encourage them to breed. The "couple" at Rio de Janeiro Zoo wore wedding gowns for the ceremony and had their own wedding cake.

T Set

Greg Rivera and Mike Essl are the A-Team of collectors. They are crazy about Mr. T and have more than 5,000 Mr. T items. The items include 600 Mr. T dolls, as well as lunch boxes, ceramic piggy banks, pencil sharpeners, toothbrushes, drinking glasses, and four boxes of Mr. T cereal.

Presidential Campaign

Ron Regen's goal in life was to meet his namesake, former President Ronald Reagan. "I was named after him by my parents. My mother liked him, and they thought it was kind of funny." Regen began writing to Reagan when the latter was Governor of California and he subsequently sent telegrams to every member of Congress (twice), joined various political groups, and paid to attend expensive dinners at the White House. His mammoth quest cost him more than $20,000, but the closest he ever came to meeting his hero was kissing Reagan's dog on a tour of the White House.

Face-off

Sculptor Ron Mueck exhibited his work—a lifelike sleeping face—in the Museum of Contemporary Art in Sydney, Australia, in 2002. A self-portrait, it is made from a fiberglass resin and is part of a collection of "hyper-real" figures made by the artist.

"The Ice Bear" is the first person to complete a long-distance swim in all five of the world's oceans
page 160

An Indian woman blew up a regular hot-water bottle until it burst
page 163

A puppy aged six months swallowed a 13-in (33-cm) serrated knife and survived
page 165

Despite having no movement in her arms and legs, a British woman sailed solo across the English Channel steering the boat with her mouth
page 172

PETE CABRINHA OF HAWAII surfed a 70 ft (21.3 m) wave at the break known as Jaws on the North Shore of Maui, Hawaii, on January 10, 2004. It was the largest wave ever ridden at the Global Big Wave Awards. Cabrinha set off to practice on a brand-new board to warm up before the event, but when the jet ski was removed he surfed in on this staggering wave.

IMPOSSIBLE

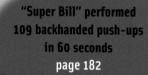

A regurgitator swallows light bulbs, coins, live goldfish, and glass eyes before bringing them back up again
page 181

"Super Bill" performed 109 backhanded push-ups in 60 seconds
page 182

An American performer had concrete blocks broken on his face with a sledgehammer and escaped from a quarter of a mile of plastic food wrap, while holding his breath
page 184

FEATS

Ice Breaker

Lewis Pugh combines extreme swimming with polar adventure. Besides being the first person to complete a long-distance swim in all five oceans of the world, British swimmer Pugh has also completed the most southern swim ever undertaken, earning him the name "The Ice Bear."

Wearing only swimming shorts, goggles, and a cap, Pugh plunged into the freezing sea off the Antarctic Peninsula in December 2005 to swim 0.6 mi (1 km) in a water temperature of only 32°F (0°C). To reach the spot just below the 65th parallel off Petermann Island, an ice-breaker ship had to cut through 25 mi (40 km) of thick pack-ice. Although it was dusk and snowing heavily, Pugh decided to undertake the swim on the night of December 14

Before Pugh entered the water, he was able to raise his core body temperature to 101.1°F (38.4°C) without doing anything other than looking at the icy water.

Pugh attributes much of his success to the rigorous mental training he undergoes, with the help of his coach, before each polar swim.

before the ice closed over again. The swim was undertaken on the 94th anniversary of the Norwegian explorer Roald Amundsen becoming the first man to reach the South Pole.

This incredible feat took Pugh 18 minutes 10 seconds.

He said, "As soon as I dived in, I had a screaming pain all over my body. After three minutes, I'd lost all feeling in my hands and feet, and after six minutes I lost all feeling throughout my arms and legs. I am not sure how I kept on going for so long. I had to concentrate all the time and swim as fast as I could to keep the cold out. I am ecstatic to have swum so close to the South Pole."

Thirty-five-year-old Pugh enjoys pushing back boundaries, many of which, he says, are ultimately mental rather than physical.

Pugh was supported by a ten-person team who were on hand at all times to collect physiological data for both research and safety purposes.

▶ Joe's Jaunts

Aged 62, Joe Bowen made his third trip across the U.S.A. He became famous in 1967 when he cycled 14,000 mi (22,530 km) on a winding route from California to his home in eastern Kentucky. Then, in 1980, he walked on stilts from Los Angeles, California, to Powell County, Kentucky, on a more direct route. It took him six months to plod more than 3,000 mi (4,828 km) through driving rain and desert heat. And, in 2005, he retraced his original cycle route, this time with 58 lb (26.3 kg) of equipment strapped to his bike.

Shark Rider

Fearless Manny Puig isn't content with getting right up close to sharks—he rides them, too! He follows hammerhead sharks in a boat off Florida Keys, then leaps on them and hangs on while they thrash about in the water. He even tackles more dangerous bull sharks, grabbing them by two holes near the gills before climbing on. Manny also dives into swamps in the Everglades and rides alligators with his bare hands. He says: "I rely on proper technique and the grace of God."

Stunt Kid

When he was just 2½ years old and still wearing diapers, Evan Wasser was an American skateboarding ace! Riding a skateboard that was almost as tall as he was, he could perform amazing jump stunts.

Mighty Molars

A 71-year-old Chinese woman pulled a car a distance of 65 ft (19 m) in 2005—with her teeth. Wang Xiaobei attached one end of a heavy rope to the car and wrapped a handkerchief around the other end before biting on the rope. Among other items she can carry in her mouth are a 55-lb (25-kg) bucket of water and a bicycle.

Courageous Swim

In September 2001, Ashley Cowan, aged 15, from Toronto, Ontario, became the youngest person and first disabled athlete to swim across Lake Erie. She managed to complete the 12-mi (19-km) swim in 14 hours, despite having had all four limbs amputated below the joints when she had meningitis as an infant.

◀ Fish School

Dean and Kyle Pomerleau teach fish to perform tricks. Sir Isaac Newton, the Betta Fish pictured here, learnt to go through a hoop after a week of training.

Quick on the Draw

German artist Gero Hilliger can produce portraits faster than a Polaroid camera. He is able to complete a portrait in just over six seconds and once rattled out 384 in 90 minutes. He can also do portraits blindfolded—purely by touch.

On Yer Bike!

★ In 2004, a German inventor came up with the Dolmette, a huge superbike powered by 24 chainsaws.

★ Argentina's Emilio Scotto rode 457,000 mi (735,500 km) on a motorcycle between 1985 and 1995. He went round the world twice and visited more than 200 countries.

★ In 2003, Swede Tom Wiberg constructed a mini motorcycle that was just 2½ in (6.4 cm) high and 4½ in (11.4 cm) long. It had a top speed of 1.2 mph (1.9 km/h), thanks to a miniscule, ethanol-powered combustion engine.

Hot Breath
Tipnis Shobha from India is able to blow up a regular hot-water bottle until it bursts. Shobha accomplished her incredible feat in Germany in 2005.

On Target

Darts player Perry Prine, from Mentor, Ohio, threw 1,432 bull's-eyes in 10 hours in March 1998. In that time, he threw a total of 6,681 darts—that is 11 darts a minute, of which on average 2.39 were bull's-eyes. He calculated that in the 10 hours, he walked more than 3 mi (5 km) to and from the dart board.

A 34-year-old Indian policeman, R. Velmurugan, **jumped** from a height of **34 ft** (10 m) into a **tub** containing just **7 in** (18 cm) of **water** in 2005.

Indian Trail

A Hungarian immigrant now based in Edgewater, Florida, 58-year-old Peter Wolf Toth traveled the U.S.A. from 1971 to 1988, carving faces into logs in each state. Sculptor Toth enjoys carving images of American Indians—so much so that his 67 towering statues (some as tall as 40 ft/12 m high) can be found in every U.S. state, as well as in Canada. This "Trail of Whispering Giants" stretches from Desert Hot Springs in California, to Springfield, Massachusetts.

Long Throw

Believe it or not, the magician and card-trick specialist Rick Smith Jr., of Cleveland, Ohio, can throw a playing card a distance of 216 ft (66 m)!

▶ Brick Lift

Eighty-seven-year-old Xie Tianzhuang from China lifted 14 bricks, weighing a total of 77 lb (35 kg), with his teeth, in Hefei in October 2005. He managed to hold the bricks suspended for 15 seconds.

Instant Art

Using only a palette knife and wads of toilet tissue, "Instant Artist" Morris Katz has created and sold over 225,000 original oil paintings in a 50-year career. In July 1987, he painted for 12 consecutive hours at a hotel in his native New York City, during which time he finished 103 paintings and sold 55 on the spot. He once painted a 12 x 16 in (30 x 40 cm) canvas of a child in the snow in just 30 seconds.

Super Size

Isaac "Dr. Size" Nesser of Greensburg, Pennsylvania, started lifting weights at the tender age of eight. As a result, it's perhaps of little surprise that he ended up boasting a 74-in (188-cm) chest, 29-in (74-cm) biceps, and the ability to bench press a massive 825 lb (374 kg). And if you ever need someone to carry 100-gal (380-l) drums filled with gas, Dr. Size is definitely the man for the job.

Slice of Luck

When veterinarian Jon-Paul Carew looked at this X ray he could hardly believe his eyes—a puppy aged six months had somehow swallowed a 13-in (33-cm) serrated knife!

Jane Scarola had been using a knife to carve a turkey at her home in Plantation, Florida, in September 2005. She put the blade on the counter away from the edge, but thinks that one of her six other dogs must have snatched it. From there it came into the possession of Elsie, her inquisitive St. Bernard puppy, who swallowed it! Elsie probably had the blade between her esophagus and stomach for four days before Dr. Carew removed it in an operation lasting two hours.

Dr. Carew admitted: "I was just amazed that a dog this small could take down a knife that big and not do any serious damage, and be as bright, alert, and happy as she was."

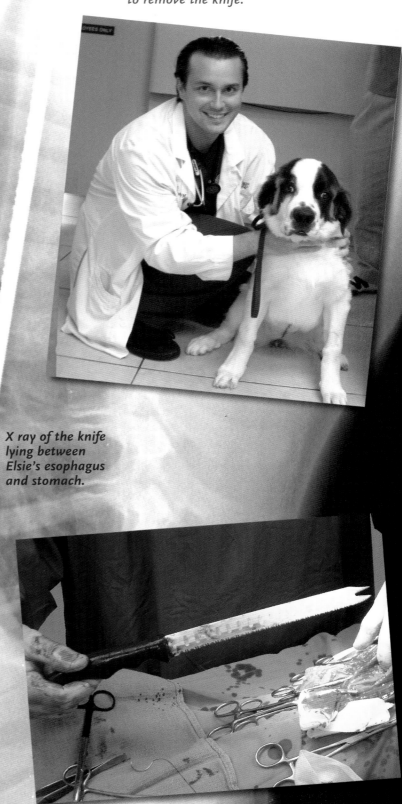

Jon-Paul Carew with Elsie after her operation to remove the knife.

X ray of the knife lying between Elsie's esophagus and stomach.

The offending knife, on the operating table, after removal.

Spinning Around

Suspended 525 ft (160 m) above the Rhine River, Germany, two German tightrope artists made a spectacular motorcycle river crossing in 2003. The bike was connected to a trapeze dangling beneath the high wire. Johann Traber sat on the trapeze, while his son, 19-year-old Johann, rode the motorcycle. They spun around the wire 14 times during the 1,900-ft (579-m) crossing, using shifts in their weight to keep revolving.

Marathon Mission

Margaret Hagerty has run a marathon on each of the Earth's seven continents—quite an achievement for a woman of 81. The elderly athlete, from Concord, North Carolina, completed her mission by taking part in Australia's Gold Coast Marathon in 2004, having previously run in locations including Greece, Brazil, and the South Pole. Asked how long she will keep going, she said: "Some days I think I am going to pick a date, run, and quit. But then I think, 'Well, they can just pick me up off the street one day.'"

Action Man

Although born without arms, Jim Goldman, from St. Louis, Missouri, can play baseball by placing the bat between his neck and shoulder. Using this method, he can hit a 60-mph (97-km/h) fastball thrown by a semi-pro ball player.

Quest

For more than eight years, Rafael Antonio Lozano has been making his way across North America—as part of his mission to visit every Starbucks coffee shop on the planet. By September 2005, the 33-year-old coffee lover from Houston, Texas (who uses the name Winter), had visited an incredible 4,886 Starbucks shops in North America and 213 in other countries including Spain, England, France, and Japan. His record for a single day was visiting 29 shops in southern California.

Hungry Eyes

This pine snake, found in Gainesville, Florida, was discovered in a chicken coop after having eaten two lightbulbs he mistook for eggs. The bulbs were three times the size of the snake's head and would have been fatal, but for a successful operation to have them removed.

Bar-tailed Godwit

The bar-tailed godwit is a migratory bird that would be hard to beat in an endurance flying contest—it migrates 7,456 mi (12,000 km) from Alaska to New Zealand in six days and six nights at speeds of up to 56 mph (90 km/h) without stopping to feed.

In **July 1998, Super Joe Reed** made a **65-ft** (20-m) leap on a **250cc dirtbike** from the **roof** of one building to another in LOS ANGELES, CALIFORNIA. The **roofs** were **140 ft** (43 m) above street level.

The High Life

Walking a tightrope 300 ft (91 m) above ground would be scary enough for most people, but Jay Cochrane has done it blindfold! In 1998, Cochrane, from Toronto, Ontario, walked 600 ft (184 m) between the towers of the Flamingo Hilton, Las Vegas. Known as the "Prince of the Air," Cochrane once spent 21 days on a high wire in Puerto Rico. In 1995, he walked a tightrope 2,098 ft (639 m) above the Yangtze River in China, and in 2001 he walked 2,190 ft (667 m) between two 40-storey buildings on opposite sides of the Love River in the city of Kaohsiung in Taiwan.

In Father's Footsteps

U.S. motorcycle stuntman Robbie Knievel (son of the famous daredevil Evel Knievel) made a spectacular 180-ft (55-m) jump over two helicopters and five airplanes parked on the deck of the Intrepid Museum, Manhattan, New York, in 2004. He had to construct a ski ramp 30 ft (9 m) high to help the motorbike build up enough speed to clear the aircraft-carrier-turned-museum.

Lug Tug

A Chinese man can pull a train with his ear! Thirty-nine-year-old Zhang Xinquan pulled a 24-ton train 130 ft (40 m) along a track in June 2005 by means of a chain attached to his right ear. After years of practice, he admits that his right ear is now bigger than his left. The previous month he had pulled a car 65 ft (20 m) with both ears while walking on eggs, without breaking them. The father of 15 children can also stand on eggs and pick up a 55-lb (25-kg) bicycle with his mouth.

❯ Cable Car Survival

On March 16, 2004, in Singapore, 36 teams of two took up the challenge of surviving seven days inside a cable car. They were allowed only one ten-minute toilet break each day. Nineteen of the couples survived the challenge, emerging on April 23 after experiencing 168 hours of stifling humidity, motion sickness, and claustrophobic conditions.

Blind Corners

Blindfolded and with a hood over his head, 19-year-old Samartha Shenoy, from India, rode a motor scooter for 15 mi (24 km) through the streets of Mangalore in 2004.

Flying Visit

In May 2004, Geoff Marshall traveled to all 275 stations on the London Underground system in just 18 hours 35 minutes 43 seconds.

Moonwalk Relay

In October 2002, a relay team comprising Adam Hall, Ramsey Brookhart, and Joshua Dodd moonwalked 30 mi (48 km) from Boulder, Colorado, to Denver.

Juggling Heavyweight

Believe it or not, Bob Whitcomb, from Ohio, juggles bowling balls. He can catch three 16-lb (7.3-kg) balls 62 consecutive times.

GALLERY
back to the archive

EYE-BLOWING FEAT
By forcing air out of the tear ducts in his eyes, Alfred Langevin of Detroit was able to blow up balloons, smoke, and even blow out candles.

BACK-WALKING
Yvonne Burkett was so flexible that she could walk on her own back. This photograph shows her performing this feat in 1934.

STRONG TEETH
Sam Marlow of Chelsea, Massachusetts could lift a barrel of beer weighing 260 lb (118 kg) with his teeth whilst doing a handstand.

TOP-HEAVY
Johnny Eck was born in Baltimore without the lower portion of his body. He got around by walking on his hands, as seen in this photo, taken in 1937.

HIGH-UP KITTY
Bob Dotzauer, a teacher in Cedar Rapids, Iowa, managed to balance a cat in a basket on top of a ladder some 24 ft (7.3 m) tall while balancing it on his chin!

HAIR-RAISING
Joseph Green, from Brooklyn, New York, was known as "the man with iron hair." His hair was so strong that he could use it to bend an iron bar.

CRAZY DRIVER
"Texas Zeke" Shumway of Dallas, Texas, drove more than 50,000 mi (80,500 km), both in cars and on motorcyles, within an almost vertical drome only 46 ft (14 m) wide.

MONSTER FISH
Herman Newber of New York caught this ocean sunfish in 1932 when it got stranded in shallow water. It weighed more than 700 lb (318 kg).

Looking Back

September 1, 1925 Charles Coghlan returned home when a flood in Galveston, Texas, washed him from his grave, took him around Florida, and up the coast to Prince Edward Island— some 2,000 mi (3,220 km) away—where he used to live. **April 27, 1939 Mrs Earl Palmer** miraculously survived when her jugular vein was slit and she didn't get treatment for 17 hours.

The Ice Man Swimmeth

Dutchman Wim Hof says that, like fish, his body contains a form of antifreeze. In 2000, he swam 187 ft (57 m) under ice in a lake near Kolari, Finland, wearing only trunks and goggles. Then, in 2004, he spent 1 hour 8 minutes in direct, full-body contact with ice.

Instant Beauty

"One-minute beautician" Uma Jayakumar can create a hairstyle using a hairpin in seven seconds. In July 2005, the Indian hairdresser created 66 hairstyles in a minute, using a chopstick.

Boat Pull

At the age of 65, Maurice Catarcio, from Middle Township, New Jersey, swam the backstroke while tugging an 80-ft (24-m) sightseeing boat across a lake. And at 72, the former wrestler dragged a 27,000-lb (12,247-kg) bus down a New York City street.

Look, No Hands!

At the 2002 X-games, Mat Hoffman, a 30-year-old BMX bike rider from Oklahoma City, performed the first no-handed 900, where the bike goes through 2½ spins.

Cold Comfort

Gilberto Cruz remained buried in ice for 1 hour 6 minutes 24 seconds at a Brazilian shopping center in 2005. The 42-year-old performed the stunt in a transparent box in the mall at Ribeirao Preto with only his head sticking out of the ice.

Religious Vision

Indian sculptor Rama Satish Shah makes intricate models of religious figures, while blindfold. Over the past five years, she has created 36,000 figures from plaster of Paris, ranging in height from ⅕ in (½ cm) to 9 in (23 cm). Each one takes her about three minutes to make.

All At Sea

★ When a Russian yacht lost its rudder in the Southern Ocean in 2005, the resourceful crew used a cabin door as a replacement.

★ In 1992, Kenichi Horie of Japan managed to steer a pedal boat 4,660 mi (7,500 km) from Hawaii to Japan. His pedal-powered voyage took him 3½ months.

★ A boat moored at Newport Beach, California, was sunk in 2005 when 40 invading sea lions piled on to it!

◄ Walking on Water

When Rémy Bricka first crossed the Atlantic in 1972, it was on board a luxury liner. For his second Atlantic crossing—16 years later—he decided to walk! The Frenchman set off from the Canary Islands on April 2, 1988, with his feet lashed to 14-ft (4.3-m) fiberglass pontoons. Behind him he towed a raft that contained a coffin-sized sleeping compartment, a compass, and water desalinators. He took no food, eating only plankton and the occasional flying fish that landed on his raft. Walking 50 mi (80 km) a day, he reached Trinidad on May 31, highly emaciated, and hallucinating, at the end of his 3,502-mi (5,636-km) hike across the ocean.

IN DEPTH
Tooth and Nail

Georges Christen, 43, is one of the world's strongest men. He can stop a plane from taking off with his teeth, pull trains, bend nails, and power a Ferris wheel—but insists he is a gentle giant.

What inspired you to become one of the world's strongest men?

"As a child in Luxembourg, I was fascinated by circus strongmen. Aged 16, I started lifting weights, and then I saw a French guy on television bending 50 iron carpenter's nails. I broke his record by bending 250 with my teeth when I was 19."

What are your most famous stunts?

"I prevented three 110-horsepower Cessna Sport airplanes from taking off at full power—one with my teeth and two with my arms. I have also pulled trucks, buses, railway carriages, and a 95,000-kg ship— all with my teeth. At Luxembourg's Schobermesse fair, I made a 45-m, 60,000-kg Ferris wheel turn by pulling it with a rope by my teeth. And I like tearing telephone books—I can rip 1,344-page books into several pieces."

Are your stunts dangerous?

"A favorite is blowing up a hot-water bottle until it bursts—the pressure could blow back into my lungs and kill me. But I train and calculate the risks."

So how do you train—and how do you protect your teeth?

"I train every day—a mixture of physical strength and mental concentration to liberate all the force you need at one special moment. My teeth aren't perfect—when I was about 20, my dentist told me not to use my teeth in this way, but I did anyway and now he often comes to my shows because I'm good publicity for him! I used to work for an insurance company, but they won't insure me because they have no way of knowing how dangerous it is to prevent a plane taking off."

What is the most difficult stunt to do?

"I can now bend 368 nails in one hour. And, although it's not as spectacular, the hardest one is tearing a deck of 120 playing cards, because they are small and hard to grip, and also because they are plastic-coated."

How do you think of new stunts?

"I have a collection of books and posters of old-time strongmen, and I try to adapt their stunts for modern times. If they were holding back horses, I make it airplanes. I might lift a table with my teeth—and have a woman sitting on top."

Has your strength ever got you into trouble?

"I try not to be a strongman in my private life—if people want to pick a fight, I tell them it's just my job. I once accidentally pulled the bumper off a car at a car show. And I also once unintentionally broke a 'test your strength' machine at a fairground."

How long will you carry on testing your strength?

"I taught the telephone-book stunt to my office worker father, and he was still doing it when he was 94! I have bought an old blacksmith's forge and I'm turning it into a small museum full of things strongmen used to use and wear. People can come and train the way they did. My main vision now is to entertain."

171

🔻 **Beer on the Brain**
A Wushu (martial arts) enthusiast performs a headstand on a beer bottle in Nanjing City, China, on May 3, 2005.

Climbing Granny

When 78-year-old grandmother Nie Sanmei accidentally locked herself out of her fifth-floor apartment in Changsha, China, in 2005, she started scaling the outside of the building! Using window grills as handholds and footholds, she reached the fourth floor before her concerned daughter-in-law arrived with the key.

Bird Man of Devon

When Jonathan Marshall goes hang gliding near his home, in Devon, England, he not only flies like a bird: he flies with birds. He has trained wild birds to join him in flight. Marshall became obsessed with the idea of flying with birds when he was eight years old and has spent the past decade training a few falcons to fly with him. "Flying with birds puts you right into their world," he says. "Up there, flying at 1,000 ft (305 m), I see everything from their point of view. How many people have that experience?"

Grape Catch

In 1991, in the town of East Boston, Massachusetts, Paul J. Tavilla, who is known as "The Grape Catcher," incredibly caught a grape in his mouth after it had been thrown by James Dealy from a distance of 327 ft 6 in (99.8 m).

Marathon Push

Rob Kmet and A.J. Zeglen, from Winnipeg, Manitoba, pushed a 2,600-lb (1,180-kg) sports car 43 mi (70 km) around Winnipeg's Gimli racetrack in 2005. At the end of the 24-hour push, the two men were hardly able to walk.

Car Jump

Believe it or not, Andy Macdonald once jumped over four cars on a skateboard! He made the jump of 52 ft 10 in (16.1 m) at East Lansing, Michigan, in 1999.

Blind Racer

Blind motorcyclist Mike Newman from Manchester, England, raced a powerful 1,000cc motorbike at speeds of up to 89 mph (143 km/h), guided only by radio instructions!

Mouth Control

Despite having no movement in her arms and legs, a British woman, Hilary Lister, was able to sail solo across the English Channel in August 2005 by steering her boat, *Malin*, with her mouth. Aged 33, Hilary controlled the boat by sucking and blowing on two plastic tubes connected to pressure switches that operated the tiller and sails. She navigated the 21-mi (34-km) voyage from Dover, England, to Calais, France, in a specially modified keelboat in 6 hours 13 minutes.

Hilary used a "sip and puff" technique to steer her boat.

Doug's Delight

In 2005, at the end of a 25-year marathon, Doug Slaughter, from Greentown, Indiana, finally achieved his goal of cycling 25,000 non-road mi (40,230 km). Doug had always wanted to bike the distance of the world's circumference, but because he was born with a mild handicap, he has never cycled on a road. Instead, he rode on driveways, parking lots, and forest trails, using an odometer to track his progress. He also used a stationary bike to cover some of the distance. Having achieved that target, Doug has no intention of stopping there: he's now aiming for 50,000 mi (80,465 km).

Juggling Jogger

Believe it or not, 33-year-old Michal Kapral, from Toronto, Ontario, ran a marathon in 3 hours 7 minutes in September 2005 while juggling three balls at the same time!

Driving **monster truck Bigfoot 14**, Dan Runte, from ST. LOUIS, Missouri, jumped **202 ft** (62 m) over a **Boeing 727** airplane at SMYRNA AIRPORT, Tennessee, in 1999.

In the Dark

Teenage bowling champion Amy Baker, from Houston, Texas, has an unusual recipe for success—she practices blindfold. As soon as she started bowling wearing a dark eyemask—at the suggestion of her coach Jim Sands—her scores improved dramatically, enabling her to become a national champion.

Backwards Bob

Known to his friends as "Backwards Bob," Canada's Bob Gray can write backward and upside down with both hands simultaneously. He can also spell backward phonetically.

Ms. Dynamite

Protected by only a helmet and a flimsy costume, American entertainer Allison Bly has blown herself up more than 1,500 times with explosives equivalent to the force of two sticks of dynamite. "The Dynamite Lady" performs the stunt inside a box she calls the "Coffin of Death," but has so far suffered nothing worse than broken bones, concussion, and powder burns.

Young Soldier

Calvin Graham, the youngest U.S. serviceman in World War II, was wounded in combat, then later discharged for lying about his age—he was only 12 years old.

Fantastic Feet

Claudia Gomez of Baton Rouge, Louisiana, can use her feet to shoot a bull's-eye with a bow and arrow while doing a handstand!

Sporting Double

In October 2003, just 22 hours after making a hole-in-one at Pleasant View Golf Course, Paul Hughes, 74, of Waunakee, Wisconsin, bowled a 300 game at Middleton, Wisconsin.

Ear Power

A Chinese man is able to blow up balloons and blow out candles with his ears. Wei Mingtang, from Guilin City, discovered more than 30 years ago that his ears leaked, after which he came up with the idea of using them to inflate balloons with the aid of a pipe. And he once blew out 20 candles in a line in just 20 seconds using a hose attached to his ears.

Speedy Seventy

Ed Whitlock, aged 72, of Toronto, Ontario, Canada, became the first person over the age of 70 to run a marathon in under three hours.

⬆ Walking on Air

An Uygur tightrope walker spent a long 37 days and nights living on a 100-ft (30-m) high wire stretched across a dam in Nanjing, China, in May 2005. Thirty-two-year-old Aisikaier comes from a family of high-wire walkers, and had spent 26 days on a wire in 2004, but this time he managed to stay up longer. He spent his nights in a makeshift shelter attached to the thick wire. To kill time and alleviate the boredom during the day, he performed daring hula-hoop, unicycle, and balancing tricks. The only contact he had with the world below was via his cell phone, which he used so that he could answer questions about his feat, or talk to fans.

Sharp PRacTice

The daredevil ethnic games that took place in Guiyang, southwest China, in May 2005, were certainly at the cutting edge of sport.

The Miao people, whose favorite pastime is buffalo fighting, used the games to demonstrate their expertise at such feats as swallowing a red-hot sword and walking barefoot on the razor-sharp blade of a giant knife. Children got in on the act too, with a 13-year-old girl balancing delicately on the tips of knives. The opening ceremony was also a far cry from the Olympics, a group of Miao kung-fu artists performing a series of amazing stunts.

Standing on broken glass and walking on a series of knife points are two of the amazing feats in these unusual games.

Instead of using his hands, this man is swinging bricks around using his chest. They are tied to a needle that pierces his body.

174

This performer can be seen swallowing a red-hot sword as spectators look on.

As this Miao man inches along the edge of a giant knife, he stretches out his arms to balance.

Marital Bliss

Zhang Jiuyu and Guo Changlan celebrate their marriage of 80 years 15 days in Shijiazhuang, China, on October 23, 2005. The 96-year-old couple have one child, three grandchildren, and three great-grandchildren.

Egg Catcher

Brad Freeman didn't end up with egg on his face in 2005. For the 25-year-old from Calgary, Alberta, caught a boiled egg in his mouth thrown from an amazing distance of 275 ft (84 m).

Karaoke King

Barry Yip, a D.J. from Hong Kong, spent 81 hours 23 seconds singing 1,000 karaoke songs.

Mule Train

Desperate to attend a 2005 Mule Days festival in Ralston, Wyoming, Pam Fedirchuck and Tara Lewis reckoned the only way to get there from their home in Rocky Mountain House, Alberta, was by mule. Riding two mules and leading a third that carried supplies, they made the 857-mi (1,380-km) trip in 52 days.

Oldest Ace

Aged 101, Harold Stilson became the oldest golfer to make a hole-in-one when he landed an ace at the 16th hole at Deerfield Country Club, Florida, in May 2001. A 27-handicap golfer, he started playing at the age of 20, but did not make the first of his six holes-in-one until he was 71.

Iron Bear

Harold "Chief Iron Bear" Collins, from Shannon, North Carolina, pulled a 22.87-ton truck 100 ft (30 m) in under 40 seconds in New York City in 1999. A full-blooded Lumbee Native American, Collins is certainly built for the part: he has a 63-in (160-cm) chest.

Viking Voyage

Robert McDonald aims to cross the Atlantic in a replica Viking ship made from 15 million ice-cream sticks held together by 2 tons of glue. The former Hollywood stuntman, from Florida, spent two years gluing together the sticks that make up the *Mjollnir* (*Hammer of Thor*), which is 50 ft (15 m) long. McDonald plans to sail the ship from Holland to Key West, Florida, via Denmark, Scotland, Iceland, Greenland, and Canada—the route the Vikings are believed to have taken to America 1,000 years ago.

The 15-ton ship will be powered by oars and a sail from a 30-ft (9-m) high mast.

Sweet Catch

One of the weirdest acts on the U.S. entertainment circuit features Scott Jeckel blowing marshmallows from his nose into the mouth of Ray Perisin, who then swallows them. The Illinois pair started performing their act with popcorn, but switched to marshmallows, as they were more aerodynamic.

Stair Crazy

Most people would take the elevator up an apartment block, but not Bernadette Hallfeld Duychak. She's crazy about climbing stairs! In August 2005, she climbed Harbor Point—her 54-storey condominium in downtown Chicago, Illinois—more than 55 times in 24 hours, making a total of around 40,000 stairs. "When I started, I could barely climb 20 floors. Now I climb at least 2,000 floors a week!"

◀ Incredible Hunk

Although he weighed only 88 lb (40 kg) at the age of 16, Dennis Rogers, from Houston, Texas, could lift twice his body weight over his head! Once the smallest boy in his class, Rogers, who weighs in at 160 lb (72.5 kg), is pound-for-pound the strongest man in the world. He can tear thick books vertically using only two fingers and can bend a solid steel bar around his neck into a U-shape. In 1995, he successfully prevented four Harley Davidson Sportster motorcycles, powered at full throttle, from moving for 12 seconds.

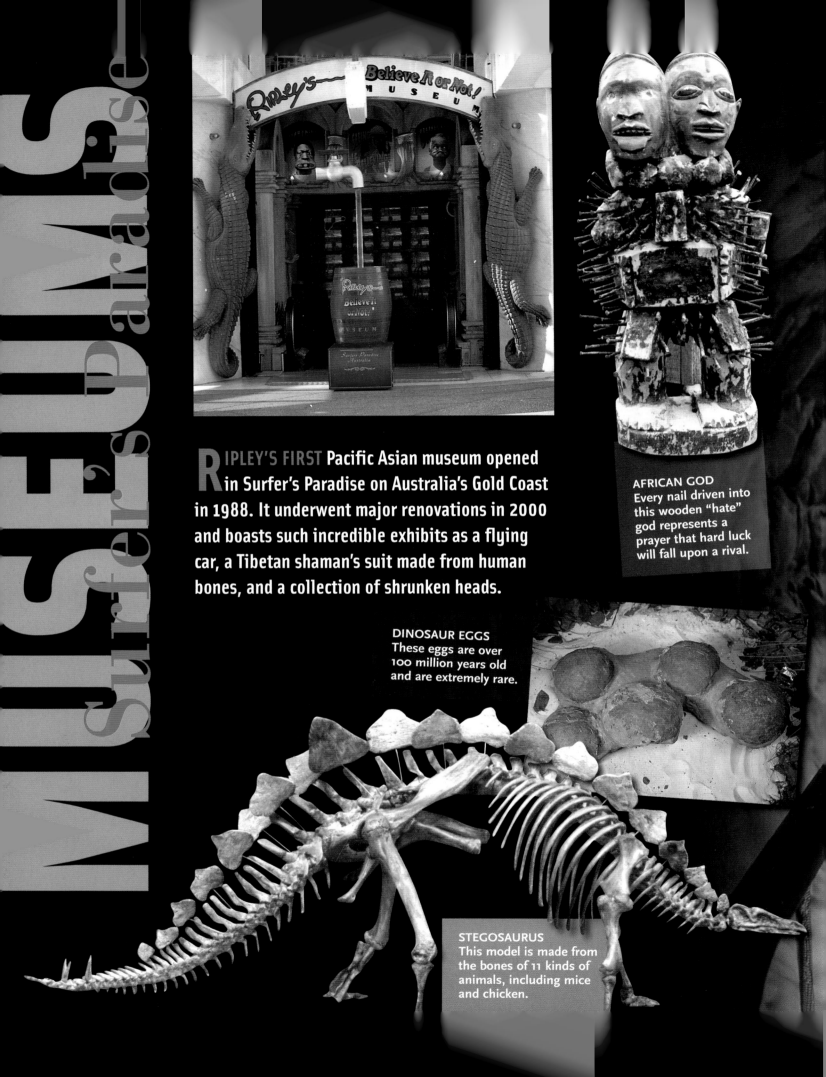

MUSEUMS
Surfer's Paradise

RIPLEY'S FIRST Pacific Asian museum opened in Surfer's Paradise on Australia's Gold Coast in 1988. It underwent major renovations in 2000 and boasts such incredible exhibits as a flying car, a Tibetan shaman's suit made from human bones, and a collection of shrunken heads.

AFRICAN GOD
Every nail driven into this wooden "hate" god represents a prayer that hard luck will fall upon a rival.

DINOSAUR EGGS
These eggs are over 100 million years old and are extremely rare.

STEGOSAURUS
This model is made from the bones of 11 kinds of animals, including mice and chicken.

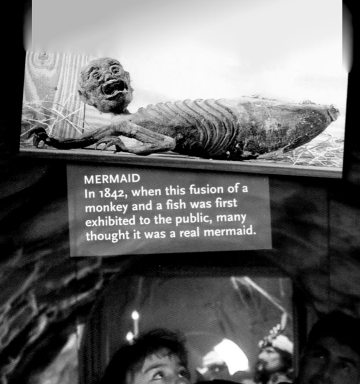

MERMAID
In 1842, when this fusion of a monkey and a fish was first exhibited to the public, many thought it was a real mermaid.

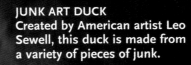

saliva is considered to be a powerful aphrodisiac.

ROTATING TUNNEL
The rotating walls of this tunnel make those walking through feel like the floor is moving, even though it is still.

JUNK ART DUCK
Created by American artist Leo Sewell, this duck is made from a variety of pieces of junk.

DON'T MISS!

▶ Triceratops dinosaur skull

▶ A large turtle that was clamped on to a sea plane and taken for an aerial ride

▶ Narwhal tusk

▶ Robert E. Lee paddlewheeler made from matchsticks

▶ Human dentures made from dolphin and crocodile teeth

▶ A flying car

▶ Portrait painted on a housefly

ASARO NATIVE DANCE MASK
Worn in New Guinea, "Mud Men" masks are believed to transform the wearer into an invincible spirit.

179

Handicap Golfer

A Florida golfer achieved three holes-in-one over a six-month period—all while swinging one-handed! Sixty-eight-year-old Bill Hilsheimer, from Nokomis, lost most of his right hand in a childhood accident, and uses only his left arm when he swings. But after waiting 50 years for his first ace, he racked up three between September 2003 and March 2004. The odds of an amateur golfer hitting a hole-in-one are 12,600 to 1. The odds of Bill's feat would be impossible to calculate.

Jill Drake of **KENT**, England, won a contest for the *loudest screamer*, with a **scream** of **129 decibels**— that's as loud as a **pneumatic drill**.

Human Cartoon

New Yorker Rob Lok is known as "The Human Cartoon" because he is able to smash a watermelon with his head!

Biker Marathon

In May 2002, British couple Simon and Monika Newbound set off from Dublin, Ireland, on a monumental motorcycle journey that would take them more than three years. By May 2005, the pair had clocked up visits to 54 countries and had ridden an amazing 105,000 mi (169,000 km). As well as circumnavigating the world, they rode north of the Arctic Circle three times on three different continents, crossed the U.S.A. from coast to coast five times, and visited every U.S. state and Canadian province. They rode 1,600 mi (2,600 km) off-road in Mongolia, had an audience with the Pope in Rome, and camped on the Great Wall of China.

Ear-lifting

Zafar Gill, from Pakistan, lifted an ear-bending 121 lb (55 kg) and held them for 12.22 seconds suspended from one of his ears! He successfully completed this amazing feat in Germany, in November 2005.

Egg-head

New Yorker Barnaby Ruhe can throw a boomerang on a 100-ft (30-m) elliptical path so that it returns to hit an egg that he has carefully placed on top of his own head! Ruhe has made more than 100 successful hits and has been whacked only a few times. He says of his eggsploits: "What you throw out is what you get back."

Globe Trotter

In three years of travel between 2000 and 2003, Charles Veley visited a staggering 350 countries, enclaves, islands, federations, and territories, spending over $1 million on journeying almost a million miles. His most difficult destination was Clipperton Island, a remote French territory 700 mi (1,126 km) off the coast of Mexico in the Pacific Ocean. Owing to a treacherous reef, his boat was unable to land, forcing him to swim to shore. "There was nothing else I could do," he smiles. "By then I was obsessed with completing my goal."

S Hard to Swallow

Having swallowed the goldfish with plenty of water, Stevie safely retrieves them.

Stevie Starr, a 34-year-old Scotsman, is a professional regurgitator. He swallows such objects as light bulbs, coins, live goldfish, and glass eyes before bringing them back up again.

Stevie also swallows butane and soap, and then blows out a gas-filled bubble. He swallows a ring and locked padlock—when the articles are returned, the ring is locked inside the padlock! When Stevie swallows numbered coins, he can retrieve them at will, and in whichever order the audience requests.

He learned his talent while living in a children's home in Glasgow, Scotland. "I used to swallow pennies to hide them from the other kids... I didn't realize that someday I'd be doing it for a living."

Stevie regurgitates dry sugar after having previously swallowed a bowlful with a glass of water.

181

Super-fit

In June 2005, at Hartford, Connecticut, Bill Kathan Jr., from Vermont, became the first person in the world to do more than 100 backhanded push-ups in one minute. "Wild Bill," as he is known, proved he was super-fit by performing 109 backhanded push-ups in the 60-second limit.

Blinding Speed

In September 2005, Hein Wagner, 33, of Cape Town, South Africa, drove a car at a speed of 168 mph (270 km)—even though he has been blind since birth.

Pacific Crossing

Steve Fisher from Toledo, Ohio, crossed the Pacific Ocean from California to Hawaii in 1997 on a 17-ft (5.2-m) windsurfer. The 2,612-mi (4,200-km) journey on *Da Slippa II* took him 47 days.

Escape Artist

Queensland-based escape artist Ben Bradshaw freed himself from a straitjacket while fully submerged in a tank of water in just 38.59 seconds in Sydney, Australia, in April 2005.

Gran Tour

A Californian grandmother completed a journey down the west coast of North America in 2002, riding solo on an 11-ft (3.4-m) watercraft. Jane Usatin, 56, from Carlsbad, set off from Blaine, Washington, and reached Mexico 28 travel-days later at the end of a 1,828-mi (2,941-km) trip.

Ball Tower

In November 1998, David Kremer, of Waukesha, Wisconsin, stacked ten bowling balls vertically without using any adhesive.

Mexican Wave

An amazing 42 Brazilian surfers rode a wave together on Macumba Beach in Rio de Janeiro on November 18, 2005.

American Odyssey

In June 2005, Jason Hill climbed on his bike in Deadhorse, Alaska, and began pedaling. By January 2006, he had reached Missoula, Montana, but his ultimate destination is Tierra del Fuego in Argentina. He reckons the 19,000-mi (30,600-km) journey, from the Arctic Circle to the very bottom of South America, will take him more than two years.

Saddle Weary

In April 2005, Randy Davisson, from Decatur, Alabama, succeeded in his mission to ride the same horse in every state in the U.S. and in each Canadian province and territory. The quest, on his faithful appaloosa Eli Whitney, took Randy nearly five years to complete and finished when he climbed into the saddle on the island of Oahu in Hawaii.

Randy and Eli stopped for pictures outside post offices along the way.

Up and Down
Robert Magniccari of Rockaway, New Jersey, made 190 take-offs and landings in 24 hours at two airports in New Jersey.

Tour of America
Don Boehly, of Grayson, Kentucky, set off in September 2004 aiming to cycle through the 50 U.S. states. He expects to complete the 25,000-mi (40,000-km) trip in 2007.

Wheelbarrow Push
In 1975, Rev. Geoffrey Howard, a priest from Manchester, England, took 93 days to push a Chinese sailing wheelbarrow 2,000 mi (3,218 km) across the Sahara Desert.

Generous Donor
Frank Loose of Germany donates blood every week and has given more than 800 times.

Sharp Practice
Red Stuart from Philadelphia, Pennsylvania, swallowed 25 swords at once in September 2005! The result of years of training, his intake consisted of a 32-in (80-cm) long broadsword plus 24 smaller swords 18 in (46 cm) in length.

Chin Up
In December 2003, David Downes, of Felixstowe, England, balanced an open ironing-board on his chin for 3 minutes 32 seconds.

Crazy Golf
When Dave Graybill said he was off for a round of golf in 2003, he wasn't planning on playing any ordinary course. The Glendale, Arizona, firefighter had designed a golf course 4,080 mi (6,566 km) long that would take him right across the U.S.A. The first tee was on Santa Monica Pier, California, and the 18th hole was in Central Park, New York. The round took seven months, through 16 states, and incorporated some of the best-known U.S. landmarks. He hit balls through deserts, across rivers, down streets, even out of an airplane!

House Hole

A family in Waihi, New Zealand, escaped without injury after their house fell into a hole 50 ft (15 m) wide in the middle of the night!

Lucky Numbers

Kris Wilson spends two hours a day writing numbers on notepads as part of his ultimate goal to become the first person in the world to write by hand every number from one to a million. Wilson, from Provo, Utah, began his challenge in February 2004. Eighteen months later he had reached nearly 600,000. His numbers are for sale—people buy anniversary and birthday numbers, and get a certificate signed by "Mr. Million" himself.

Nail Suspension

Harley Newman can suspend himself on just four nails—a variation on the normal bed of nails. Nothing seems to faze him. The U.S. performer can pick combination locks with his teeth by feeling the numbers with his tongue, and has had concrete blocks broken on his face with a sledgehammer. He has also supported a 1,700-lb (771-kg) human pyramid while lying on a bed of nails, and can even escape from a quarter of a mile of plastic food wrap, while holding his breath.

Baby Walker

Believe it or not, a four-year-old Chinese girl can walk 300 ft (91 m) along a tightrope, suspended 100 ft (30 m) above ground level! Yin Feiyan, from Anhui province, has been tightrope walking since she was two.

Australia's **R.J. Brunow** performed **64** **consecutive** **360**-degree **spins** (donuts) in a Holden Gemini car at Queensland Raceway in May 2005. He **destroyed** a brand new set of tires in the process.

Dancing Feet

U.S. entertainer David Meenan managed to tap dance 32 mi (52 km) in 7½ hours at Red Bank, New Jersey, in October 2001.

Ancient Wheel

Archeologists in Slovenia have discovered a wheel that is between 5,100 and 5,350 years old—it is believed to be the oldest ever found.

Back Flip

Josh Tenge from Incline Village, Nevada, performed a back flip measuring 44 ft 10 in (13.7 m) in length on a sandboard in 2000.

Jumping Granny

Thelma Tillery believes in keeping her word. She promised her grandson that she would make a parachute jump when she turned 85, so she did just that. In September 2005, the skydiving grandmother landed safely at Kearney, Nebraska.

Fjord Rescue

Inge Kavli, age 73, dove into a fjord in Norway and swam out 66 ft (20 m) to rescue a baby boy after his mother accidentally crashed her car into the water.

My Left Foot

When Tad Lietz, from Appleton, Wisconsin, plays the cello, it is a considerable achievement—not only because he's an accomplished cellist, but also because he is missing his left arm and bows with his left foot.

Wheelie Fast

In March 2005, Australia's Matt Mingay reached a speed of 140 mph (225 km/h) doing a motorbike wheelie over a distance of 0.6 mi (1 km) at Temora Aerodrome, New South Wales.

IN DEPTH
Paintball Wizard

Australian martial-arts expert Anthony Kelly, 41, has such quick reactions that he can catch flying arrows and punch faster than Muhammad Ali in his prime—as well as catch speeding paintballs blindfold.

How did you first develop your quick reactions?

"I grew up watching martial-arts star Bruce Lee and boxer Muhammad Ali and was fascinated by how fast people could move. I have trained all over the world and have black belts in seven martial arts. I developed the world's first electronic device for testing reaction speeds, based on a traditional Chinese wooden dummy. My reaction time was under three hundredths of a second."

When did you start to catch things?

"In 1999, I saw an old kung-fu movie where the hero had to catch an arrow. I learned how to do this within a week. I can now catch 38 arrows from three archers in two minutes at a distance of eight meters."

How did you get the idea to catch paintballs?

"A student at my martial-arts center in Armidale, New South Wales, owned a paintball field. He said 'Okay, you can do arrows, how about paintballs?' My record now stands at 28 caught unbroken at 20 meters in two minutes, and 11 caught blindfold in the same conditions."

How dangerous is it?

"They shoot the paintballs through a paintball gun at a minimum speed of 240 feet per second—around 70 balls in two minutes. They're really painful, like a cricket ball coming at you at speed, and when I go for a record I'm black and blue. Once an arrow nearly went through my head—it took everything I had to block it. It's stupid to do it, I guess."

Do you have a special technique?

"I'm very in tune with sound. I can get a stopwatch and tell you if it is two or three hundredths of a second between the beeps. So when I catch paintballs blindfold, I can tune into the noise and then bring the ball towards me, slowing its velocity down in milliseconds."

How fast can you punch?

"I hold the record for most punches in one minute, which is 347, and the most in one hour, which is 11,856. I punch on average ten punches per second—Bruce Lee could supposedly do eight, Muhammad Ali six or seven."

How do you train?

"Every day I do crazy things, like trying to slide into a shop door as it's closing. My diet is quite strange in that I only eat meat and potatoes and have never eaten fruit or vegetables—I don't know if that makes a difference!"

Do you use your skills in other areas?

"I travel the world doing T.V. appearances of my skills, and am the world's leading reaction training coach. I am also a full-time martial arts instructor."

Do you have any future projects?

"I'm working on how fast the body can go. I have taken the old martial-arts stunt of breaking a board one step further—I suspend three boards together, and can break the middle board while the outside boards stay intact. Experts can't work out how! The old masters believed noise could implode human organs, but that's a difficult one to test—so far I'm sticking to breaking balloons!"

185

Backwards Biker

Roger Riddell, from Charlotte, North Carolina, jumped over six cars while sitting backwards on his Harley Davidson motorcycle, in the town of Yakima, Washington State, in 2003.

In Reverse

American Steve Gordon unicycled backwards for an amazing 68 mi (109 km) in Springfield, Missouri, in June 1999.

Sew Clever!

Despite being unable to use her arms and legs, American Sapna Goel still manages to paint and sew unassisted. Sapna, who contracted polio when young, has developed the amazing ability to thread a sewing needle with her tongue.

High Jump

New Zealander A.J. Hackett jumped 764 ft (233 m) from the Macau Tower on August 17, 2005. He is estimated to have hit speeds of more than 95 mph (150 km/h) during the 20-second descent. Hackett was tied on to a special cable that dramatically slowed his rate of descent once he was just 33 ft (10 m) above the ground, to allow for a safe landing.

▶ Living Underwater

Two Italian divers spent ten days living underwater in September 2005. Stefano Barbaresi and Stefania Mensa endured cold, fatigue, and, ironically, dehydration to live at a depth of 26 ft (8 m) on the seabed off the island of Ponza, Italy. They slept beneath bedframes, which were turned upside down to stop the sleeper floating upward, and spent most of their time in their underwater "house," that contained two sofas, an exercise bike, books, and a waterproofed television.

Cast Adrift

Fishermen Lafaili Tofi and Telea Pa'a from Western Samoa, survived for six months after drifting 2,480 mi (3,990 km) in the Pacific Ocean in a small metal boat.

Scientists in **AUSTRALIA** used a **laser** to **sculpt** a replica of the **Sydney Opera House** that was so **small** that it appears as a **speck of dust** to the naked eye.

Camel Vaulting

At the 2004 Yemeni Traditional Sports Festival, Ahmed Abdullah al-Abrash was crowned world camel-jumping champion after using a trampoline to vault over a line of camels 10 ft (3 m) long.

World Trek

On June 20, 1970, brothers David and John Kunst set off from their hometown of Waseca, Minnesota, aiming to become the first people to walk around the world. Four years, 3 months, and 21 pairs of shoes later, David completed the 14,450-mi (23,255-km) trek (he flew across the oceans), arriving back in Waseca with mixed emotions. Sadly, his brother had been killed by bandits in Afghanistan only halfway through the expedition.

All of a Quiver

Terry Bryan from Colorado Springs, caught an arrow traveling 135-mph (217-km/h) with his bare hands on an edition of the *Ripley's Believe It or Not!* TV show. Not only did he successfully complete the challenge, he went on to do it again—blindfold!

Bit by Bat

Jeanna Giese of Wisconsin became the first documented person to survive rabies without being given a vaccination! A bat bit the 15-year-old girl in September 2004.

Chopper Bike

Believe it or not, Las Vegas stunt rider Johnny Airtime once jumped his motorcycle over the spinning blades of four helicopters!

Speed Jumping

Forty-seven-year-old Jay Stokes from Arizona made no fewer than 534 successful parachute jumps in 24 hours at Lake Elsinore, California, in November 2003. With the help of three pilots working in two planes in rotating two- to three-hour shifts, he was able to average just under 2 minutes 45 seconds per run.

BOONTHAWEE SEANGWONG and Kanjana Kaetkeow tied the knot on Valentine's Day on February 14, 2006 at Pattaya beach resort in Thailand. The highlight of the Thai wedding, complete with chanting monks, centipedes, and scorpions, was that the "wedding room" took the shape of a coffin. The bride's 32 days spent in a plastic cage with 3,400 scorpions in 2002 can only be matched by the groom's 28 days in a cage with 1,000 centipedes in 2003.

SIMPLY

UNBELIEVABLE

SouNds CRaZy

IF KEN BUTLER'S COLLECTION of musical instruments doesn't strike a chord with some listeners, it's hardly surprising. Ken dismisses conventional instruments in favor of the toothbrush violin, the golf-club sitar, or the hockey-stick cello.

New Yorker Ken created his first hybrid instrument in 1978 by adding a fingerboard, tailpiece, tuning pegs, and a bridge to a small hatchet, which he then played as a violin. The success of his ax violin led him to create more than 200 additional wacky instruments from such diverse objects as bicycle wheels, umbrellas, shotguns, and snow shovels. He usually chooses objects that are of roughly similar shape or proportion to the instrument that they then become.

The American musician and visual artist, who studied the viola as a child, has seen his creations displayed in museums and galleries in Peru, Europe, and Tokyo, as well as in several Ripley's museums. In 1997, he released an album—*Voices of Anxious Objects*—and he has performed with ensembles playing 15 of his instruments.

Ken can conjure up a tune out of just about anything. Here he demonstrates his prowess playing the bicycle wheel.

Musician Ken Butler, surrounded by some of his wacky instruments, including a hockey-stick cello in the top row.

To decide what would make a good instrument, Ken Butler seeks out objects that are relatively strong, but also relatively lightweight, and that allow for the placement of tuning pegs and strings.

Lightning Conductor
With Carl Mize, lightning doesn't just strike twice—it's struck four times already! In 2005, Mize was hit for the fourth time, while working on the University of Oklahoma campus. Mize was hospitalized for four days before being discharged.

Bulletproof Case
British manufacturers have devised a special bulletproof briefcase. If the user is fired at, the brown leather case can be flipped open and used as a shield able to withstand handguns up to a .44 Magnum.

Pumpkin Paddlers
Howard Dill grows pumpkins partly for their seeds and partly for carving out for racing. He cultivates an oversized variety of pumpkin called Atlantic Giant, and after selling the seeds he donates the hollowed-out fruit for use in the famous annual pumpkin paddling regatta at Windsor, Nova Scotia, Canada. In the 2005 event, 40 competitors paddled their way across Lake Pesaquid while sitting in pumpkins that weighed more than 600 lb (272 kg). The winner usually manages to get round the course in about 10 minutes.

Mitch Maddox, of DALLAS, Texas, legally changed his name to "DotComGuy" and lived for an *entire year* by buying everything he needed off the Internet!

Lifted Car
Despite fracturing her spine and damaging two vertebrae in a car crash near Washington, England, Kyla Smith managed to lift the one-ton car—about 20 times her own weight—6 in (15 cm) off the ground in the attempt to free her trapped friend.

Uninvited Guest
When Beverly Mitchell returned to her home in Douglasville, Georgia, after two weeks' holiday, she discovered that the lights were on and a strange car was parked in her driveway. Another woman, a stranger, had moved in, redecorated the rooms, and was even wearing Mitchell's own clothes.

Flying Nun
Madonna Buder has definitely got the triathlon habit. As well as being a Canadian record-holder and Ironman legend, she leads a quieter life as a Roman Catholic nun. Now in her seventies, Sister Madonna, from Spokane, Washington, has completed well over 300 triathlons. She took up running in 1978. Before entering her first Boston marathon, she sought permission from the local Bishop to take part.

Mind-bender
Magician Paul Carpenter, from Houston, Texas, performs the art of psycho-kinetics, or metal bending, wowing audiences across the United States.

Strong Boy

When Rique Schill, from Jamestown, North Dakota, was pinned under the family Ford in 1984, his nine-year-old son Jeremy lifted the 4,000-lb (1,814-kg) car despite weighing only 65 lb (30 kg) himself.

Caught on Camera

Michael Adams, from Manchester, England, chose an unwise target to rob—a shop specializing in security cameras. His raid was caught on eight different CCTV cameras!

Car Plunge

In 2004, a car containing four teenage girls plunged over a 108-ft (33-m) cliff in Britain and flipped over three times before landing upright on rocks just a few feet from the swell of a raging sea. Incredibly, the girls' worst injury was a broken ankle.

Static Spark

In 2002, Bob Clewis, 52, of San Antonio, Texas, survived a gas station explosion after a simple spark of static electricity from his jacket ignited and engulfed him in flames.

Long-life Bread

Vivien Anderson from Cambridgeshire, England, holds a bread roll that dates from World War I! It was given to her grandfather in a ration pack while he was serving in the conflict. Handed down through the family, the roll is estimated to be about 90 years old.

Ice Fall

Although it was a warm summer's day, a cricket match near Faversham, England, was interrupted in 2005 when a huge chunk of ice fell from the sky and exploded onto the field. At the time, the sky was cloud-free and there were no aircraft in sight.

Perfect Present

Helen Swisshelm received the best Christmas present in 2001—a class ring that she had lost 53 years earlier! She last saw the gold-and-onyx ring in 1948 while swimming with friends in the Hudson River near her home in Cohoes, New York. She gave up hope of ever seeing it again until, over half a century later, she received a call at her home in Lutz, Florida, from a nun at the Catholic school she had attended in Albany. A man with a metal detector scouring the Hudson had found a 1948 class ring bearing the school's shield and, via initials on the ring, the nuns matched the year and letters to Mrs. Swisshelm.

High and Dry

A seal was left high and dry when he found himself stranded on top of a post off the coast of Scotland. He had to wait nine hours before the tide came back in sufficiently for him to roll back into the water.

Bullet Surprise

After waking up with a headache, swollen lips, and powder burns in June 2005, Wendell Coleman, 47, of Jacksonville, Florida, went to hospital, where doctors found a bullet embedded in his tongue. Coleman didn't even know he'd been shot.

House Spared

A houseowner in California must be the luckiest in the world. When the fires that devastated 663,000 acres (268,300 ha) of southern California in 2003 reached the wealthy suburb of Scripps Ranch, 16 mi (26 km) from San Diego, flames destroyed every house in the street except one.

Smoking Nest

Fire chief Donald Konkle, of Harrisburg, Pennsylvania, decided that a house fire had been started when a bird picked up a smoldering cigarette while building its nest!

Two Lauras

In June 2001, when Laura Buxton, from Staffordshire, England, released a balloon at her tenth birthday party, it traveled 140 mi (225 km) before being found in Wiltshire, England, by another ten-year-old girl, Laura Buxton! Not only did the girls share the same name and age, but they discovered they also had the same hair color and owned the same kinds of pet— a dog, a guinea pig, and a rabbit.

When **Harry Dillon**, aged 71, sent out a letter addressed with **nothing** but a former comrade's **name** and a **guessed city**, the British ex-soldiers were **reunited** after **50 years**!

Missing Pen

In 1953, Boone Aiken lost his engraved fountain pen in Florence, South Carolina. Three years later, while in New York City, Mrs. Aiken spotted a pen on the street next to their hotel. It was the lost one.

Wallet Recovered

When James Lubeck's wallet slipped from his pocket into Marblehead Harbor, Massachusetts, in 1966, he never expected to see it again. But in August 2005, he heard from Antonio Randazzo, who had hauled in the wallet's collection of credit cards in a netful of cod, flounder, and haddock 25 mi (40 km) away from where Lubeck had lost it.

Same Birthday

Four generations of one family from Brisbane, Australia, share the same birthday—August 1. Norma Steindl was born on August 1, 1915; her son Leigh on August 1, 1945; Leigh's daughter Suzanna on, August 1, 1973; and Suzanna's son Emmanuel on August 1, 2003.

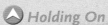
Holding On

Skydiver and sky-surfer, Greg Gasson regularly performs amazing stunts in the air. Here he hangs precariously over Eloy, Arizona, holding on by only one strap of his parachute, thousands of feet above the ground.

Christmas Cheer

When Matilda Close was born on Christmas Day 2003, in Victoria, Australia, believe it or not, she was the third generation of her family to be born on December 25! Her mother Angela and her grandmother, Jean Carr, were both born on Christmas Day.

Heart-stopper

While remodeling his bathroom in 2005, Nigel Kirk, from Burton-on-Trent, England, came within 0.04 in (1 mm) of dying after accidentally shooting himself in the heart with a nail gun. As he worked, 53-year-old Nigel slipped and managed to fire a 2-in (5-cm) steel tack straight into his heart. Luckily, the tack hit hard scar-tissue that had built up from an illness he had suffered from 30 years earlier and just missed his vital heart vessels.

Chewing Chalk

Rena Bronson, of Macon, Georgia, has a weird food craving—she eats chalk every day! She has been devouring chunks of the white clay called kaolin since 1992. Although it has made her constipated, she says that she likes the creamy consistency in her mouth.

Desert Ordeal

Max, a one-year-old golden retriever, survived after spending 3 weeks and 3 days stranded in the Arizona desert in 2005. Max ran off after his owner Mike Battles's truck was involved in a road accident. The dog was eventually found lying under a bush.

Double Birth

Twins Mary Maurer and Melanie Glavich gave birth to sons 35 minutes apart in 2005. They had the same due date, May 27, but both sisters went into labor early. They delivered in adjoining rooms at the same hospital in Middleburg Heights, Ohio.

HEADLESS FOWL

ON SEPTEMBER 10, 1945, farmer Lloyd Olsen chopped off 5½-month-old Mike's head with an ax in readiness for the cooking pot, but the headless rooster continued pecking for food around the farm at Fruita, Colorado!

Olsen visited Los Angeles, San Diego, Atlantic City, and New York working the sideshows with his "Wonder Chicken" Mike.

Olsen decided to spare Mike and began feeding him grain and water with an eyedropper. Although most of Mike's head was in a jar, part of his brain stem and one ear remained on his body. Since the majority of a chicken's reflex actions are controlled by the brain stem, Mike was able to function relatively normally.

Over the next 18 months, the chicken's weight increased from 2½ lb (1.1 kg) to 8 lb (3.6 kg) and, insured for $10,000, Mike toured the U.S.A. as the "Wonder Chicken," with Lloyd charging 25 cents for a peek. Finally, he choked on his way back from an appearance in Arizona. Olsen was unable to find the eyedropper used to clear Mike's open esophagus and Mike died.

Mike the Headless Chicken would "peck" for food and "preen" his feathers, just like the other chickens on the farm.

Surprise Mail

Former Polish soldier Karol Brozda, 79, now living in the Czech Republic, holds up a letter he sent to his parents from a U.S. prison camp in France in February 1945, assuring them that he was alive. His parents received the letter in March 2005!

Brozda's letter took a staggering 60 years to arrive.

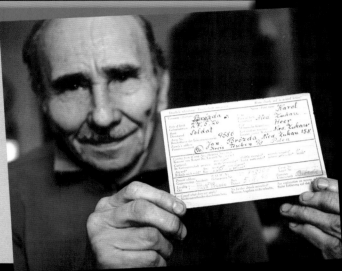

Croc Attack

Shelly Hazlett has had 29 operations since being savaged by a huge crocodile during a show at her uncle's croc park in Australia. When Shelly slipped in mud, the reptile clamped its jaws on her lower torso and let go only when her father gouged out its eyes.

Magnetic Power

Erika zur Stimberg is irresistible—to forks, spoons, and frying pans, which for the past 12 years have been flying toward her and sticking to her body. Doctors, in Brakel, Germany, are at a loss to explain her magnetism.

Insect Invasion

In November 2004, tourists holidaying in the Canary Islands, which lie off the northwest coast of Africa, received a shock when they were joined on the beach by a swarm of approximately 100 million pink locusts. Many of the migrating insects didn't live long enough to enjoy the scenery, however, having suffered broken legs and battered wings while crossing the sea in high winds and heavy rain.

Unwanted Gifts

Horst Lukas, of Iserlohn, Germany, was sent 12 bicycles, four boats, a mobile home, and dozens of tickets for rock concerts after a hacker spent $500,000 on eBay using his name.

Fruit Fight

Every year, villagers at Ivrea in northern Italy re-enact a medieval battle by dressing up as soldiers and pelting each other with oranges!

Bendy Bodies

Contortionists with the State Circus of Mongolia perform extraordinary feats by bending their bodies into seemingly excrutiating shapes. Their limbs and joints are so flexible that they are able to bend into extreme positions.

Favorite Drink

A family in Cheshire, England, are so addicted to the fruit-cordial drink Vimto that they have a subterranean tank of the stuff in the garden. Pipes carry the liquid from the tank to the kitchen, where it is available on tap.

Experiencing **blurry vision**, **Patrick Lawler**, of **DENVER**, Colorado, went to a **dentist** in **January 2005**, only to learn that he had **shot** a **4-in (10-cm) nail** through his mouth into his skull with a **nail gun!**

Shrimp Shower

It rained shrimp on Mount Soledad, California, in April 2005. Hundreds of the tiny crustaceans fell from the sky during a storm. Experts said that juvenile shrimp frequently gather together in large numbers in shallow water during rough weather out at sea and that they had probably been carried inland by a sea spout.

Angel Camera

Laurie Robinson is no ordinary photographer. She likes to take pictures of tombstones in cemeteries in Los Angeles, California. And when she has her prints developed, ghosts and angels mysteriously appear in the photographs. She believes that the spirits show up in her pictures because of the positive energy she sends out.

Crushing Blow

Two men escaped from a Kentucky jail in 2005 and hid in a garbage truck—only for their bodies to be discovered in a nearby landfill the following day. The jailbirds hadn't realized that, to prevent exactly this kind of escape, the prison requires that all garbage be compacted twice before it leaves the grounds.

Lion Guard

Believe it or not, a 12-year-old Ethiopian girl owes her safety to a pack of lions. The girl was abducted in June 2005 by seven men who wanted to force her into marriage, but the kidnappers were chased away by three lions that amazingly then stood guard over the girl for at least half a day. A police sergeant said: "They stood guard until we found her and then they just left her like a gift and went back into the forest. Everyone thinks this is some kind of miracle." A wildlife expert suggested that the girl's crying might have been mistaken for the mewing sound of a cub, which would explain why the lions didn't eat her.

▶ Not Strictly Ballroom

MS DanceR is a robotic dance partner that has been manufactured in Japan. The robot's memory holds the waltz pattern, predicting the next step of the dance and following a human lead, but it can also sense pressure in its arms and back in order to stay in sync with its human partner.

Shocking Experience

A man built up at least 30,000 volts of static electricity in his jacket simply by walking around the Australian city of Warrnambool, Victoria, in September 2005. Frank Clewer left a trail of scorch marks, carpet burns, and molten plastic behind him.

MUSICAL MAESTRO
Mort Mortensen of New York could perform two different piano pieces on two pianos, at the same time. At his peak, he could do this trick blindfold with a cloth over each keyboard and wearing gloves.

ARMLESS HUNTER
Despite being born without either of his arms, J. Oscar Humphrey became the best bird-hunter in the state of Arkansas.

ALL BUTTONED UP
Professor Leo Kongee could sew buttons to any part of his body, including his tongue, as seen here, as well as put skewers through his chest, cheeks, and ears. This photograph was taken in 1932.

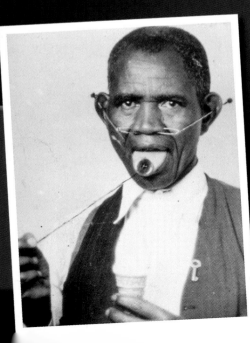

BACKWARD HOOLA
At the age of just ten, Joyce Hart, of New Jersey, could do a backward somersault through two hoops.

CORN LADY
In 1938, Virginia Winn, of Texas, stitched 60,000 grains of corn onto an evening dress, one by one. The gown weighed 40 lb (18 kg).

TIGHTROPE FLYER
Aviator Gus Manhart got himself stuck on some high-tension wires shortly after take-off, but, luckily, he was able to climb out unharmed.

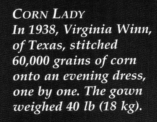

WATER-LOGGED
A tree spouting water was found in Fort Defiance, Virginia. This photograph was taken in 1932.

Looking Back

January 26, 1917 **Matilde Kovacs** burned her 500 million kronen legacy the day before she died just to spite her heirs. **October 20, 1927** **Susan D. Marcich**, of Chicago, lost all her hair in one night—she had gone to sleep with a full head of hair, but when she awoke there was no trace of it. **May 14, 1849** **Black rain** fell over an area of 400 sq mi (1,036 sq km) in Ireland.

◄ **Ghost Radar**
This pocket-sized gadget aims to help people avoid "other-world" spirits. Shown here being used in a Tokyo cemetery, it claims to detect "unknown energies, ghosts, and spirits," by sensing tiny variations in magnetic turbulence, light, and temperature, and then giving position and movement. Instructions contain details on eight types of specter that range from harmless lost souls stuck in this world to evil spirits.

Dozed Off

A cargo plane circled for more than half an hour in March 2005 because an air-traffic controller at Nice Airport, France, had fallen asleep.

Old Neighbor

Gilbert Fogg of Nettleham, England, discovered that his neighbor Tom Parker was actually a long-lost comrade from World War II, whom he thought had died in battle!

Bail Blunder

After being arrested for possession of counterfeit money in 2005, fraudster Darrell Jenkins from Springfield, Massachusetts, tried to pay his $500 bail using fake notes!

Dog's Dinner

A man from Schaarbeek, Belgium, set his apartment on fire in April 2005 after trying to cremate his pet dog on a barbecue and using too much gasoline!

Tea Thief

A man who stole a tractor-trailer truck in Washington State in 2005 had to call 911 for medical help after drinking from a cup he found in the cab. What he thought was a refreshing drink was in fact the truck driver's tobacco spit!

Happy Accident

Eddie May Jr., of Georgia, choked on a piece of food while driving, blacked out, then hit a passing car. The impact knocked the food from his throat and he awoke uninjured!

Pot Shot

While sitting on the toilet in April 2005, an off-duty Texan police officer accidentally shot a man. Officer Craig Clancy was answering a call of nature in San Antonio when his gun fell from its holster as he pulled down his pants. In trying to catch the gun, he grabbed the trigger and fired two bullets, one of which went through the cubicle wall and grazed the leg of a man who was washing his hands at the time.

▶ King of Cubes

Believe it or not, 14-year-old Shotaro Makisumi, of Japan, can solve a "3 x 3 x 3" Rubik's cube puzzle in a mere 13.72 seconds.

Incriminating Evidence

After ordering a pizza and asking for a job application form, a man suddenly produced a gun and robbed a Las Vegas pizza parlor of $200 in June 2005. But police didn't have to do much detective work to catch him. He left behind the partially completed form, which included his name and address.

IN DEPTH
The Great Escape

The Dark Master of Escape, Canadian Steve Santini, 42, also known as "The World's Most Extreme Escape Artist," puts the fear back into escapology with his blend of heavy metal and medieval torture.

How did you become interested in escapology?

"I did a book report for school on Houdini, and then started to experiment on my own. There were no instruction books—my parents kept getting calls: 'Your kid's jumping into our pool wrapped in bike chains.'"

How did it develop?

"I broke out of my first jail cell at a police station when I was 14 (I was put in there voluntarily!). I used to buy up old cuffs and locks, rip them apart, and see how they worked. I didn't know trick locks existed—I just learned how to defeat normal mechanisms."

Have you ever feared for your life during a stunt?

"On New Year's Eve 2005, when I performed the Cremation Chamber. It was watched by an audience of 35,000 people and 15 million live on television—the most ever to witness a single escape. I was in a vault with walls just one-eighth of an inch thick, and I was handcuffed and padlocked to a chain welded inside the door. On three sides of the vault were propane flame throwers—I was supposed to be out within one minute, when the temperature hit 400°F and the air became unbreathable. But one of the cuffs jammed, and I had to hold my breath until I could break free."

What other escapes have you performed?

"Lots—my favorites include escaping from a nailed and padlocked coffin submerged under 30 ft of water, and breaking out of a maximum security cell on Canada's Death Row, which had held the last man to be publicly hanged in that country."

What makes your shows different?

"I got tired of the image of escapologists in the glitzy suit in Vegas. I wanted to remove the magic from it—by doing all escapes in full view of the audience. What really grabs people has to involve pain and danger. I use sinister heavy-metal music to play that up."

Why "Dark Master"?

"I came up with that not because I'm Satanic or because I'm portraying an evil person, but because I'm facing devices from people's nightmares, from the darkest periods of human history. I combine modern technology—like being pulled towards a chain saw—with ancient devices, like thumb screws and iron maidens."

Do you use hypnotism or contortionist techniques?

"I'm not a contortionist—I'm not a svelte guy! I use hypnotism techniques to focus. But it basically comes down to extreme stubbornness and an incredibly high pain tolerance."

Do you get nervous beforehand?

"Terribly. Every time I do these things, there's genuinely the chance that something will go horribly wrong. Once you're in, you can't panic though—if you do, you're done."

Are you working on any future projects?

"I want to be stretched on a medieval rack and have that lowered under water. No-one's ever got off a rack, let alone a submerged one. No, I'm not a masochist—I just know what will make people go 'whoa!'."

Black Spot

In 1966, Christina Cort narrowly escaped death when a truck smashed into her home in Salvador, Brazil. She was still in the same house 23 years later when another truck crashed through the wall— driven by the same man.

Train Spotting

★ Russian Vladimir Rasimov drank so much vodka that he fell asleep between train tracks and didn't wake up even when a 140-ton cargo train passed over him.

★ A Jack Russell terrier named Sam survived after being hit by a train in Cheshire, England.

★ In 2002, a train driver delayed hundreds of passengers for over an hour near Birmingham, England, after admitting he didn't know the route.

Potato Ring

Forty years after losing her wedding ring in a potato field, a German farmer's wife found it again while eating—it was inside a potato!

⬆ Screen Damage

When four horses broke out of their field in Hausen, Germany, in April 2003, only three survived. One horse was killed instantly when he raced across the road and was hit by a car, crashing through the windscreen. Miraculously, the 26-year-old driver was unhurt.

In the Stars

Born in 1835, the year of Halley's comet, U.S. writer Mark Twain said that as he had come into the world with the comet, so he would pass with it. The comet returned in 1910 and Twain died that April, aged 74.

⬆ Perilous Putt

Harold Parris, who has been playing golf regularly for 55 years, made the mistake of teeing off without his glasses in April 2005. Parris managed to land the ball on the back of an alligator while playing a round at the Robber's Row golf course, South Carolina!

Clip Chain
Eisenhower Junior High School in Taylorsville, Utah, is a school with a difference. The pupils have a habit of setting themselves amazing challenges. On March 26–27, 2004, the students created a "Mega Chain" that measured 22.17 mi (35.68 km) long and used 1,560,377 paper clips. They took 24 hours and divided the team into different roles to achieve this incredible feat.

Dog Train Ride

When Archie the black Labrador became separated from his owner at a Scottish railway station in 2005, he decided to take the train, not only choosing the right one, but also getting off at the correct station! When the Aberdeen to Inverness train pulled in to the station, Archie, having lost sight of his owner and perhaps fearing a long walk home, trotted aboard. The clever dog got off 12 minutes later at the next stop, Insch, his local station.

Delayed Revenge

In 1893, Texan Henry Ziegland jilted his girlfriend, as a result of which she killed herself. Bent on revenge, her brother shot Ziegland in the face, but the bullet only grazed him before lodging in a nearby tree. A full 20 years later, Ziegland was using dynamite to uproot that same tree when the explosion blasted the bullet from the trunk. The bullet struck Ziegland in the head, killing him.

Bermuda Triangle

While riding a moped in Bermuda in 1975, a man was killed by a taxi. A year later, his brother was killed riding the same moped after being hit by the same taxi, driven by the same driver. The taxi was even carrying the same passenger.

A **baby** hurled from a car during a MASSACHUSETTS road accident in 2004 went **flying through the air,** landed on the **pavement,** and was nearly struck by another car, but **miraculously survived** with just a few bruises.

Elvis Relics

Among the many Elvis Presley relics that have sold on eBay are a branch from a tree ($900) and a hanging plastic fern ($750), both from his Graceland home, and a ball from his pool table ($1,800). However, a tooth said to be from Elvis's mouth failed to sell when no one bid the asking price of $100,000.

Wave Rider

Brazilian surfer Serginho Laus achieved a lifetime's ambition in June 2005 when he rode one continuous wave for 33 minutes, and a distance of 6.3 mi (10.1 km). He was able to ride the wave up the mouth of the Araguari River in northeast Brazil thanks to a "bore" created by a change in the tides.

Underwater Mail

The island nation of Vanuatu in the Pacific Ocean has opened the world's first underwater post office, which is manned by postal workers in diving gear!

Super Seller

Bargain hunter Suzie Eads, of Rantoul, Kansas, has sold so many items on eBay that she has been able to build a house for her family with the proceeds. She has auctioned more than 17,000 items altogether, including a discarded beer can for $380. She even drives with the licence plate EBAY QUN.

ShiNinG ExAmPLe

THE AVERAGE LIGHTBULB lasts no longer than 1,000 hours. But a carbon filament bulb has been burning in the fire department at Livermore, California, for more than 100 years!

Since being installed in 1901, the four-watt bulb has burned through the birth of powered human flight, women being granted the vote, two world wars, space exploration, 19 U.S. presidents, and 25 Olympic Games. Visitors come from as far away as South Africa and Sweden to check out the famous

Such is the worldwide interest in the Livermore lightbulb that it has its own official website, complete with a live webcam that allows browsers to see that it is still burning.

bulb. Engineers attribute its longevity to a combination of low wattage and filament thickness.

What makes its survival all-the-more remarkable is that before a local reporter uncovered its history in 1972, Livermore firefighters often batted it for good luck as they clung to the side of the departing fire truck. It has also experienced countless near

misses from footballs and Frisbees. Now it is treated like a precious stone. As Tim Simpkins, Inspector with the Livermore-Pleasanton Fire Department, says: "I don't want to be on duty when and if it ever goes out."

Appropriately, the town slogan—adopted in the 1920s because of the area's clean air—is "Live Longer in Livermore."

| Wright Brothers Flight 1903 | Ford Makes Model-T 1908 | Television Invented 1927 | Nuclear Age Begins 1945 | Pres. Kennedy Assassinated 1963 | Pres. Nixon Resigns 1974 | PC's Sold By IBM 1981 | Internet Growth 1993 |

Flagpole Raised 1906 · WW I 1914 · Women Get The Vote 1920 · WW II 1941 · Disneyland Opens 1955 · Man Lands On The Moon 1969 · Titanic Found 1985 · Berlin Wall Falls 1989

Light Bulb Installed 1901 · Livermore 1st Rodeo 1918 · Stock Market Crashes 1929 · Lawrence Livermore Lab 1952 · Woodstock & Altamont 1969 · Lightbulb Moved 1976 · LPFD Formed 1996 · Lightbulb Century 2001

1901 — 1920 — 1940 — 1960 — 1980 — 2001

As the world's oldest-known working lightbulb, when the Livermore fire department bulb was moved to its new home in 1976, it was handled with the greatest care. The bulb was granted Code 3 status and transported with truck lights flashing and sirens wailing.

Animal Artist
Koopa the turtle, owned by U.S. artist Kira Varszegi, has sold more than 100 pieces of his own artwork. He creates the paintings by covering his underbelly in paint and sliding around on a canvas. The works usually sell for around $135 a piece.

Shot by Dog
Bulgarian hunter Vasil Plovdiv was shot by his own dog in 2005 when he tried to knock a bird out of its mouth with the butt of his rifle. The German pointer refused to drop the quail and instead leaped at Plovdiv, knocking the trigger and peppering his chest with shot.

Poetic Justice
After two U.S. thieves stole a checkbook from the home of Mr. and Mrs. David Conner, they went to a bank with a $200 check made out to themselves. The female teller asked them to wait a minute, then called security. The teller was Mrs. David Conner.

Heavy Breathing
Three police cars raced to answer an emergency at a house in Lake Parsippany, New Jersey, one night in August 2005, only to be told by the owner that she had been teaching her German shepherd dog to make 911 calls. The 911 operator heard only "heavy breathing."

Tight Squeeze
Contortionist Hugo Zamoratte—"The Bottle Man"—can dislocate nearly every bone in his body and squeeze into a bottle!

Smith Party
In Vermont, all 57 of the David Smiths listed in the state's phone books got together for a "David Smith Night!"

Bright Spark
After locking himself out of his still-running car in Glen Burnie, Maryland, in 2005, an 82-year-old man had the idea of stopping the engine by removing all the gasoline. Unfortunately, he used an electric vacuum cleaner to siphon the fuel and when a spark ignited the vapors he was taken to hospital with burns.

Church Afloat
In 2003, the 2,000-sq-ft (185-sq-m) Malagawatch United Church was moved by water and road 20 mi (32 km) to its new home in Highland Village, Iona, Nova Scotia.

Hidden Bullet

For 25 years, Adrian Milton of New York had a bullet in his skull but didn't know it. He remembered an incident back in 1976 when blood had suddenly spurted from his head, but he always assumed that he'd been hit by debris from a building site. In fact he'd been shot in the head. His secret emerged in 2001 during a routine visit to the doctor.

Cash Flow

Two motorcyclists lost $20,000 in cash in 2005 when their backpack burst open on a highway near Winchester, England. Although drivers stopped to help, strong winds blew the notes across the road and only a small portion of the money was recovered.

Physicists from **MANCHESTER, England**, and **CHERNOGOLOVKA, Russia**, have created a *flat fabric* called "*Graphene*," which is only **a single atom thick**!

What's in a Name?

Even by the standards of Martha Stewart's colorful career, the U.S. kitchen goddess came up with a moment to remember in September 2005. On her TV show, she gathered no fewer than 164 Martha Stewart namesakes. They included Martha Stewarts who were married to men with equally famous names—a Jimmy and a Rod—and even a bulldog named Martha Stewart.

Head Space

Karolyne Smith, of Salt Lake City, Utah, offered her forehead for sale on eBay as the site for a permanent, tattooed advertisement. The winning bid of $10,000 was made by the Golden Palace online casino.

Body Talk

Believe it or not, an Indian man lived with his mother's corpse for 21 years. Syed Abdul Ghafoor kept the embalmed body of his mother in a glass casket at his home in Siddavata and even consulted the corpse before making important decisions.

Future Vision

One of the most popular crazes in Las Vegas is the "morph booth," where as many as 300 couples a day line up to see what their virtual reality child would look like. The fotomorphosis machine merges you and your partner's images to produce a supposedly accurate simulation of any future offspring. Some couples are reportedly using the machine before deciding whether or not to get married!

Toad Toxin

Dogs in Australia's Northern Territory are getting high by licking toxins from the backs of cane toads. Local veterinarian Megan Pickering said that some dogs were becoming addicted to the hallucinogens and she had treated more than 30 that had overdosed on bufo toxin.

Drawbridge Drama

A 79-year-old grandmother had an incredible escape in 2005 after she was left dangling 100 ft (30 m) in the air from a drawbridge. Retired teacher Helen Koton was crossing a canal in Hallandale Beach, Florida, when the drawbridge began to rise. She clung on to the railing as the bridge rose to its full height, leaving her hanging in the air, her handbag swinging from her ankle. Drivers alerted the bridge operator, who lowered Helen back to the ground.

Two-headed peacock
This two-headed peacock was raised on a farm in Texas, and lived to be almost two years old. It was taxidermied by Tim Dobbs of Midland, Texas, in 2003. Ripley has yet to perform DNA testing to determine if the two heads do indeed belong to the same bird.

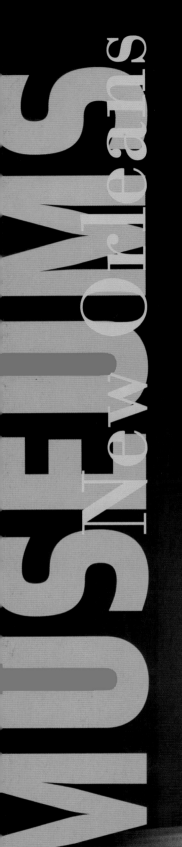

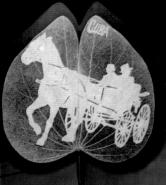

TOBACCO LEAF
An image is etched onto the skeleton of this tobacco leaf.

HAVING SURVIVED the terrors of Hurricane Katrina relatively unscathed, this museum located in New Orleans' historic French Quarter is now open. It features a display on JFK's killer, Lee Harvey Oswald, that includes a lock of his hair and his mortuary toe tag.

LION COFFIN
The man for whom this coffin was created in Ghana was especially proud of his hunting prowess.

SKULL BOWL
Made from the skull of a Tibetan monk, this bowl was used by monks to drink from.

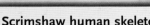

DON'T MISS!

- Scrimshaw human skeleton
- Mortician's toe tag with hair lock from the body of Lee Harvey Oswald
- Camel bone carving
- Matchstick London Tower Bridge
- Mummified head of American cannibal Alferd Packard
- Giant tire

LOUIS ARMSTRONG
This portrait of the jazz artist is made up of 21,000 individually cut crystals.

O-KEE-PA TORTURE RITE
The Mandan held a festival each summer to placate the spirits by practicing self-mutilation.

CHINESE SLIPPERS
These 19th-century "Golden Lily" slippers were made for women with bound feet.

ASSASSINATION CAR
Lee Harvey Oswald was a passenger in this car on the day of President Kennedy's assassination. On the back seat, wrapped in papers, lay the $12 rifle that he used to shoot Kennedy.

VAMPIRE KILLING KIT
A 14-piece traveling vampire killing kit used in Europe in the 19th century.

ROTATING TUNNEL
In this interactive room, the eye deceives the brain into thinking the floor is moving.

Mountain Fall
Martin Tlusty from Prague, Slovakia, was climbing with friends in 2005 when he lost his footing, slipped, and fell 1,000 ft (305 m) down the side of a mountain. He escaped with just cuts and bruises.

Rope Jumper
James Thompson from Willow Glen, California, can jump rope while bearing the weight of four adults on his back! He can also jump rope both in a squat position with a 170-lb (77-kg) person on his back, and in a standing position with a 250-lb (113-kg) person on his shoulders.

Frazzled Cat
When a cat climbed a 40-ft (12-m) power pole to reach a bird's nest in 2005, it got a nasty electric shock. Yet despite plunging from the 25,000-volt pole in Gardnerville, Nevada, and sparking a fire that left its fur singed from head to toe, the frazzled cat survived.

Brace Yourself
An English teenager discovered in 2004 that he had been living with a broken neck for at least ten years. Liam Careless was told by doctors in Manchester that just one push in that time could have killed him.

First Word
After a 1984 Arkansas car crash left him paralyzed and in a coma, Terry Wallis lay silent for 19 years. Then, in June 2003, aged 39, he came out of the coma and spoke his first word since the accident—"Mom."

Deadly Dream
While away for the weekend in April 2005, Chicago schoolteacher Charisse Hartzol had a dream that foretold her death. Worried, she packed her bags and headed for home. Halfway there, her car was involved in an accident and she died.

Deep Blue Sea
The Poseidon Undersea Resort is a new hotel in the Bahamas where you can spend $1,500 a night on a room that is situated 65 ft (20 m) below the sea. Alternatively, you can rent Poseidon's Lair—a two-room private bungalow "hung" over the edge of the aquatic shelf and accessible only by submarine. The $20,000 room rate includes a private submarine captain and a butler.

Weighty Problem
Steven Newell, of London, Ontario, Canada, was hospitalized in 2005 after putting his wading pool, which was 8 ft (2.4 m) in diameter, on the balcony of his house and filling it with 640 gal (2,423 l) of water. The balcony collapsed under the 2½-ton weight.

Explosive Laundry
Daphne Jones, of Great Yarmouth, England, went to work leaving her washing machine on. The vibrations from the spin cycle knocked over a can of spray paint, followed by a pair of scissors, which punctured the can. The can was then ignited by the furnace, causing an explosion that tore the roof off the house.

Woolly Wonder
A sheep was found alive after being buried in a snowdrift for 50 days in the Scottish highlands in 1978.

Feet First
A 26-year-old Croatian woman fell 40 ft (12 m) from her apartment window in Zadar in 2005, but survived after landing on her feet.

Cypriot **Kively Papajohn**, 76, was **trapped** in an elevator from **December 28, 1987,** to **January 2, 1988**. She survived by *eating the food* in her **shopping bag**.

What a Sucker!
Fleeing with a case of brandy from a liquor store in Buffalo, New York, in 2005, Thomas L. Hunter dropped the case, shattering the bottles on the sidewalk. He was arrested when he returned to the scene of the spillage and began sucking up the brandy with a straw!

PickLed DraGoN

The dragon was actually built by BBC model makers and turned out to be part of an elaborate publishing hoax.

SCIENTISTS AT BRITAIN'S Natural History Museum could hardly believe their eyes in 2003 when confronted with a pale baby dragon, preserved in a jar of formaldehyde.

The dragon had apparently been discovered by David Hart, the grandson of a former museum porter, during a garage clear-out in Oxfordshire.

Accompanying the find were documents suggesting that the dragon had originally been offered to the Natural History Museum in the late 19th century by German scientists, but that the museum had rejected it as a hoax.

While modern scientists began to re-examine the tale, it emerged that the 19th-century museum curators were right—the dragon was a hoax. But, the current story was also a hoax! Hart had invented it in order to promote a novel written by Allistair Mitchell. The dragon had been made for a BBC TV series *Walking With Dinosaurs*.

Hoaxers claimed that the dragon was more than 100 years old, and was preserved in a jar of formaldehyde.

Dancer the Dog

The latest craze for America's dog owners is "doggie dancing." Although essentially a fun event, competitors take it very seriously, with judges rating the couples on technical merit and artistic impression. "You need to go from move to move with flow and transition," says Patie Ventre, seen here with Dancer.

The dogs are allowed to wear a decorative collar during their dance routines.

Long Overdue

A book was returned to a Californian library in 2005—78 years late! Jim Pavon said he discovered the copy of Rudyard Kipling's *Kim* in a box belonging to his late aunt, who had borrowed it from a library in Oakland in 1927. The library waived the fine of around $600, which had accrued on the overdue book.

False (Teeth) Alarm

Three years after losing his dentures in a fall, a Taiwanese man discovered in 2005 that they had been stuck in one of his bronchial tubes all the time. The 45-year-old complained to a doctor of breathing difficulties, leading to the discovery of the missing dentures.

▶ Knitted Art

The Canadian artist Janet Morton's Domestic Interior, *a piece that includes this knitted telephone and table, is just one of her hand-knitted wool creations. In another work, entitled* Cozy, *she covered a cottage situated on Toronto Island in more than 800 recycled sweaters!*

Nice Surprise

When a landslide destroyed Albert Trevino's home in Bluebird Canyon, California, in 2005, all he had time to salvage was his passport, a few important papers, and his wife's favorite painting, which she had bought for under $100 in a garage sale back in the 1980s. However, the 74-year-old later learned that the rescued painting was in fact a $500,000 masterpiece by U.S modern artist Joseph Kleitsch!

Sting for your Supper

A Chinese man not only catches wasps, he also eats them! Zhong Zhisheng, from Shaoguan City, does not charge people for removing wasps nests from their homes, on condition that he is allowed to take the insects home and fry them.

Corn Zeppelin

In August 2005, a church in British Columbia, constructed an airship made entirely of popcorn! Members of Prince George's First Baptist Church used 2,865 lb (1,300 kg) of popcorn kernels (and a similar amount of syrup to hold them together) to create an airship 20 ft (6 m) high. The pre-made moulds for the body, nose, 10-ft (3-m) long wings, and 3½-ft (1-m) barrel-shaped engines needed two forklifts and a tower of scaffolding to move them.

Grab a Grape

Whenever Steve Spalding opens his mouth, there's a fair chance a grape will drop into it. "The Grape Guy" from Carrollton, Texas, specializes in catching as many as 60 grapes a minute in his mouth, usually thrown by his brother Scott. Steve is deadly serious about his art. When he first met his wife Denise, he got her to drop grapes into his mouth from the 22nd floor of the Sahara Hotel in Las Vegas, Nevada. His ambition is to catch a grape dropped from the top of Las Vegas's towering Stratosphere Hotel—a distance of around 900 ft (274 m).

Extra Fingers

Devender Harne, an 11-year-old boy from Nagpur, India, has a total of 25 fingers and toes. The five extra digits are functional and normal in size and do not prevent Devender playing his favorite sport of cricket.

Twin Tragedies

In March 2002, Finnish twin brothers, aged 71, were killed in identical bicycle accidents along the same road, two hours apart. Both men were hit by trucks, the second twin's fatality occurring half a mile from the first's.

When stranded in the **Andes**, **Leonard Diaz** from Colombia was **rescued** after a phone company employee called him on his **expired cell phone** to ask if he wanted to **buy more time**!

Yak-skiing

Yak-skiing is the new extreme sport that is catching on in Manali, India. A person on skis stands at the foot of a hill holding a bucket of nuts while attached by a long rope fed around a pulley to a yak at the top of the hill. When the bucket is rattled loudly, the yak charges down the hill, yanking the skier up the slope.

Desperately Seeking ...

The Lutheran Church of Landeryd, Sweden, put a "wanted" ad in a local newspaper asking for churchgoers.

Ironic Theft

Among items stolen from All Souls Church in Peterborough, England, in July 2005, was a 2-ft (0.6-m) high statue of St. Anthony of Padua, who is the patron saint of lost and stolen items.

Name Check

On business in Louisville, Kentucky, in the late 1950s, George D. Bryson registered at room 307 at the Brown Hotel. When he jokingly asked if there was any mail for him, the clerk gave him a letter addressed to the previous occupant of the room, another George D. Bryson!

Totally Barking

Mark Plumb, aged 20, of Houma, Louisiana, was arrested in August 2005 after he allegedly ran barking from a house and bit the local mailman on the shoulder.

▶ Playing with Food

The Vienna Vegetable Orchestra is seen here performing in London, England, at a concert that included only vegetables! Formed in 1998, the orchestra consists of musicians playing instruments made almost exclusively of vegetables.

Sniff and Tell

A German telecommunications company is presently developing the world's first cellular phone that will alert users when their breath is bad!

Timely Delivery

After accidentally locking herself out of her home in Berkeley, California, in 1974, Mrs. Willard Lovell tried several ways to get back in. Just when she was about to give up, the mailman arrived with a letter from her brother who had stayed with her a few weeks earlier. In the letter was a spare key that he had forgotten to return before he left.

Pig Saviour

Joanne Altsman owes her life to Lulu, her Vietnamese pot-bellied pig. When Joanne suffered a heart attack while on a trailer home holiday on Presque Isle, Pennsylvania, in 1998, Lulu squeezed out of the trailer's dog flap, pushed open the gate and waddled out into the middle of the road where she lay on her back with all four trotters in the air to stop the first passing car. Sure enough, a driver stopped, followed Lulu back into the trailer and found Mrs. Altsman semi-conscious. Doctors later said Joanne would have died within 15 minutes but for the pig's actions. Lulu received a bravery award and a big jam doughnut.

▼ Lick Art

Fifty-year-old Wang Yide from Jianyang, China, uses his tongue and fingers to make paintings. He is one of the few artists still making traditional Chinese paintings using this method.

Hidden Mineshaft

When Pete Taviner offered to repair an uneven kitchen floor at a media training center in Bristol, England, in 2001 he discovered an old 40-ft (12-m) deep mineshaft under the linoleum. The floor had rotted away and the only thing covering the hole was the linoleum.

Registered Hair-do

The "comb-over," in which a partially bald person grows hair long on one side and then combs it over the bald spot, is a U.S. patented invention!

Shock Factor

The Great Voltini, Welsh electrocution artiste Sebastian Vittorini, 39, loves nothing more than sending half a million volts of electricity through his body until lightning shoots from his fingers.

How did you become interested in electricity?

“ I saw a cabaret act with an electric chair and I was fascinated to know how it worked, so I started building one myself. It went from there! ”

What is your most famous act?

“ The 'Lightning Man' act. I stand or sit on top of a huge Tesla coil—a 14ft-high column of wire named after its inventor Nikola Tesla and made by manufacturer HVFX. It transforms electricity into about half a million high-frequency volts— my body basically becomes a human conductor, and sparks and lightning strands shoot out through my fingertips. ”

Does it hurt?

“ Actually, when you do it right, it's a pleasant kind of tingly feeling. It's only when you do it wrong that it hurts. ”

What are the dangers involved?

“ When you get it wrong, your muscles contract involuntarily, which is very unpleasant—it's the same effect as when a person who has got an electric shock is thrown across the room. It can also cause cardiac arrest—people have died doing this kind of act. Long-term, it can cause partial paralysis owing to long-term nerve damage. ”

Why do you take the risk?

“ So far, I've been shocked only a few times and had minor burns from the sparks. The most frightening thing is that when I'm on the machine, I can't control it myself—so my safety is in someone else's hands. But when I'm doing it, it's amazing. The lightning strands are constantly waving about in front of me. It's the most beautiful thing I've ever seen—I absolutely love it. ”

Why doesn't the shock kill you instantly?

“ It is believed that the frequency is so high—300 kHz as opposed to the 50 Hz of regular household electricity—that the nerves can't sense it, like you can't hear a dog whistle. It would kill me if I was in a complete circuit—if a bolt of lightning connected with something grounded, like a curtain rail, I would die instantly. ”

Do you do other work with electricity?

“ My show features lots of electricity and static stunts—I spend quite a lot of time electrocuting my beautiful assistant Nurse Electra, who is also my girlfriend! I can light a gasoline-soaked torch with the sparks from my hands—I've done that one on national television. ”

Has it ever got you into trouble?

“ In the early days I practiced on machines in my kitchen. When I was building my first coil, I got a knock on my door from my next door neighbor —it had destroyed his computer. ”

What will you do next?

“ I'm working on a character called Sir Voltalot for a show loosely based on the Arthurian legends. He will use a huge Tesla coil and electricity to rescue damsels in distress and find the Holy Grail. ”

▶ Amazing Meditation

In December 2005, Ram Bahadur Bomjon, aged 15, from southern Nepal, claimed to have mastered the art of meditation to such an extent that he had gone without food and water for more than seven months. He plans to meditate for six years to achieve enlightenment.

Unlucky Clover

Despite spending more than half his life in U.S. jails, George Kaminski has collected nearly 73,000 four-leaf clovers. He found all of them in the grounds of various Pennsylvania prisons, but when he was moved to a minimum-security facility in 2005, he was horrified to find that there were no clovers to be found anywhere in the grounds. Kaminski feared that his great rival, Edward Martin Sr., a retiree of Soldotna, Alaska, would seize the opportunity to expand his own collection of 76,000 four-leaf clovers.

Night Stalkers

★ Ian Armstrong from Cheshire, England, got up to mow the lawn in the middle of the night while sleepwalking.

★ Stephen Hearn crashed his car at 70 mph (113 km/h) while sleepwalking near Birmingham, England. When he was found, he was in his pajamas and still snoring.

★ Sleepwalker Thomas Manninger climbed out of the first-floor window of his house in Eltville, Germany, shimmied up a drainpipe, and walked across the roof. Upon waking up, he lost his balance and fell 20 ft (6 m) to the ground.

Slice of Fortune

A slice of singer Justin Timberlake's half-eaten French toast (complete with fork and syrup) sold on eBay for a staggering $4,000.

Mad Leap

A man was injured in 2005 when he jumped from a car traveling at 60 mph (96 km/h) in an effort to retrieve a cigarette that had blown out of the passenger-side window. Jeff Foran suffered trauma to his eyes, nose, and chin.

Bank Folly

Thomas E. Mason was charged with robbing a Winona, Minnesota, bank in June 2005, having been arrested nearby and identified by bank staff. The main evidence against him was his hold-up note, which began: "Hi, I'm Thomas Mason."

Park Patrol

In an incredible feat of endurance, Christopher Calfee, a 38-year-old schoolteacher from Richmond, Virginia, ran around a park for nearly 92 hours in September 2005 without stopping for sleep. For four days and four nights he lapped Chesterfield's Pocahontas State Park. Apart from a three-hour halt to recover from the effects of dehydration, Calfee's only other breaks were for food at the end of each 25-mi (40-km) stint. But he never slept during the 316-mi (508-km) run. The pain was so intense that he had to protect his blistered toes with duct tape.

Packed Church

Canadian bride Christa Rasanayagam didn't exactly want her wedding in Ontario in 2004 to be a quiet affair. She was accompanied up the aisle by no fewer than 79 bridesmaids, aged from one to 79, who jostled for room with the groom's 47 best men.

Bumpy Landing

A German driver who was using an airport runway to practice high-speed driving had a lucky escape in 2005 when a plane landed on his roof! The 55-year-old Porsche driver was traveling at more than 100 mph (160 km/h) near Bitburg when the bizarre collision occurred.

In 2005, Sasha Gardner advertised a **bucket of seawater** from BOURNEMOUTH, England, *for sale* on eBay at $100. A London man **snapped it up** within a week.

Short Term

Believe it or not, there was a man who was president of the U.S. for just one day! When James K. Polk's term ended at noon on Sunday, March 4, 1849, and his successor, Zachary Taylor, refused to be sworn in until the following day, David Rice Atchison, the president pro tem of the Senate, technically ruled the country in the intervening period. Asked what he did on that historic day, Rice admitted that he mostly slept after a succession of late nights.

▶ Human Dart Board

Evgeny Kuznetsov, from Dzerzhinsk, Russia, set himself up as a human dartboard in Moscow in January 2006. Darts were hurled at his back—amazingly, without drawing a drop of blood.

Young at Heart

Although she is an impressive 96 years old, Peggy Barrett regularly takes to the skies in a glider. She and other 90-and-over pensioners from Gloucester, England, have formed the Gliding Nonagenarians.

Peggy in her glider at the Cotswold Gliding Club, England.

Niagara Plunge

In October 2003, Kirk Jones, of Canton, Michigan, went over Niagara Falls without safety equipment and lived. Tourists saw Jones float by on his back in the swift Niagara River, plunge over the 180-ft (55-m) Horseshoe Falls on the Canadian side, then drag himself out of the water onto the rocks below.

Parachute Ahead

Parachutist Maria Ganelli, aged 40, had a fortunate escape in August 2005 when she landed in the middle of Italy's busy Adriatica Highway. She had planned to come down in a nearby field, but gusting winds pushed her off her chosen course and stunned drivers were forced to swerve to avoid hitting her.

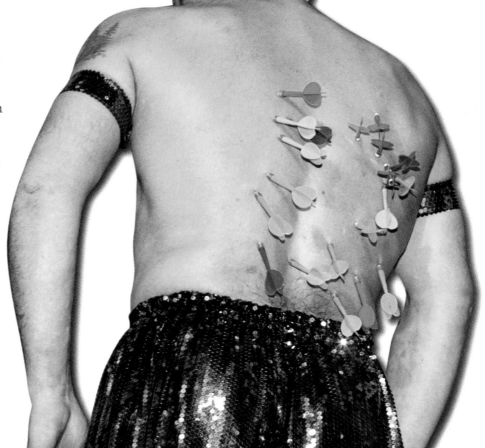

THE ANNUAL LEMON FESTIVAL in Menton, France, is a world-famous carnival with a difference. All the decorations and carnival floats are constructed out of lemon and orange sculptures. An incredible 500,000 elastic bands and 130 tons of citrus fruits are used each year with more than 300 people spending 20,000 man hours to get the festival ready for its opening day.

THE FINAL

A hotel room was redecorated using 1,000 lb (454 kg) of melted cheese
page 235

The only car to be seen driving around Venice is a floating wooden Ferrari
page 240

Leon, a pet two-year-old lion, is taken on a leash for a daily walk out on the streets
page 242

Charlie a 17-year-old chimpanzee is a black belt at karate
page 244

RECKONING

Full of ENteRprise

TONY ALLEYNE has boldly gone where no interior designer has gone before by converting his apartment into a replica of the starship *Enterprise*.

Star Trek fan Tony, from Hinckley, England, watched hours of *Star Trek* videos to help him recreate the transporter console from the *Enterprise.* When he was unable to find a home for it, he redesigned his apartment to accommodate it.

Between 1999 and 2004 he worked to give the small apartment a futuristic feel, complete with voice-activated lighting, realistic console panels, and an infinity mirror above the toilet. Where most people have a bedroom, Tony has a replica of the transporter unit that beams crew members to far-flung locations. Speakers in the rooms replay sound effects from *Star Trek*, and there is a cardboard cut-out of Patrick Stewart as Capt. Jean-Luc Picard, the commander from *Star Trek: The Next Generation.* "If you're going to do something, you have to go all the way," says Tony.

Tony and the cardboard cut-out of Capt. Jean-Luc Picard in his main living room space, which also houses his transporter console.

Every detail, from this screen, which faces into the kitchen, to the windows of the apartment, follows the Star Trek theme.

Tony in his converted kitchen, complete with futuristic white units and specialist lighting underneath the cupboards.

These panels show Alleyne's amazing craftsmanship, as well as his fidelity to the Star Trek original.

TACTICAL/SECURITY

◄ **Pencil Passion**
Emanuel Petran, aged 62, from the Czech Republic, has collected an amazing 3,333 pencils over almost 30 years. He plans to combine his collection with another to form a museum dedicated to the graphite wooden pencil.

Horn Haul

A Chinese pensioner can lift up to 14 bricks with a "horn" that has grown on his forehead. When doctors told him that they couldn't operate on the tumor—which is 2 in (5 cm) long—because of its location, 74-year-old Wang Ying decided to incorporate it into the strong-man act he had been performing since the age of eight. He lifts the bricks by means of a length of rope looped around the protruding facial growth.

Sketch Wizard

George Vlosich III, of Lakewood, Ohio, produces detailed portraits of famous people—from The Beatles to baseball star Mickey Mantle—all on an Etch-a-Sketch®. He spends up to 100 hours on each picture and sells the best as unique works of art. He has even had an Etch-a-Sketch® signed by President Clinton.

Human Robot

A Japanese company has enabled human movement to be operated by remote control. A headset sends a low-voltage current through the wearer's head, affecting the nerves that help maintain balance.

Full Facial

Three teams of scientists, from the U.S.A., France, and Egypt, have created incredibly detailed facial reconstructions of the ancient Egyptian king, Tutankhamun. The teams each built a model of the young Pharaoh's face based on approximately 1,700 high-resolution images taken from CT scans of his mummy. They reveal what King Tut looked like on the day he died nearly 3,300 years ago. The scans, which are the first ever of an Egyptian mummy, suggest that he was a healthy, yet slightly built 19-year-old, standing 5 ft 6 in (1.67 m) tall.

Escape Relay

In October 2005, more than 50 escapologists in different venues from Australia to California took part in the Worldwide Escape Artist Relay—the largest ever coordinated performance by escape artists. One of the most daring feats was that of Paul Sautzer (a.k.a. Dr. Wilson) who, in Mount Desert Island, Maine, escaped from a combination of padlocks, manacles, and chains, and an iron collar called the Chrysalis.

Boy Racer

While his father was in a shop buying a chocolate bar, three-year-old Oliver Willment-Coster, of Bournemouth, England, managed to release the handbrake of the family car, take the car out of neutral gear, and steer it one-handed down the street, until he smashed into a parked police van.

Oliver had been strapped into the passenger seat of his father's car when he managed to drive off.

Field Trials

Nova Scotia farmer Andrew Rand proposed to his girlfriend by hopping onto a tractor and using a harrow to carve the words "LISE MARRY ME" in huge letters in a rye field. His efforts probably inspired Chris Mueller from North Dakota to use a plough to pop the question to Katie Goltz in a soybean field. He had almost finished his message when he realized there wasn't enough room for all the letters. Fortunately, "Katie will you M-A-R-Y me?" still won her heart when she viewed it from the air.

Married 162 Times

Believe it or not, a 75-year-old Bosnian man claims to have married 162 times—and counting! Nedeljko Ilincic says he first got married when he was 15 and since then it has been "just one wife after another."

▲ Lawful Wedded Dolphin

In 2005, Sharon Tendler married Cindy the dolphin at a special ceremony in Eilat, Israel. She got down on one knee and gave Cindy a kiss and a piece of herring. Sharon met Cindy 15 years ago and has since visited the dolphin two or three times a year.

Hanging Around

Scottish artist David Mach has definitely got the hang of sculpture—he makes lifelike models out of wire coat hangers! First he makes a plastic mold of the model shape, around which he shapes the coat hangers. Each coat hanger is individually formed and bent, then welded several times to its neighbor. He leaves the hooks protruding out to create a ghostly fuzz around the object, which he says gives the final sculpture a kind of aura and makes it more enticing to look at.

Depressing Date

Psychological researchers in the U.K. claim that January 24 is the most depressing day of the year.

A TOKYO department store has a pair of slippers inspired by the **Wizard of Oz.** They glisten with **690 rubies** and are worth **$2 million!**

Odd Love

When political activist Regina Kaiser was arrested at her Berlin apartment in 1981 and taken to the Communist Stasi security police headquarters for questioning, she feared the worst. However, to her surprise, she fell in love with her interrogator, Uwe Karlstedt, and the couple are still together 25 years later.

▶ A Lot of Hot Air

Hot-air balloons prepare to take off (left) at an air base in Chambley, northern France, on July 23, 2005. The 261 balloons lined both sides of the road as they aimed to float into the air at the same time—and in a line.

Tenpin Pong

For the bowler who can sniff victory, Storm Products, based in Brigham City, Utah, manufactures a range of scented bowling balls, including cinnamon, orange, amaretto, and cherry. They cost between $150 and $250.

Ice-cream salesman **Derek Greenwood**, of **ROCHDALE, ENGLAND**, had a **funeral cortege** that consisted of **12 ice-cream vans** all playing jingles on their way to the cemetery!

Surprised Patriarch

Mick Henry of Yorkshire, England, discovered at the age of 59 that he is a tribal chief of the Ojibway Tribe of Manitoba, Canada.

Big Order

After Gita, a 47-year-old Asian elephant, resident at Los Angeles Zoo, California, had infected portions of a toe removed from her left front foot in September 2005, orthopedic shoemaker Cesar Lua was asked to create a boot to keep the wound clean while it healed. Working from photographs and measurements supplied by the zoo, Lua took a full 12 hours to craft the $450 circular shoe. Made mostly of brown leather, ½ in (1 cm) thick, the finished shoe measured 53 in (135 cm) in circumference and 19 in (48 cm) in diameter. It was held to the elephant's ankle by means of a strap.

Alcatraz Swim

A nine-year-old boy succeeded in 2005 where many before had failed—by escaping from Alcatraz. Johnny Wilson, from Hillsborough, California, swam 1.4 mi (2.2 km) from the island to San Francisco in less than two hours in October 2005 to raise money for the victims of Hurricane Katrina.

Hippo Sweat

In 2005, Professor Christopher Viney, of the University of California, collected and studied hippopotamus sweat, hoping that the ingredients would help develop new human sunscreens!

WOLF BOYS

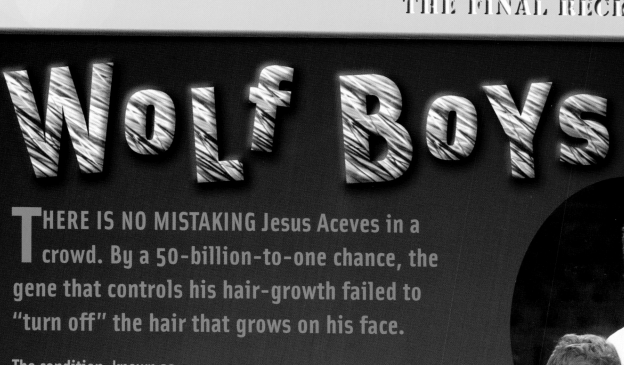

THERE IS NO MISTAKING Jesus Aceves in a crowd. By a 50-billion-to-one chance, the gene that controls his hair-growth failed to "turn off" the hair that grows on his face.

The condition, known as hypertrichosis (meaning "extra hair"), has left his face covered in dark hair and has earned him the nickname "The Wolf Boy." The condition is hereditary— 24 members of his family have had it, including his sister, and his great-uncle, Manuel the Wolf Man. Although unable to get a regular job in his native Mexico, Jesus has traveled the world with circuses and sideshows. He considers his hirsute appearance to be a gift from God and mostly enjoys the attention he receives for it. "I like it when children look at me in wonderment," he says. "It makes me feel like a star."

Larry and Danny Ramos Gomez, who also suffer from hypertrichosis, are performers in the Mexican National Circus.

A rare genetic condition means that Jesus Aceves has his face covered in dark hair, earning him the nickname of "The Wolf Boy."

⏶ Ear Hole
Venezuelan tattoo-artist Constantino has stretched his earlobe so much that he can place a shot glass in it.

Screw Loose
When Etienne Verhees, from Antwerp, Belgium, started coughing in October 2005, he coughed up a metal screw! It was one of four screws that had been used to hold a metal plate in place in his neck after he had broken two vertebrae falling from a ladder in 2001. Doctors said that the screw must have moved following an infection.

> Linda Dagless and **Brad Wheeler,** of NORWICH, ENGLAND, named their baby daughter "**Ikea**" after the Swedish furniture company!

Potter Potty
Fifteen-year-old Harry Potter fan Sandra Luchian, from Moldova, spent over a month of her 2005 summer vacation writing out the latest book, because she couldn't afford to buy it. She borrowed a copy of *Harry Potter and the Half-Blood Prince* from a friend and wrote down the 607-page story word for word in five notebooks.

Giant Bunny
Visitors to a northern Italian mountain could be forgiven for thinking they were seeing things. In 2005, a huge pink rabbit was erected on the side of the 5,000-ft (1,524-m) high Colletto Fava mountain. The soft toy, which is 200 ft (61 m) long, is expected to stay in place until 2025, and was designed by Austrian artists.

Dead Chrysler
Angry because his car wouldn't start, a Florida man pulled out a gun and shot it! John McGivney, 64, fired five rounds into the hood of his Chrysler outside his home in Fort Lauderdale. When startled neighbors asked him what he was doing, he calmly replied: "I'm putting my car out of its misery."

Touch Test
A blind German woman can distinguish between colors simply by touch. Gabriele Simon, from Wallenhorst, uses her fingertips to recognize the different colors of various items of clothing. She says it has taken her 20 years to master the skill, which gives her greater independence, as she no longer has to ask her mother what to wear.

⏶ Free-falling
"Jump for the Cause," a nonprofit organization that specializes in skydiving fund-raisers, succeeded in performing an amazing 151-person formation skydive. The skydivers were made up of women from 24 different U.S. states, 15 different countries, and varied occupations.

Greedy Thief
A 308-lb (140-kg) thief, who ransacked a pie store near Fagaras, Romania, was caught after getting stuck on his way out. When the owner arrived to open the store the following morning, he found a pair of legs hanging out of the window!

Fake Cow Stolen

Believe it or not, a full-size, fiberglass cow was stolen from a roadside billboard in eastern Virginia, in October 2005. One of a pair valued at $3,200, the 500-lb (227-kg) black-and-white cow was removed from the billboard along Interstate 464 in Chesapeake.

Love Letters

Every year, in the build-up to February 14, the tiny post office in the small Texas town of Valentine becomes one of the busiest in the world. Postmaster Maria Elena Carrasco and her lone part-time assistant suddenly have to deal with a flood of mail as more than 7,000 romantics, from all corners of the globe, dispatch cards to be stamped with the postmark of Valentine.

Queasy Rider

Millard Dwyer from Pulaski County, Kentucky, was fined $225 in 2005 for "driving" a horse under the influence of alcohol. Dwyer, who was stopped by police as he tried to steer his horse Prince around a street corner, was three times over the legal limit after downing a 12-pack of beer. Kentucky state law classes a horse as a vehicle.

Foxy Thief

After frolicking in the waves in the summer of 2005, beachgoers on Prince Edward Island, Canada, returned to the shore only to find that their sandals had been stolen—by a marauding family of foxes.

Unplanned Landing

On a forced landing, Mark and Mercedes Davies landed their single-engine plane atop a moving semi-truck before crashing onto the highway. Incredibly, both of them emerged unharmed!

Roses are Red

★ For Valentine's Day 2005, Brazilian teenager Frederico Skwara bought girlfriend Juliana Magalhaes a pregnant sheep called Waffle.

★ Special "flirt" carriages were created on the subway in Vienna, Austria, for Valentine's Day 2003 to encourage all single passengers to find love.

★ The most popular Valentine's gifts in China are not chocolates or flowers, but tropical fish!

Testing Times

Seo Sang-moon finally passed the academic part of his driver's licence examination in South Korea in 2005—on the 272nd attempt.

Walking Underwater

Lloyd Scott, from Rainham, England, completed a marathon underwater (26.2 mi/42.2 km) starting in Lochend, Scotland, in October 2003, while wearing a lead-booted early diving suit weighing 120 lb (54 kg). It took him 12 days to finish the walk emerging at Loch Ness.

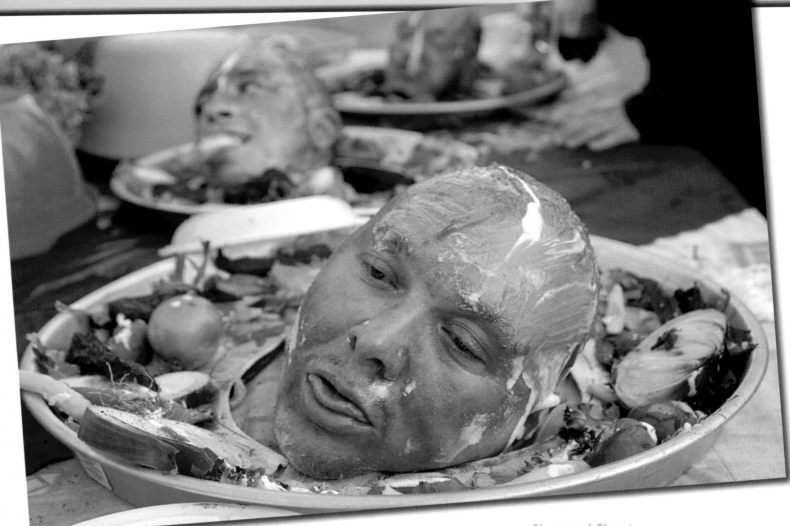

▲ Served-up Heads!
Villagers dressed as heads on plates during the New Year's Carnival in the village of Vevcani, Macedonia, in 2006. The 1,300-year-old carnival features the villagers performing in a variety of events.

Whopper Chopper
Mark Henry is altogether a little young to be long in the tooth. But the nine-year-old Canadian stunned dentists with a top right front tooth that measured nearly 1 in (2.5 cm) long. Dr. Gabriela Gandila of Owen Sound, Ontario, who had to pull out the tooth, said it was like a horse's.

The Quicker Flicker
In August 2005, Sheeshpal Agarwal was officially declared the fastest dentures remover in India. The 51-year-old can remove and reinsert his teeth with a single flick of his tongue 176 times in 5 minutes.

Wide Awake
Silvio Jarquin Rostran and Janeth Margarita Cerrato from Nicaragua won a no-sleep marathon in 2005 by staying awake for 51 hours.

Believe it or not, a **100-year-old** Belgian motorist, **Cyriel Delacauw**, was given an **insurance discount** in 2005 because he *hadn't* had an **accident** in more than **80 years** of driving!

Lying Low
A 6-ft (1.8-m) tall man on the run from police was found four months later in a bizarre hideout—curled up inside a TV set in a mobile home near Bainbridge, Georgia. The fugitive had escaped from Florida police in September 2004.

Cheerers' Chant
A man who left the scene of a road accident in Ann Arbor, Michigan, in August 2005, was tracked down, not by police but by local cheerleaders. Members of the Lincoln High School varsity cheerleading squad witnessed the crash, and turned the man's licence plate number into a cheer so that they would be able to remember it.

Car Possessed
We've all heard of cars being repossessed, but Christine Djordjevic is convinced that her car is possessed. In March 2005, the driverless vehicle started itself and reversed into a neighbor's home, at South Haven, Indiana, causing damage worth several thousand dollars. Police officers were sceptical of the story until they saw the 1995 Mercury Tracer Trio start itself again and head down the road. They stopped it before it hit anything.

GLowiNG PiGS

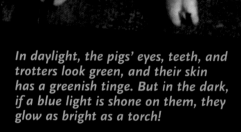

WHAT'S GREEN, grunts and glows in the dark? A Taiwanese pig, of course!

Scientists in Taiwan have bred three fluorescent green pigs by adding genetic material from jellyfish into normal pig embryos. Although other countries have created partially fluorescent pigs, these are the first to be green from the inside out. Even each pig's heart and internal organs are green.

DNA from jellyfish was added to around 265 pig embryos, which were implanted in eight different sows. Four of the female pigs became pregnant and gave birth to three green male piglets in 2005.

Two years earlier, Taiwanese scientists had created the world's first glowing green fish. Now researchers hope that the pigs will be able to help in the study of stem cell research to combat human diseases.

In daylight, the pigs' eyes, teeth, and trotters look green, and their skin has a greenish tinge. But in the dark, if a blue light is shone on them, they glow as bright as a torch!

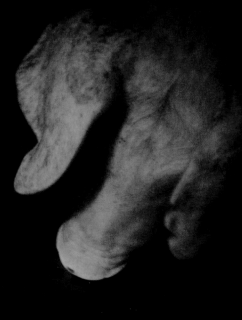

Making a Splash
Underwater hockey was invented in 1954 by field hockey players looking for a way to keep fit during winter. Here, a team from Roger Bacon High School in Cincinnati, Ohio, take on Michigan State University in a nationals match.

Isak and the Beanstalk
When nine-year-old Isak Spanjol planted a squash seed in the family yard in Brooklyn, New York, in 2004, he had no idea that it would grow into a monster plant. The rare species of gourd coiled around cable lines and stretched over fences into neighboring yards. Some of the vegetables hanging from it were 6½ ft (2 m) long, nearly 2 ft (0.6 m) bigger than the botanist himself!

Driving Green
Mali Blotta and David Modersbach drove 11,000 mi (17,700 km) from California to Argentina in 2004, in a station wagon that ran on recycled vegetable oil instead of gas!

Prize Pumpkin
When Ron and Sue Boor paraded their prize pumpkin at the 2005 West Virginia Pumpkin Festival, it took five men and a forklift to get it onto the scales! The Boors, who have been raising large pumpkins since 1990, had produced a 1,082-lb (492-kg) monster. At its peak, the pumpkin grew 35 lb (16 kg) a night and "drank" 198 gal (750 l) of water a day.

Self-healing
Pedro Lopez, a 39-year-old Mexican, amazed physicians by successfully performing complex surgery on himself. By inserting a needle through his navel, he drained fluid from his lungs that was hampering his breathing. Specialists described it as a miracle. "We do this kind of surgery draining liquid in small quantities," said one, "but this man drained three liters of liquid—and without anesthesia!"

Young Juror
Nathaniel Skiles, of Kirkland, Washington, has been summoned for jury duty three times in two years—and he's only six years old! The blunder occurred after his birthdate was listed incorrectly on a state identification card.

Jumbo Treadmill
Finding that Maggie, an African elephant, was 1,000 lb (454 kg) overweight, officials at Alaska Zoo introduced a specially made treadmill to help her exercise off the excess pounds. The treadmill is 20 ft (6 m) long, 8 ft (2.4 m) wide, and weighs 15,972 lb (7,244 kg). It is believed to be the first treadmill in the world built specifically for an elephant.

Ghost Guard

Dave Davison has one of America's most unusual jobs—he guards a bonafide ghost town. Built during the late-19th century by prospectors looking for silver and gold, Silver City, Idaho, is a ghost town in the winter. Its 40 homes (which are owned by summer vacationers) become deserted and the town is usually cut off by road from the outside world because of snow. As watchman, Davison thwarts thieves on snowmobiles to ensure that Silver City doesn't disappear from the map altogether.

Pretty in Pink

When 700 prisoners had to walk 2 mi (3.2 km) to be transferred from their old overcrowded jail to a brand new, bigger facility in Phoenix, Arizona, in 2005, Sheriff Joe Arpaio came up with a surefire way to prevent the convicts from escaping—he dressed them in fluffy pink underwear and flip-flops! He reckoned that the hardened criminals would simply be too embarrassed to run.

Late Mail

Evelyn Greenawald, of Anamosa, Iowa, received a postcard from her daughter Sheri in Germany in October 2005—27 years after it had been mailed. At the time of writing the postcard, Sheri was beginning her opera career in Europe. She now lives in San Francisco, California.

Cookie Lady

Merry Debbrecht, of Rose Hill, Kansas, has been baking up to 480 cookies a day and sending them to U.S. soldiers who are stationed in Iraq. By the summer of 2005, she had sent more than 30,000 cookies and said that she wouldn't stop until the war was over.

Seal of Disapproval

A man from Colorado was arrested in 2004 when he tried to board a plane at Logan Airport, Boston, Massachusetts, carrying the severed head of a seal. Security staff discovered the head in a small canvas cooler.

Bike Tree

Most people keep their Harley motorcycle on the driveway or in the garage. But Richard Woodworth keeps his in a tree outside his home in Raleigh, North Carolina. He insists that hanging the bike from the branches is art.

After a **television** belonging to **Chris van Rossman,** of **CORVALLIS, Oregon,** began emitting an international satellite **distress signal**, police and military rescue units showed up to save it!

Name Game

A man called Pete set up a website in 2005 with the aim of getting another 1,999 Petes to attend a gathering in London, England! Pete Trainor started his quest as a bet.

Flip-flop Sculpture
Australian John Dahlsen puts the finishing touch to his sculpture made from hundreds of flip-flops on Sydney's Bondi Beach in 2004 as part of the "Sculptures by the Sea" exhibition. Dahlsen scours Australian beaches for plastic objects washed up by the ocean to make into artworks.

WRITTEN IN SKIN
Rosa Barthelme of Kansas picked up the name "The Human Slate" because messages written lightly on her skin stood out and remained for about 30 minutes.

WHAT A HANDFUL!
Julius B. Shuster, of Pennsylvania, perfected the art of holding 20 baseballs in one hand!

OPEN PRISON
People of the city of Anna Maria, Florida, were so proud of their lack of crime that they bragged their jail had no bars, roof, doors, or windows.

LARGE LUMP
This 6,725-lb (3,050-kg) piece of solid coal from Dawson, New Mexico, was paraded proudly at a Cowboys Reunion on July 4, 1930.

CROSS-LOG SKIING
The log-packed Androscoggin
River was crossed in 1955 by
Kenneth Lambert on a pair of
snow skis.

FAMILY TRANSPORT
In 1938, the Harriman family rode
from Portland, Oregon, to Toledo,
Ohio, on a motorcycle. The total
weight of the four people and their
dog was 590 lb (268 kg).

WELL RISEN
In Ravenna, Kentucky, a well
that had previously been sunk
into the ground gradually rose
out of it. In 1932, it had risen
8 ft (2.4 m) above the earth.

OFFICE PET
Mrs. Brodie's boss, although a car
dealer by day, was also a game
hunter. Mrs. Brodie is pictured
here in 1941 with a tame lion that
her boss captured as a cub, and
whom she raised in her office.

Looking Back

April 29, 1927 **Bobby Leach,** who survived going over Niagara Falls in a barrel in 1911,
died from injuries received when he slipped on a banana skin while walking along the street.

December 2, 1927 Little **Marie Finster** jumped from the roof of a building and was saved
miraculously by falling into her mother's arms, who happened to be passing at that very minute.

Toilet Snake

Going to the bathroom will never be the same for Alicia Bailey of Jacksonville, Florida—not since she was bitten by a venomous snake hiding in her toilet bowl. As she lifted the toilet lid, a water moccasin bit her on the leg. She survived the ordeal, but admitted that she had become "toilet shy."

Hopelessly Lost

In 2005, three elderly U.S. ladies took 24 hours to get home after becoming lost on their 20-mi (32-km) journey home from church. What should have been a short drive to Upson County, Florida, turned into an A.P.B. from worried relatives, as 72-year-old Alice Atwater took Florence King and Ruthelle Outler on an unintentional detour through Birmingham, Alabama, and the Georgia cities of Atlanta and Macon.

Mature Mother

Adriana Iliescu, aged 67, claims to be the oldest recorded woman to give birth. A university professor and children's author, she is from Bucharest, Romania. Adriana gave birth to a daughter after doctors reversed the effects of the menopause and then used in-vitro fertilization and the sperm and eggs from younger people to impregnate her.

Adriana Iliescu with her one-year-old daughter Eliza Maria, on January 16, 2006.

Stop Thief!

Having cut through a security fence at a shop in Durham, North Carolina, in 2005, a thief stole 50 red, octagonal stop signs valued at $1,250. He was arrested after being spotted pushing a shopping cart filled with signs and trying to sell 16 of them for $28.

Blooming Great!

In Vienna, West Virginia, Brenda Wilson lovingly tends a rosebush that just won't stop growing. The bush was planted in 1966 and stands more than 16 ft (4.9 m) tall— over four times the usual height for a rose bush.

◀ Extra Tongue

Delores Whittington's cat is truly unique in the feline world. Not only was she born with five toes on each paw (hence her name Five Toes), but the black Burmese mix also has two tongues! Delores, from Dobson, North Carolina, noticed the twin tongues for the first time back in December 2004.

Hiss-terical

A woman was attacked by a 4-ft (1.2-m) long python while watching a movie at a cinema in the United Arab Emirates, in June 2005. A friend uncoiled the snake from the hysterical woman's leg and removed the serpent from the cinema. Both women continued watching the film.

Believe it or not, **Stormy,** a *groundhog* at CHICAGO'S BROOKFIELD ZOO, had braces fitted to his **lower teeth** in 2005 to enable them to grow straight and help him eat!

Odd One Out

Debby Cantlon, from Seattle, Washington, couldn't help noticing that there was something unusual about one of the pups being fed by Mademoiselle Giselle, her Papillon dog. The strange "pup" was actually an orphaned newborn squirrel, who was happily being allowed to feed from the dog right alongside its canine "brothers and sisters."

Big Knit

By the spring of 2007, Darlene Rouse hopes to have knitted a scarf that is a mile long! With help from a close-knit group of friends and family in Opelika, Alabama, she has been working on the inspirational Hope Scarf, a garment that will carry each knitter's name, along with a short, life-affirming message.

Mother Love

Reggie the hamadryas baboon was the star attraction at England's Paignton Zoo in 2005—but for all the wrong reasons. After being born with a normal covering of hair on his head, Reggie had it all licked off by his overly attentive mother, leaving one bald baby baboon!

Smoking Chimp

A chimpanzee at a zoo in China has finally managed to quit smoking—after 16 years of nicotine addiction. Ai Ai, a 27-year-old chimp at Qinling Safari Park, started smoking cigarettes given to her by visitors after her mate died in 1989. When a second mate died and her daughter was moved to another zoo, in 1997 the lonely Ai Ai began chain-smoking. Worried about her deteriorating health, keepers tried to get her to kick the habit by giving her earphones and allowing her to listen to music on a Sony Walkman. At first Ai Ai still squealed for cigarettes but, ultimately captivated by her new interest, she soon forgot about her smoking habit altogether.

▶ A Bit Cheesy!

Room 114 at the Washington Jefferson Hotel in New York City was redecorated by the artist Cosimo Cavallaro, in May 1999, using 1,000 lb (454 kg) of melted cheese! Cavallaro explained that he did it to show his joy for life. The installation of "cheese art" remained on display for a month.

Rock Champions

One of Canada's more unusual sporting events is the Rock Paper Scissors World Championships, held in Toronto. Although originally a children's game, there are now more than 2,200 members of the World Rock Paper Scissors Society, and players travel to Toronto from Oslo, Prague, Sydney, London, and all over the U.S.A. The victor collects $7,000 in prize money.

Hamster Power

A 16-year-old boy from Somerset, England, has invented a hamster-powered cellular phone! Peter Ash attached a generator to the exercise wheel of Elvis the hamster and connected it to his phone charger. He said: "Every two minutes Elvis spends on his wheel gives me around 30 minutes of talk time on my phone."

Lucky Jim

Jim McClatchey died 100 times on November 20, 2004, but still came back to life! Doctors at the Piedmont Hospital, Atlanta, Georgia, were stunned as McClatchey suffered repeated cardiac arrests needing immediate shock treatment. In the first hour alone, his heart stopped 50 times. He had to be shocked so frequently that he sustained second-degree burns to his chest.

Hard Cheese

A year after intentionally sinking 1,760 lb (800 kg) of cheese into the water off the Saguenay fjord, north of Quebec City, Canada, a cheese company finally gave up hope of its recovery when divers and high-tech tracking equipment failed to locate it to bring it back to the surface. Leaving the $50,000 cheese in 160 ft (50 m) of water for months was supposed to produce a unique flavor.

Jackpot!

Once jailed for lottery fraud, when freed, Romanian Stancu Ogica won $33,000 playing the lottery!

Christmas Bonus

In December 2004, Richard and Donna Hamann paid that month's electric bill for all of Anthon, Iowa!

Heart Beats

★ A human heart beats 100,000 times a day and during an average lifetime it will beat more than 2.5 billion times.

★ Blood pumped out from your heart travels 60,000 mi (96,560 km) around your body each day—that's 20 times the distance across the U.S.A. from coast to coast.

★ The human heart pumps about one million barrels of blood during an average lifetime—enough to fill more than three super-tankers.

Metal Skyline

Chinese artist Zhan Wang chose kitchen utensils as his medium to recreate London's urban landscape. He even included a dry ice machine to give the work an atmospheric London fog.

Junior Filmmaker

Nine-year-old Kishen from Bangalore, India, made history in 2005 by directing a full-length feature film. The movie is called *Care of Footpath* and is about slum children. Kishen has been acting since the age of four and has appeared in 24 movies and more than 1,000 TV shows.

Chat Tomb

Driven by a desire to speak to his late mother, Juergen Broether from Germany has devised a $1,940 mobile phone and loudspeaker device that can be buried next to a coffin. The device enables people to talk to the dead for up to a year.

Home Is Where Your Car Is

After being evicted from her London, England, home, Ann Naysmith lived in her car for 26 years. When health inspectors confiscated her old Ford, community members bought her a Mercedes!

Cannon Fodder

Missouri daredevil David "The Bullet" Smith, 28, calls himself a "human cannonball" and is blasted from his cannon 500 times a year worldwide.

How did you become a human cannonball?

My parents were circus performers and my father David Smith Sr. became a human cannonball himself more than 30 years ago. All of my nine siblings have done it, and when I was 17 my father said I was ready. A year or so later he hurt his back and asked me to stand in for him, and that was that.

What happens when you are "fired?"

I can't tell you how the cannon is ignited—it's a family secret. But there is a tremendous force on my body— 10 Gs, which is ten times my bodyweight. I start off at the bottom of the 34-ft-long barrel—before I get to the end I've already traveled 30 ft. I then go from 0 to 50 mph in a fifth of a second. The whole flight of about 150 ft takes under 4 seconds.

How do you land?

I fly about 80 ft up in the air, somersault, and land on my back in a net which is usually about 20 x 50 ft big.

What do you feel when you are in the air?

I'm very aware—it's like slow motion. I think about what direction the wind is hitting me from, where my netting is, whether I need to correct my flight path, if I have clearance of obstacles above, and below me. I even occasionally wonder what we're having for dinner! It all happens so fast, my mind's just along for the ride.

What unusual places have you been fired over?

I was shot over part of the Grand Canyon. I also shoot over Ferris wheels, and was once shot into slime for a world record. I stood in for Ewan McGregor in Tim Burton's movie Big Fish.

Who makes your cannons?

My father has built seven cannons himself. I'm just putting the wheels on my first. We've got cannons ranging from 18 ft long to 36 ft.

Does your father still perform?

Yes, he's 63. He was recently shot from Tijuana, Mexico, into the U.S.A.—the first person to be shot over an international border. He held his passport in his hands as he went. We also once performed in cannons side by side—I broke my father's previous distance record as I came out, and he landed one second later and broke mine. He holds the current record of 201 ft 4 in.

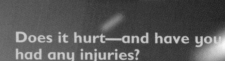

Does it hurt—and have you had any injuries?

It hurts your whole body. I've never missed the net—I wouldn't expect to live through that. I did blast a hole in the net once—I woke up eight minutes later surrounded by paramedics, but miraculously I wasn't badly injured.

Will your own young daughters follow you into the act?

My six-year-old isn't interested, but my youngest is nearly two and is a daredevil, so she might. Her mother would shoot me—but then she shoots me anyway: she pulls the trigger on the cannon!

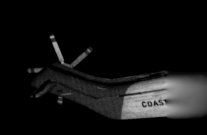

ONE OF RIPLEY'S latest museums, Key West opened in 2003. Among its varied unbelievable exhibits are a Jivaro Indian shrunken torso, once owned by Ernest Hemingway, and a portrait of Vincent van Gogh made from butterfly wings.

PHURBU DAGGER
Tibetan monks use these daggers to exorcise evil spirits.

RAMA STATUE
This Thai statue of Rama, a Hindu god, was set in rice fields to assure a good harvest.

DON'T MISS!

▶ Collection of multi-leaf clovers

▶ Giant tree climbing coconut crab

▶ Spiked torture chair

▶ Human bone rosary

▶ Toast art: "Adam" (from Michelangelo's Creation)

▶ Woman's bolero cape made from human hair

▶ A pair of gold lamé panties autographed by Madonna

▶ Three-legged chicken

prehistoric relative of the elephant—its tusks were up to 10 ft (3 m) long.

MATCHSTICK MODEL
Made by a prisoner serving a life sentence since 1979 in England.

FANTASY COFFIN
In Ghana, coffins reflect the status of the deceased. Paa Joe carved this lobster coffin.

GUMBALL PORTRAIT
Chewing one gumball a day, it would take you 27 years to chew the 10,000 gumballs used to make this portrait of Robert Ripley.

EXECUTIONER'S SWORD
Ripley brought this weapon from China where it was used to behead criminals.

CANNIBAL SKULL
Now extremely rare, cannibal trophy skulls used to be worn as amulets by warriors in New Guinea.

Wood You Believe It!

THE RESIDENTS OF VENICE are used to watching gondolas navigating the city's famous network of canals, but to see a Ferrari floating along the waterways is a different matter altogether.

But, this is no ordinary car—it is made entirely from wood, right down to the steering wheel, upholstery, and mirrors. The Ferrari F50 is one of several full-size wooden cars created by Italian artist Livio De Marchi, a man who combines skill, wit, and panache to design lifelike sculptures from wood.

This soft, leather flying jacket may look authentic, but it's actually made from the same material as the hanger—wood.

In De Marchi's bathroom is a wooden dress that has been "washed and hung up to dry."

De Marchi uses around a hundred different chisels and a 1964 wooden hammer to carve works of intricate detail. One of his first pieces was an enormous wooden hat in the style of origami, the Japanese art of paper-folding. The hat is situated alongside another of De Marchi's creations, a wooden dove of peace, in a park in Himeji, Japan.

Among his other wooden sculptures are a 26-ft (8-m) high vase, containing a dozen flowers, and a house of books, where hundreds of individually carved volumes line the shelves.

Everything in this wooden closet is made of wood—including the tie, hat, trousers, and a jacket, complete with lifelike creases.

In Livio De Marchi's "House of Books," the shelves hold hundreds of individually carved wooden books.

Livio De Marchi navigates the canals of Venice at the wheel of his wooden Ferrari. His other wooden cars include a 1937 Jaguar, a Fiat Topolino, a Mercedes, and a VW Beetle.

Lion on a Leash

Whenever Jaroslav Kana ventures out from his home in the Czech Republic, he takes a walk on the wild side. Accompanying him is his pet, Leon, who is a two-year-old lion! Jaroslav obtained the lion from a private breeder two years ago and has trained him so that he will perform in advertisements and TV shows.

Rotating Car

A new Japanese electric car could make parking problems a thing of the past. The Nissan Pivo, with its 180-degree rotating cabin, always faces forward—so there's no need to reverse!

Eyes Tight Shut

Trying to moisten her eyes in January 2005, 78-year-old Australian Terry Horder accidentally grabbed a wrong container and glued her eyes shut. Doctors were able to get them open and her eyes were unharmed.

Roller Ride

Richard Dickson, a 37-year-old father-of-five, won a new car in May 2005 by riding the "Twister Two" roller coaster at Denver, Colorado, for nearly 53 hours, in the process covering a total of 757 mi (1,218 km).

It's **not** only your car that goes in for a wash at a **Madrid, Spain,** gas station. A coin-operated **pet-washing** machine enables animals to get a *soapy wash and dry* for approximately **$5**.

Cat Theater

Yuri Kuklachev is founder of the Moscow Cats Theater, which boasts around 30 trained housecats in its company. The cats' tricks include front-paw stands, "tightrope" walking on a pole, and traversing the pole from underneath by grasping it with four paws.

Divorce Cake

Baker Georgius Vasseliou from Berlin, Germany, has introduced a new line at his cafe—personalized divorce cakes. To celebrate a split, he has devised cakes with a large smiley face or a torn up photo of the "ex" iced on the top. And with over 10,000 divorces a year in the city, he thinks he's on to a winner.

Artistic Ape

Tama Zoo Park, in Tokyo, Japan, has discovered a new talent among its residents. Gypsy, a 50-year-old orangutan, is just one of three orangutans who have taken to drawing with crayons. Her favorite colors are yellow and blue.

IN DEPTH
Jumping for Joy

Austrian B.A.S.E. jumper Felix Baumgartner, 37, has thrown himself off some of the world's most challenging structures—and has even mastered the art of flying.

What does B.A.S.E. mean?

"It stands for Building, Antenna, Span (or bridge), and Earth (or cliffs). You have to jump off all four, with a parachute, to register as a B.A.S.E. jumper."

How did you start?

"As a kid, I used to hang out at the airport watching the guys jumping out of airplanes, and as soon as I was 16, and could get my parachute license, I started skydiving. Ten years later, I made my first B.A.S.E. jump from a bridge in West Virginia, and a year after that I had become the first European to win the international championships."

What is the highest jump you have made?

"The Petronas Towers in Kuala Lumpur in 1999. At the time they were the highest buildings in the world, and hard to get into—my preparations took two months. I put my parachute and a hand-held camera in a little suitcase and sneaked to the 88th floor disguised as a businessman. I climbed onto a window-cleaning platform and jumped from 451 m—eight seconds in freefall at 170 km/h before the parachute opened."

What is the lowest jump you have ever made?

"The Christ the Redeemer statue in Rio de Janeiro. I saw it on a documentary and thought the right arm was far out over the mountain and that it would be a high jump—in fact I had just 29 m, which gave me only 1½ seconds to open the parachute. I didn't want to sneak up the inside stairs, so I used a crossbow to shoot an arrow over the right arm with a steel cable attached and pulled myself up. I stepped off the 25-cm wide hand and pictures of it went across the world."

When and where did you learn to "fly"?

"In 2003, I was the first person to "fly" across the English Channel unaided. I have always dreamed of flying—we spent years preparing, with a team of 40 people working on different types of wings. Eventually, we found the perfect wing—a 6-ft carbon-fiber fin—and I jumped out of a plane over Dover at 30,000 ft and "flew" 22 mi at speeds of up to 225 mph until I reached the other side."

Did you fear you might not make it?

"There was a big chance of losing my life if something went wrong with the oxygen tank I was wearing. At that altitude you need every breath, and if there's no oxygen you die in less than a minute. But I was well-prepared—I trained in a wind tunnel, and was even strapped onto the roof of a Porsche car speeding down an airport runway to see how it feels at that speed."

Was it the scariest thing you've done?

"No. That was jumping into the Mamet cave in Croatia's Velebit National Park. Usually I can see when I jump, but that was totally dark and I had to use an MP3 player to give a countdown of when I'd get to the bottom, 190 m down at 170 km/h."

What makes you jump—and how long will you carry on?

"I like to be in the air—it's like my second home. I have made more than 2,600 parachute jumps and 130 B.A.S.E. jumps, and I think I'll be doing it for a long while yet."

> ▶ **No Ordinary Chimp**
> Charlie the chimpanzee is a black belt at karate! The 17-year-old chimp, who weighs 200 lb (90 kg) and stands 4½ ft (1.4 m) tall, is seen here practicing with his owner Carmen Presti of Niagara Falls, New York.

Baby Driver
A four-year-old boy drove his mother's car on a late-night trip to a video store. Although he was too small to reach the accelerator, the boy put the car into gear and the idling engine took him to the shop 400 yd (370 m) away in Sand Lake, Michigan. Unfortunately, the video store was shut and on his return journey the youngster hit two parked cars, and then reversed into a police car. His mother said that he had learned how to drive the car while sitting on her lap.

Time Warp
A gas-station manager, in Lincoln, Nebraska, accidentally turned back the clock 50 years in October 2005 by selling premium gasoline for 32 cents a gallon instead of the usual $3.20. Drivers could hardly believe their luck as they pulled into Kabredlo's Convenience Store. The mistake with the decimal point was corrected after 45 minutes.

Satanic Turtle
For Bryan and Marsha Dora, Lucky the turtle is the devil in a half-shell. The only survivor of a fierce fire that killed 150 other animals at their pet shop in Frankfort, Indiana, in 2005, the red-eared slider turtle emerged from the inferno with the face of the devil on his shell. The heat gave the shell a new pattern, with Satanic eyes, lips, goatee, and devil's horns.

Flushed Fish
Some of the oldest public lavatories in Paris, France, have been transformed into havens of wacky chic by introducing live goldfish into the fake plumbing!

Lofty View
Katya Davidson has a different view of the world than most people—the 15-year-old walks about her house on 32-in (80-cm) stilts, jumps rope on a bouncy ball 3 ft (1 m) high, and unicycles down to her local grocery store in Roseville, California. Her love of circus apparatus began when she was aged nine, and she got her first unicycle for Christmas.

Street Skiing
Olympic ski champion Jonny Moseley helped transform one of San Francisco's streets into the venue for a king-of-the-hill contest in September 2005. Trucked-in snow was dumped on two blocks of Fillmore Street, a section so steep that the sidewalks have staircases. The skiers raced down the run, which measured 400 ft (120 m).

On **November 25, 2004**, a robber took **$14,500** from a bank in FUKUOKA, JAPAN, but was so **overcome with guilt** that he *mailed the money back* with an *apology note* a week later!

Pension Imposter

After a Turkish mother died in 2003, her 47-year-old son, Serafettin Gencel, buried her in his basement and disguised himself as her for the following two years so that he could collect her retirement pension. He regularly visited the bank dressed in a woman's overcoat, headscarf, and stockings until employees became suspicious of his voice.

Serafettin Gencel, dressed as his dead mother, sitting in the bank where he drew her pension.

Pug Dressers
At Naples, Florida, there is an annual beauty contest, although it is not for people, but for pug dogs. The Pug o'ween event was started in 1998 by pug-owner Karen Coplin for those who like to dress up their pugs in fancy costumes.

Still Alive
Dona Ramona, from Sampues, Colombia, was still very much alive in October 2005, despite being wrongly declared dead on four separate occasions. Doctors defended their prognoses, saying that they were fooled because the 97-year-old kept slipping into a diabetic coma.

▶ Cyclops

A kitten named Cy, short for Cyclops, was born on December 28, 2005, in Redmond, Oregon, with only one eye and no nose. A ragdoll breed, sadly it survived for only a few hours.

Kicking Out

Twelve-year-old Michael Hoffman, a taekwondo black belt from Ann Arbor, Michigan, managed to kick a cushioned pad 2,377 times in a single hour in October 2005. He alternated between using his right and left leg every minute.

Key to Success

After a joke backfired and Arthur Richardson, of North Platte, Nebraska, ended up swallowing the key to his friend's truck, a doctor X-rayed Richardson's stomach and said that the key posed no danger to his health. But his friend still needed to use the truck. So they took the X rays to locksmith John Somers, who used the pictures to fashion a new key. Amazingly it worked in the truck!

Sand Painting

In October 2005, 70 schoolchildren created a sand portrait, measuring 85 x 59 ft (26 x 18 m), of Lord Nelson and the HMS *Victory* on the beach at Scarborough, England, to celebrate the 200th anniversary of the Battle of Trafalgar. They used half a ton of pigment, a quarter of a ton of sand, and over a mile of string to create the sand painting in ten different colors. Painting began at 9.30 a.m. and had to be completed before high tide at 7 p.m.

Slow Way

Paul Kramer took the slow way to his niece's wedding. He hopped onto his bicycle at his home in southern California on April 12, 2005, and pulled into his brother's driveway at North Olmsted, Ohio, 71 days and 4,250 mi (6,840 km) later.

Honey Trap

An estimated one million bees were living inside the walls of St. Mark United Church of Christ in Knox, Pennsylvania, in 2005. The problem became so serious that honey was oozing through the walls!

The entire town of **KIRUNA, SWEDEN**, is being *relocated* at a cost of more than **$2.5 billion** to save it *sliding* into the **abandoned iron mines** below.

Hypnotic Robber

A crook in Moldova found a new way of robbing banks in 2005—he put cashiers into a trance before making them hand over the money. With the hypnotist still at large, the country's bank clerks were warned not to make eye contact with customers.

Pigeon Fancier

In 2005, a Los Angeles, California, man was found to be sharing his house with 300 birds—dead and alive—including 120 dead pigeons. The man was reportedly often seen walking with his favorite pigeon.

◀ Inverted Feet

Wang Fang, from Chongqing, China, has inverted feet. She can still walk and run and successfully manages her own restaurant business.

Underwater Juggling
American performer Ashrita
Furman juggles in an aquatheater
in Kuala Lumpur among nurse
sharks and 3,000 other marine
animals. His personal best is
juggling continuously for
37 minutes and 45 seconds at a
depth of more than 13 ft (4 m).

INDEX

ACKNOWLEDGMENTS

FRONT COVER AND TITLE PAGE Kevin Kolczynski/Universal Orlando/Reuters; 8–9 John Gress/Reuters; 10–11 (dp) DPA/Empics; 10 (b/l) & 11 (t/r, t/l, c, b/r & b/l) Crazy Horse memorial photos by Robb DeWall; 12 Hrywniak Bogdan/Empics; 13 (c) Paul Pikel; 14 (t, c/l & b) Masatochi Okauchi/Rex Features, (c/r) www.fuerrot.at/Rex Features; 15 David Lin/Reuters; 16 Norm Betts/Rex Features; 17 (t) Norm Betts/Rex Features, (b/l) Australian Customs Service/Reuters, (b/r) Rex Features; 20 Gavin Hansford/Image courtesy of Charles Robb and the Dianne Tanzer Gallery, Melbourne; 21 Fredrik Schenholm/Ultimate Freedom Photography; 22 George Whiteside; 23 (t) Yuriko Nakao/Reuters, (b) Phil Noble/Empics; 24–25 David Giles/Camera Press; 26 Randy Finch/Derek Maxfield/iceguru.com; 27 (t) Luray Caverns, (b) John Paul Brooke/Rex Features; 30 Solent News/Rex Features; 31 Skip Snow, The United States National Parks Service; 32 Dani Cardona/Reuters; 33 (t) Scott Wishart/Rex Features, (b) Camera Press; 34 (t) Paul Pikel, (b) Pacific Press Service/Rex Features; 35 Action Press/Rex Features; 36 (t) Simon Jones/Rex Features, (b/l & b/r) Lars Stroschen/Rex Features; 37 Sean Dempsey/Empics; 38–39 Sukree Sukplang/Reuters; 40 (c/l) Chaiwat Subprasom/Reuters, (r) Leon Schadeberg/Rex Features; 41 (l) Leon Schadeberg/Rex Features, (r) Chaiwat Subprasom/Reuters; 42 (t) Ben Phillips/Barcroft Media, (b) Craig Barritt/Barcroft Media; 43 (t) Malissa Kusiek/Empics, (b) Mark Mirko/Rex Features; 45 Moses Lanham; 46 (t) Indranil Mukherjee/AFP/Getty Images; 47 Will Burgess/Reuters; 50 (t) Barcroft Media, (b) John Gress/Reuters; 51 Natasha Veruschka; 52 (t) Camera Press, (b) Kimimasa Mayama/Reuters; 53 (t) Francois Lenoir, (b) Alexander Demianchuk/Reuters; 54–55 (dp) Jim McNitt; 54 (b/l) Jim McNitt; 55 (b/c) Jim McNitt, (b/r) CLY Creation; 56 (t) Ma Qibing/Camera Press, (b) Stuart Clarke/Rex Features; 57 Kai Pfaffenbach/Reuters; 60 (t) Chinafotopress/Camera Press, (b) Gary Roberts/Rex Features; 61 Simon Burt/Rex Features; 62 Incredible Features/Barcroft Media; 63 Doug Hall/Rex Features; 64 (t) Chip East/Reuters, (b) Claro Cortes IV/Reuters; 65 JulianCash.com; 66 Ben Phillips/Barcroft Media; 67 (t/l & t/r) Heather Insogna, (b) Toby Melville/Reuters; 68–69 Camera Press; 70–71 Norm Betts/Rex Features; 72 James Bodington/Reuters; 73 (t & c/r) John Gress/Reuters, (b/l) Arko Datta/Getty Images; 74 (t) Reuters, (b) Konstantin Postnikov/Camera Press; 75 Deborah Ann Duschl; 76–77 (dp) Ando Art; 76 (t/r) Aamir Qureshi/AFP/Getty Images, (c) Ando Art; 77 (t/r) Rex Features, (c/r) Ando Art; 78 (t) Historical Photo Archive Collection/Niagara Falls Public Library; 80 (c/l & b/l) Caricato/Rex Features, (r) Vano Shlamov/Getty Images; 81 (t/r) Laure A. Leber, (b/l) Dale Rio; 82 (t) Dibyangshu Sarkar/AFP/Getty Images, (b) J.P. Moczulski /Reuters; 84 (b/l & r) China Photos/Reuters; 85 Sipa Press/Rex Features; 86 East News/Getty Images; 87 (t & c) Shannon Stapleton/Reuters, (b) Alessia Pierdomenico/Reuters; 90 (t) China Newsphoto/Reuters, (c/r & b) Tobias Schwarz/Reuters; 91 Seth Wenig/Reuters; 92 China Newsphoto/Reuters; 93 (t) Michael Fresco/Rex Features, (b) Anthony Devlin/Rex Features; 94 Bobby Hunt; 95 Jim Mouth; 96 Rex Features; 97 (b/l) Emily Baron/Barcroft Media, (t/r) Tim Winborne/Reuters; 98–99 Mary Schwalm/Empics; 100–101 Paul Pikel; 102 (t) China Newsphoto/Reuters, (b) Anna Kelly; 103 (t) Romeo Ranoco/Reuters, (b) Rex Features; 104 (b) Stephen Hird/Reuters; 105 Rex Features; 106–107 (dp) M. Usher/Rex Features; 106 (t/l) Reuters, (t/r) Stringer/Reuters; 107 (t) Sam Barcroft/Barcroft Media; 110 (t) Sukree Sukplang/Reuters, (b) Incredible Features/Barcroft Media; 111 aCaseofCuriosities.com; 112 The United States National Parks Service; 113 (b) Gary Roberts/Rex Features; 114–115 Eliana Aponte/Reuters; 116 (t) Masatoshi Okauchi/Rex Features, (b) Christian Charisius/Reuters; 117 David Gray/Reuters; 120 (t) Rex Features, (b) Stewart Cook/Rex Features; 121 Claro Cortes IV/Reuters; 122 Thierry Roge/Reuters; 123 (t) Erik S. Lesser, (b) Fernando Cavalcanti/Reuters; 124–125 Claro Cortes IV/Reuters; 126 (t) China Newsphoto/Reuters, (b) Camera Press; 127 Henry Lizardlover; 128–129 Azulai/Rex Features; 130–131 www.robosaurus.com; 132 Joe Klamar/AFP/Getty Images; 133 (t) Iberpress/Barcroft Media, (b) Owen Humphreys/Empics; 134 Steve Holland/Empics; 135 Sam Barcroft/Barcroft Media; 136 (t) Mike Segar/Reuters, (b) Owen Humphreys/Empics; 137 Jason Kronenwald; 140 Toby Melville/Reuters; 141 seanwhite.net; 142 (t) Sam Barcroft/Barcroft Media, (b) Toru Yamanaka/Getty Images; 144–145 Nino Fernando Campagna; 146 Paul Ortiz; 147 (t) Barcroft Media, (b) Sam Barcroft/Barcroft Media; 149 (c/l) Paul Pikel; 150 (t) Bill Graham/Empics, (b) Fabrizio Bensch/Reuters; 151 Matt Slocum/Empics; 152 Thorsten Persson/Barcroft Media; 153 (t) Sebastian Derungs/Reuters, (b) Chris Ison/Empics; 155 Octane Creative; 156 (t) Tom Pringle/Cardiff SF, (b) Sena Vidanagama/AFP/Getty Images; 157 David Gray/Reuters; 158–159 Erik Aeder/Empics; 160–161 Terje Eggum/Camera Press; 162 (t) Joe Bowen, (b) Camera Press; 163 Michaela Rehle/Reuters; 164 China Newsphoto/Reuters; 166–167 (dp/t) Deutsche Press-Agentur/Empics; 167 (b) Camera Press; 170 Vince Bucci/AFP/Getty Images; 171 (t) Georges Christen, (b) Mirgain & Huberty and Georges Christen; 172 (t) Cheng Jiang/Camera Press, (b) Chris Ison/Empics; 173 China Newsphoto/Reuters; 174–175 China Newsphoto/Reuters; 176 (t) China Newsphoto/Reuters; 177 Dennis Rogers; 180 Michaela Rehle/Reuters; 181 Stevie Starr/Mike Malley; 182 (t) Bob Child/Empics, (b & dp) Sergio Moraes/Reuters; 183 (t/l & t/r) Randy and Mary Ellen Davisson; 184 James Keivom/Getty Images; 185 (t) Christine Shing-Kelly, (b) Tim Barnsley/Armidale Express; 187 Emiliano D'Andrea/Empics; 188–189 Sukree Sukplang/Reuters; 190 (l) Jerilyn Tabor, (r) Alison Slon; 191 Doug Levere; 192 Paul Carpenter; 193 (t/l) Chris Radburn/Empics, (b/r) Dougie Hendry/Rex Features; 194 Joe Jennings/Barcroft Media; 195 Troy Waters; 196 (t) Drahoslav Ramik/Camera Press, (b) China Newsphoto/Reuters; 197 Chie Morifuji/Reuters; 200 (t) Sutton-Hibbert/Rex Features, (b) Noah Berger/Empics; 201 (t) Scott Stewart, (b) Ken "Spear" Flick and Steve Santini; 202 (t) Deutsche Press-Agentur/Empics, (b) Andy Reed/Barcroft Media; 203 R. Clayton Brough and Eisenhower JHS; 204 Steve Bunn; 205 Dick Jones; 206 (t) Camera Press; (b) Canadian Press/Empics; 210 Poseidon Resort/Rex Features; 211 Allistair Mitchell/Reuters; 212 (t) Courtesy Patie Ventre/WCFO, Inc., (b) Ben Phillips/Barcroft Media; 213 David Bebber/Reuters; 214 Feature China/Barcroft Media; 215 www.voltini.com; 216 Gopal Chitrakar/Reuters; 217 (t) Barry Batchelor/Empics, (b) Thomas Peter/Reuters; 218–219 Eric Gaillard/Reuters; 220 www.24thcid.com; 221 (t/l), (t/r) & (b/r) www.24thcid.com, (b/l) Camera Press; 222 (t) Czech News Agency/Empics, (b) Richard Crease/Rex Features; 223 Israel Sun/Rex Features; 224 Jean-Christophe Verhaegen/Reuters; 225 (t) Rex Features, (b) Tao-Chuan Yeh/AFP/Getty Images; 226 (l) Jorge Silva/Reuters, (r) Norman Kent/Jump for the Cause/Reuters; 227 Jeff J Mitchell/Reuters; 228 Ognen Teofilovski/Reuters; 229 (t) Jay Cheng/Reuters, (b) National Taiwan University/Reuters; 230 (t) Marsha Ruff, (b/l) & (b/r) John Gomes/The Alaska Zoo; 231 David Gray/Reuters; 234 (t) Bogdan Cristel/Reuters; 235 Mark Lennihan/Reuters; 236 Alastair Grant/Empics; 237 www.humancannonball.us; 240 (t) & (dp) Livio De Marchi, (b/l) Barcroft Media; 241 (t/r) & (c/r) Barcroft Media; 242 (t) Czech News Agency/Empics; (b) Noboru Hashimoto/Reuters; 243 Reuters; 244 (t/l & t/r) Christie Presti/The Karate Chimps (sm); 245 (t/l) & (t/r) Xavier Lhospice/Reuters, (b) IHLAS News Agency/Reuters; 246 (t) Traci Allen/Empics; (b) Chinafotopress/Camera Press; 247 Vincent Thian/Empics.

Key: b = bottom, c = center, dp = double page, l = left, r = right, t = top

All other photos are from MKP Archives, PhotoDisc, and Ripley's Entertainment Inc.
Every attempt has been made to acknowledge correctly and contact copyright holders and we apologize in advance for any unintentional errors or omissions which will be corrected in future editions.

The front cover shows Ryan Oman taking part in a preview of the "Fear Factor Live," which is based on the hit NBC TV show "Fear Factor," at Universal Studios theme park in Florida.